"*The Modern Larder* is a thoughtful study of the most oft-neglected space in our kitchens: the pantry. Michelle provides a treatise on stocking your shelves with consideration and then invites home cooks to enjoy the gratifying practice of utilizing those ingredients in everyday cooking—for example, the Fried Shishitos with Dancing Bonito lives up to the poetry of its name. Both useful and inspirational, this book feels made for this moment."

—Tara O'Brady,
author of *Seven Spoons*

"Michelle McKenzie's new book delights in the everyday celebration of diverse cultural flavors, beauty, and deliciousness. Her recipes are lucid and encourage exploration. I was thrilled to find more than a dozen Japanese ingredients in the pages of *The Modern Larder*, including bonito flakes, miso, shio koji, and umeboshi, along with useful tips for incorporating these flavors into your everyday cooking. This book, enhanced by Rick Poon's breathtaking photography, is definitely one that I will return to again and again."

—Sonoko Sakai,
author of *Japanese Home Cooking*

"It's no surprise that Michelle McKenzie has applied her considerable smarts to this brilliant, beautiful tome. Minimalist and deeply alluring at once, *The Modern Larder* is the kind of book I will not only proudly display like art, but dip into again and again for inspiration, wisdom, and recipes so good I want to make every one."

—Sarah Copeland,
author of *Every Day Is Saturday*, *Feast*,
and *Instant Family Meals*

lar • der | \\'lär-dər

The area in the house used for storing food.
This includes pantries, refrigerators, cupboards, and
any other areas that hold culinary ingredients such as
dry legumes, nuts and seeds, cultured dairy, canned
goods, pickles, ferments, spice blends, cured meats,
preserved fish, and grains both whole and milled.

THE MODERN LARDER

Michelle McKenzie

PHOTOGRAPHS BY RICK POON

ROOST BOOKS

Roost Books
An imprint of
Shambhala Publications, Inc.
2129 13th Street
Boulder, CO 80302
roostbooks.com

Cover art: Kara Plikaitis

9 8 7 6 5 4 3 2 1

First Edition
Printed in China

♾ This edition is printed on
acid-free paper that meets the
American National Standards
Institute Z39.48 Standard.
♻ Shambhala makes
every effort to print on
postconsumer recycled paper.
For more information please
visit www.shambhala.com.

Roost Books is distributed
worldwide by Penguin
Random House, Inc., and
its subsidiaries.

Library of Congress
Cataloging-in-
Publication Data
Names: McKenzie, Michelle,
1983– author. | Poon, Rick,
photographer.
Title: The modern larder
/ Michelle McKenzie;
photographs by Rick Poon.
Description: First edition.
| Boulder, Colorado: Roost
Books, [2021] | Includes
bibliographical references.
Identifiers: LCCN
2020011082 | ISBN
9781611805703 (hardback)
Subjects: LCSH: Quick and
easy cooking. | Cooking,
American. | LCGFT:
Cookbooks.
Classification: LCC
TX833.5 .M445 2021 | DDC
641.5/12—dc23
LC record available at https://
lccn.loc.gov/2020011082

For Mike and Luke—

whose hearts and bellies

inspire me every day

CONTENTS

INTRODUCTION

What Is the Modern Larder?

Before my son was born, most of my waking hours were spent shopping for, prepping, and cooking food. It was my job, my pleasure, the way I cared for and connected with others. My first cookbook, *Dandelion & Quince*, reflected this passion. In it I set about showcasing all the unusual produce—remarkable fruits, vegetables, and herbs—that are increasingly accessible but often overlooked by the everyday shopper. On every page I aimed to compel readers to take risks with new foods and techniques. It was invigorating, a teaching high. And then, halfway through the writing, I realized I had a parallel story to tell about my larder—the oils, vinegars, sauces, syrups, spices, and preserves I rely on every day. Items such as capers, crème fraîche, miso, shio koji, preserved lemons, date syrup, fish sauce, rice flour, ghee, yuzu, and so on.

This was a larder I'd been expanding most of my adult life. But when I spoke to culinary students and friends about it, they blanched. "Michelle, I wouldn't know what to do with chickpea flour or kefir," they said. Their reactions convinced me I was on to something, specifically cookbook number two. For my students, friends, and readers, I would take each of my larder favorites and give it a 360-degree treatment. For example, I'd show readers how shio koji can be used as a dressing, a marinade (that transforms meat and fish), a pickling medium, or simply liquid supersalt.

Then I had that baby boy I mentioned. Everyone told me he'd change everything. He did. Now, the constraints of motherhood have shown me another reason why this cookbook is needed: mining the larder is the ultimate efficiency. It saves time. It saves my family every day.

I revere the traditional French and Italian approach of bottom-up cooking: an initial sear of meats and sweating down of vegetables; the subsequent deglazing of the pan; careful tending. These methods create fully developed flavor and provide a dependable foundation on which to build a dish. While cooking remains a redemptive pleasure and I look forward to my time in the kitchen, nowadays I'm prone to bypassing a lengthy building process and instead employ hardworking ingredients from my larder. I sauté in umami-rich schmaltz, toss dried limes into simmering beans, shower homemade spice blends on roasted vegetables, bake with cultured dairy and charismatic flours, and spike many things with fish sauce. In this way, I get maximum impact for minimal effort.

1

By offering you a fresh and freeing perspective on some powerful ingredients while arming you with pro tips and solid techniques, I aim to loosen up the cook in you. Instead of big weekend or monthlong projects like preserving lemons, infusing vinegar, or making jam, I have spent my ink on less intimidating matters, demystifying kitchen keystones from a cross section of cultures and influences, and showing that there's no authentic or inauthentic usage—if a combination makes sense to the palate, it's right. I dispose of sacrilege entirely (I braise my holiday brisket with mole spices, mix fish sauce with olive oil, and pair miso with dill) and encourage you to use everything at your disposal—because when you do, magic is made. These recipe ideas are meant to free you from monotony and guide you in finessing already fine ingredients into inspired versions of themselves.

If *The Modern Larder* came with a thesis, it would be: "one ingredient can change the nature of a dish, elevating it from flat to transcendent." Many of the featured ingredients are those secret somethings in the dishes at your favorite restaurants. Some have recently become—or are likely to become—mainstream in American food culture and available to all home cooks. Most can be easily found online or, especially if you're near a big city, at a brick-and-mortar. This list is certainly not exhaustive, but it contains the ingredients I find the most compelling, those that have most changed and improved my cooking.

HOW I COOK AND SHOP

Before I became a multitasking mom in need of great efficiency, I believed that a single fat, a single acid, and a soupçon of salt were enough to make really good meals. That is the first principle of my cooking and shopping and that hasn't changed. This book isn't a shopping list of must-haves that you should run out and buy all at once. Rather, I intend it as a guide for giving more value to what's already on your shelf and an enticement to explore. If you want a roasted cauliflower salad but lack barberries, or you have beans but no curry leaves, the recipes here will still produce fine dishes—just focus on seasoning well with salt, acid, and fat, and enjoy your meal without thinking you fell short of "perfect." Perfect meals are the ones that suit the moment perfectly. It is true, however, that once you have preserved lemons and fish sauce on hand—and understand what they're capable of—your cooking will be more exciting and irreversibly better.

Second, I still champion that which might otherwise be taken for granted in a culture of excess. I hoard herb stems, freeze bean-cooking liquid, and make oils, syrups, and ferments as much for the sake of preservation as playfulness. I hold dear utility, resourcefulness, efficiency, wellness, and pleasure. Whether I'm creating something new, cooking a tried-and-true dish, or reimagining leftovers for their third show, these are the principles that drive how I work in my kitchen on a daily basis.

Third, what I cook and eat is dictated by what is available at my farmers market on any given week. For me, it's the most pleasurable and rational approach to food. I want to encourage you to eat seasonally too. Exceptionally fresh and well-tended produce, pristine and sustainable seafood, and meats raised according to the highest standards of animal husbandry invite less doing. Along these lines, I also urge you to seek out equitably sourced imported products (especially spices, sugars, chocolate, tea, and coffee). Fair-trade products are not only good for the growers, they're often more carefully produced and delivered to our kitchens via shorter supply chains—this means a higher quality and more exceptional flavor.

Fourth, as I write this, Elizabeth David's adage keeps rollicking through my mind: "Good food is always a trouble and its preparation should be regarded as a labor of love." I do think this is still true today—and always, I imagine. So, while this book is optimized for the efficiency and fun of the modern cook, we can't ignore that food that tastes good and is good for us requires thought, effort, and enthusiasm. Some of the recipes require a soaking, a salting, or some other step the night before you plan to cook. I promise I wouldn't include it if I didn't think the step's contribution was significant. Spend time selecting the best products you can find and afford—a grilled whole fish garnished with nothing more than olive oil and shiso salt needs to be a very fresh fish, and ideally that olive oil is one you don't mind slurping from a spoon. You'll also want to take time, once your larder is stocked and fresh ingredients gathered, to pause and enjoy the process of matching this thing to that. I like sketching recipe and menu ideas in a notebook.

Fifth, and connected to the above, I prefer to plan ahead so that the "labor" doesn't seem so laborious. I simmer beans before I know I need them and habitually rinse and soak rice. Make cooking a part of your life routine—well beyond mealtimes—and salting meat before bed can seem as effortless as brushing your teeth (most nights). I urge you to prepare some of the oils, sauces, spice blends, and broths in the back of book (page 333)—when you have time—so that when you *don't* have time, they can be employed with speed. Having some of these homemade goods on hand is like having a quiver of wizards' wands, each enabling breezy, beautiful weeknight meals with a shake, stir, or squeeze. If you see fresh yuzu at the market and get excited, don't just buy a few; buy a glut, with plans to preserve their flavor in the form of Yuzu Kosho (page 343), Yuzu Ponzu (page 342), Yuzu Ice Cream (page 314), and Yuzu Salt (page 352). Yuzu kosho, for example, requires about 20 minutes of active time, but two weeks later, when you are short on time, half a teaspoon will transform a salad into something special.

Sixth, my cooking style is personalized with a few trinkets. Called out in recipes as "optional embellishments," these recurring ingredients aren't required for the dish to be fantastic but are there because I tend to enjoy a dish more if it's served with one or a few of them; a tangle of delicate herbs, a drizzle of some nut or seed oil, a scattering of radish shavings, or a few drops of homemade chile vinegar make some dishes seem complete to me. But they are definitely optional.

Seventh, I'm a fan of substitutions. If you can't find or don't want a particular ingredient, in most cases you can omit or use an ingredient of equivalent character in its place. Consider the flavor and nature of what you need, then seek out something similar. For instance, Meyer lemon can masquerade as yuzu, vinegar-washed currants can stand in for barberries, salt can replace fish sauce, and buttermilk can be used instead of kefir. The big exception to this improvisational approach is baking. Unless you are a highly experienced baker, it's wise to adhere to the measurements and ingredients in a recipe. (A tangential but important note: all flours, but especially gluten-free flours such as rice and buckwheat, vary from brand to brand and from one milling to the next. And our measuring techniques differ too. I highly recommend using a scale when baking, and, as such, have chosen to provide weights before customary units of measurement in the cases where it matters most.) This same spirit of flexibility and experimentation goes for the recipe variations I provide. I see these options (see Many Ways to Season a Chicken, page 264, for an example) as jumping-off points for your own exploration. Again, I urge you to keep in your canon what has worked for you before, but—with this book as your counsel—travel in new directions.

Eighth, if you bought every single item pushed in this book, you'd have no room to cook. I don't keep all these things in my kitchen at any given time. There is a rotation of specialty goods based on my mood when shopping, and there are certain products I'm never without. In time, you'll personalize your pantry too, determining your own essentials. And once it's well stocked to your preferences, you might find it easier to shop a market without a list or menu in mind. The dishes that emerge from that freedom will be very much your own. With a foundation in place, you can purchase whatever produce catches your eye and trust you'll be able to get home and figure things out later.

Ninth, I'm cautious of trends. It is sometimes fashionable to use too much. People get excited and, understandably, go wild for a thing. But I feel strongly we need to temper the intensity. Black pepper can overpower food, and so can flavors such as anchovy, dried lime, and black garlic. Lighten up on both the amount and number of these ingredients in your cooking. Remember the pleasures of simplicity and subtlety.

Tenth, and last, I always taste a dish throughout the cooking process and again right before serving.

1

INGREDIENTS, A–Z

ANCHOVIES

Pictured on page viii.

Home cooks are often reluctant to incorporate anchovies into their cooking. I understand that this is mostly due to the fear of an overly fishy flavor ruining their hard work, possibly traumatizing their kids and putting them off the taste forever. However, when used judiciously, good anchovies will transform a ho-hum dish into something truly spectacular. When used in the right proportion to other ingredients, anchovies can make food taste extraordinary without tasting at all like fish. To create **a briny, behind-the-scenes booster** from anchovies, use your knife to finely mince salt- or oil-packed fillets until a paste forms (alternatively, use a mortar and pestle). This paste is basically a strong-armed condiment. Use it to accent a lemon vinaigrette, dressing raw leaves such as the classic romaine, of course, but also those pleasantly bitter beauts like radicchio, escarole, and puntarelle. Add it to marinades. Stir a bit into soupy things—particularly good candidates are shellfish stews, just about anything bean based, braised lamb shanks, and tomato sauce. Watch that *same* paste—it's so versatile!—melt into warm ghee, schmaltz, or olive oil, creating an instant pan sauce for fish, chicken, beans, noodles, eggs, asparagus, and every cruciferous vegetable.

There are two types of anchovies I use most often:

Salt-packed anchovies are a preserved product that require two modifications before use: a 15- to 20-minute soak in water or milk, and the removal of the backbone and tail. Agostino Recca is the brand most readily available in my area. Packed in salt, whole anchovies will keep indefinitely (refrigerate in a closed container and add more fine sea salt to cover with each use).

Oil-packed anchovy fillets are also a preserved product, but they are quite different in size, texture, and flavor to the salt-packed kind. Good oil-packed anchovy fillets are plump, meaty—never mealy—and taste of clean sea. The best I've had are from Ortiz; the company catches the fish in the spring—when they are at their fattest—and clean, salt, and cure them in barrels for six months before packing them in olive oil. These, too, can be chopped or pounded and used as a condiment in many dishes, yet they are also phenomenal whole, as a primary ingredient—consider them **a swipe of bold, bursty flavor** for simple canvases of pasta, toast, pizza, eggs, beans, and lettuces. If you are only going to purchase one anchovy product, this would be my choice for both versatility and deliciousness.

Anchovies, regardless of whether they're packaged in salt or olive oil, are best stored refrigerated. While they're fine out of the fridge for an extended period— they won't go bad—they'll lose their firmness more quickly at warm temperatures.

BANYULS VINEGAR

A good vinegar is like a highlighter on an already standout dish. Acid being one of the primary ways I season, I have many different types of vinegar at home, and I enjoy experimenting with each. But the vinegar that meets my needs more than any other is Banyuls vinegar.

Hailing from the French seaside town Banyuls-sur-Mer, Banyuls vinegar is made from the naturally sweet red wine of the region. Many red wine vinegars are too acidic for my palate and lack all depth of flavor. Banyuls is made from a fortified port-like wine and is produced slowly, allowing for the flavors of the fruit to remain and evolve. Approximately six years of aging in wood yields the smoothest, most feathery flavor I've ever tasted in a vinegar: subtly sweet, with hints of almond, vanilla, and fine aged sherry. It's a special product made in relatively small quantities, and its price reflects that, but it's a worthy expense considering the dimension it adds to a dish.

As an ingredient **in vinaigrettes and dressings**, Banyuls is in almost every salad I dress—just in different ratios to other ingredients. Even if lemon is my primary acid, I'll often add a few drops of vinegar. **As a finishing touch**, I keep Banyuls in a fine-tipped squeeze bottle so that I can easily, quickly, and precisely add a few drops to food right before it is served. **To deglaze a pan**, with the heat still on high, souse a skillet or pot with a splash of Banyuls—cook, stirring and scraping, just until all the sticky, crispy bits get juiced up and release. **As a counterpoint to sugar**, used in moderation, the acidic kick of Banyuls balances the sweetness of many desserts. In addition to the recipes in this book, stir a dash into caramel, chocolate cake batter, roasted strawberries, strawberry ice cream, or poached peaches and pears.

I use Banyuls so often in my kitchen and throughout this book, it would be impractical to list all relevant recipes below. Instead, I've included those that best illustrate its use and showcase its special flavor.

BAKED EGGS WITH LENTILS, SPINACH, AND SPICED GHEE 160 • BASIC BANYULS DRESSING 335 • BETTER BITTER GREENS 222 • BLACK LENTILS 161 • BLISTERED TOMATOES WITH PRESERVED LEMON 201 • CHILE VINEGAR 348 • CUCUMBERS WITH CRÈME FRAÎCHE AND CRISPY CAPERS 121 • HARISSA 342 • HEARTY CAULIFLOWER AND RADICCHIO SALAD WITH FRIED PINE NUTS, BARBERRIES, AND SUMAC 190 • IMPERFECT FRUIT WITH VINEGARED HONEY AND BEE POLLEN 147 • MARINATED BEETS 213 • ORANGE SALAD WITH ALMONDS AND ALEPPO-STYLE PEPPER 197 • QUICK-PICKLED SHALLOTS 348 • UME DRESSING 335 • WATERMELON AND CUCUMBER SALAD WITH FETA AND SUMAC 197 • YUZU KOSHO DRESSING 335

BARBERRIES

Occasionally I'll use dried cherries, cranberries, and raisins for sweet treats such as granola, "power" bars, and the like. But the dried fruits I use most often in my kitchen are those that serve an important role in savory dishes: currants, barberries, and prunes. Their sweetness and concentrated jammy flavor balance richness, bitterness, bite, and boredom. Barberries, with their captivating hue and unique tart flavor, are my favorite.

Use barberries **as a garnish** for rice dishes, braised meats, and creamy soups or **as a balancing element** in dishes such as the otherwise bitter and cruciferous Hearty Cauliflower and Radicchio Salad (page 190). Keeping that in mind, consider using them a bit **like a spice** in anything in your repertoire or in need of sweetness and a little zing: marinated lentils, farro with greens and pine nuts, stuffed cabbage, chicken salad sandwiches, frisée with duck (page 278), and so on.

CARAMELIZED CABBAGE FOR MANY OCCASIONS 226 • HEARTY CAULIFLOWER AND RADICCHIO SALAD WITH FRIED PINE NUTS, BARBERRIES, AND SUMAC 190 • LABNEH: THE TWO-MINUTE MEAL 59 • LEMONY FRIED RICE WITH GREENS AND HERBS 253 • VITAMIN C TEA 328

BEE POLLEN

Once exclusive to tiny natural food stores, bee pollen is now more widely available. It is touted as a superfood, valued for its healing properties, but it also adds dimension to the experience of a dish.

Bee pollen is the product of an intricate, wondrous performance by a honeybee, who scrapes the loose pollen from a flower's stamen while simultaneously moistening it with nectar. As she departs the flower, she uses comblike structures on her legs to brush the just-gathered gold powder from her body mid-flight, pushing it into concave basketlike structures that tamp it down into a single grain, or bee-pollen granule. Beekeepers collect the pollen by setting up a screen through which the bees must pass when returning to the hive. The screen gently scrapes the pollen off their legs (responsible beekeepers make sure there is still enough pollen to sustain the hive).

It's no surprise that bee pollen—the food of the baby bee—is one of nature's most completely nourishing foods, rich in amino acids and vitamins. But it also looks gorgeous—delicate, powdery grains in an arresting canary gold—and is uniquely fragrant. Its flavor is sweet, floral, and pleasantly waxy—as we'd expect— yet also very fruity. Used judiciously, it is a fascinating counterpoint to salty, bitter, nutty, and gamey ingredients. However you use it, don't expose raw bee pollen to the heat of an oven—it burns easily.

Raw, fresh bee pollen has a shelf life, particularly if it hasn't been refrigerated or frozen. Kept at room temperature, you likely have six months to consume it; the refrigerator will double or triple its shelf life. Frozen bee pollen will keep for several years.

Use it **as a main ingredient or supplement** by adding it to blended drinks, ferments, and vinaigrettes. And use it **as a garnish**—the saturated and striking hue makes people pause, and its ready-to-go granular texture makes sprinkling a snap.

BLACK GARLIC

Black garlic is *the* darling of chefs worldwide. Their adoration makes sense—these inky-black cloves boast an earthy, molasses-like sweetness, a complex sourness, and that umami factor that keeps a fork returning to the plate. Luckily for home cooks, black garlic is also easy to procure—and make—and can be effortlessly incorporated into anyone's cooking repertoire, no matter how narrow or expansive it may be.

Black garlic is made by heating whole bulbs of garlic over several weeks in a carefully controlled, warm, humid environment, such as a rice cooker. The enzymes that give fresh garlic its sharpness break down and the Maillard reaction—the chemical process of browning—occurs. The result is soft, slightly sticky, chewy, black cloves that lack all the harshness of fresh garlic.

You can make your own black garlic or purchase it from specialty shops and gourmet food retailers online. It generally keeps for up to six months in the refrigerator.

While it is typically associated with ramen, consider black garlic in a wider framework. It is a shortcut to adding a subtle sweetness, a little tang, an earthy depth, and a dark color. Because it is essentially precooked, use it as you would garlic confit or roasted garlic.

As a paste-like condiment: Black garlic cloves can be bashed to a puree with a sharp knife or mortar and pestle. Incorporate black garlic paste into dressings, sauces, marinades, wet rubs, dips, and spreads. Or serve it straight up, loosened with a bit of oil and seasoned with salt; spread on toast or crostini, swirl through labneh, or serve under a fillet of crispy-skinned fish (page 258).

As an aromatic: Create black garlic infusions by blitzing whole cloves with or steeping them in olive oil, ghee, cream, stock, or water. This basic black garlic water broth—which is as easy as steeping tea—can be employed as a base for grains, beans, soups, stews, and the like. Or, set a foundation of flavor by adding chopped cloves to a skillet or saucepan slicked with hot fat—then build a dish from there.

As a garnish: Slice cloves and scatter them across a dish to finish. Think eggs, noodles, pizza, grilled shrimp, and roasted meats.

As a spice: You can purchase black garlic as a powder. Sprinkle it on anything that wants some sweetness, earthiness, and depth.

BLACK LENTIL HUMMUS 124 • MAYONNAISE VARIATIONS 339 •
PAN-SEARED RIB EYE WITH BLACK GARLIC GHEE 293

BLACK VINEGAR

Dark and full-bodied, a few drops of black vinegar add a lot of complexity and mystery to a dish. There are many different types of black vinegar—from many different places, comprising different ingredients. Those most readily available have similar characteristics: they taste of tamarind, coffee, and smoked raisins and have the consistency and color of brewed espresso. They're neither overly tart (like distilled vinegar) nor tame.

Chinese Chinkiang—or Zhenjiang—black vinegar is regarded by many as the best. It is fermented from primarily glutinous rice and wheat bran (it usually contains yeast and sugar as well), and it's aged in earthenware crocks for at least six months. There are many brands of Chinkiang black vinegar on the market, but the recipes in this book were all tested with the basic, easy-to-find, yellow-labeled bottle.

Kurozu is a black vinegar made in Japan. It is harder to find, and many bottles are more expensive. Aged kurozu, if you can find one, is relatively rich, full-bodied, sweet, and softly acidic. I use this for finishing but rarely for cooking.

In vinaigrettes: Black vinegar can replace regular vinegar in salad dressings and marinades. I recommend adding a little something sweet—a pinch of muscovado or a tiny spoonful of honey—along with it. A classic use is the smashed cucumber salad, but it also works well drizzled on a salad with crispy eggplant or thinly sliced celery.

For basting: If I want an acid to flavor a piece of meat or seafood but I don't have time (or don't want) to marinate it, I'll baste it with vinegar. Black vinegar is great for this. Try the technique on chicken, pork, lamb, mackerel, and kebabs of all shapes and sizes.

For pickling: Put julienned ginger and a pinch of salt (and muscovado, if you'd like) into a bowl and add black vinegar to cover. After about 30 minutes, you have a quick pickle that works well alongside meat, atop fatty fish, in a salad (try it with seaweed), or stirred into fried rice.

For braising: Much like the ume vinegar in the Ume-Glazed Pork Ribs (page 283), black vinegar can be used as a braising medium for meat, tofu, or hearty vegetables like cabbage. The sugar-spiked liquid cooks down to a mellow sweetness, bright with acid, and imbues the ingredient with the dark, complex flavor of the vinegar.

To accent or finish: Add a few drops of black vinegar to sauces, caramelized vegetables, and stocks. Try adding a ½ tablespoon or more to a 3-cup batch of caramel or use instead of vanilla extract in ice cream.

In a dipping sauce: This is perhaps black vinegar's most common use. Mix equal parts black vinegar and soy sauce, add sugar and/or chile to taste, and use as a dipping sauce for things like dumplings and savory pancakes.

BLACK VINEGAR CHICKEN 263 • EASY PUMPKIN DUMPLINGS WITH BLACK VINEGAR AND PARMESAN 128 • SPICED LAMB CHOPS WITH BLACK VINEGAR AND HONEY 288

BONITO FLAKES

Let a good fish sauce (page 45) or some anchovies (page 10) be your gateway to the world of fishy flavor boosters, then buy some bonito.

Bonito—a Japanese product also known as *katsuobushi*—is skipjack tuna that has been dried, fermented, and smoked. It's commonly sold shaved into flakes, and they bring a remarkable—and, for a cured fish product, relatively mild—oceanic flavor, umami, and smokiness to anything they touch. **Infuse into dashi** and other stocks, or **sprinkle on rice, noodles, grains, eggs, and cooked vegetables or meats** right before serving.

BOTTARGA

Bottarga is the roe sac of gray mullet that has been salted, dried, and pressed until hard. It's briny, with a creamy, almost caviar-like flavor. It will **add salt and umami to the simplest of dishes** (scrambled eggs, sautéed broccoli, blanched asparagus, braised beans, roasted brussels sprouts, butter-sauced bucatini, crisp, cold lettuce, and so on).

Look for bottarga that is firm but not dry—it should be moist, almost creamy on the palate. It is sold either vacuum-packed or sealed in beeswax, and it can be kept in the fridge for a few years, as long as it remains sealed or wrapped tightly in plastic. When you open the packet, peel back the membrane of only as much as you think you're going to use. After use, rewrap well.

My mantra when using bottarga or any other product that is expensive and/or contributes a highly concentrated flavor is "less is more." The simpler you keep things, the better. The dish that is being finished with bottarga should be an elemental one: a few pristine ingredients, simply and thoughtfully prepared. So, if you decide to indulge, take care to store it properly and use it well. Have a sharp Microplane in the house so that you can apply it gently and precisely.

LITTLE GEM SALAD WITH LEMON AND BOTTARGA 181 • **SAVORY TOAST** 150 •
SHAVED FENNEL WITH LEMON AND BOTTARGA 134 • **SKILLET-CHARRED BEANS** 136

BUCKWHEAT

Unrelated to wheat, buckwheat is unusual in that it's neither grass nor grain. It's actually an edible fruit seed—a relative of rhubarb—that possesses a robust, grassy, nutty, bitter, slightly sour flavor. When most people hear the word *buckwheat*, kasha, crepes, or soba noodles pop to mind. But the usefulness of this little three-sided groat far exceeds that short list.

Like quinoa, buckwheat can masquerade **as a soft grain**, on its own or in a mix, fluffy or porridge-like. For this use, buckwheat can be purchased in various forms: as whole groats—raw or toasted, hulled or unhulled; ground for hot cereal; and ground for polenta (often combined with corn). Regardless of which kind you buy, I recommend toasting buckwheat in a dry (no fat, no water) skillet over low heat as you would whole spices, stirring and swirling often, until it's a shade darker—about 4 minutes. Then add hot water and simmer until the desired consistency is reached.

Uncooked whole buckwheat groats can be **used as topping** for everything from salads and pasta to banana bread and meringues—really anywhere nuts typically tread. For this use, look for pretoasted buckwheat groats found at Japanese tea shops under the name *soba cha*; usually roasted to perfection and cracked until coarse, these perfectly nutty and crispy morsels are ready to go. Otherwise, groats need a quick fry at home to come to life. To use raw buckwheat groats **as a garnish**, sauté whole groats in 1 tablespoon of fat (ghee, schmaltz, or any oil) over medium heat for 4 to 5 minutes before tossing with a pinch of fine sea salt. These crunchy little pyramids taste delightful and, stored in an airtight container once cool, keep for up to three days. I use them whole or pound them in a mortar until they are a coarse powder—a sort of buckwheat gomasio. Because toasted buckwheat dissolves in the mouth more quickly than toasted nuts, they can land more places—on top of scrambled eggs or tartare, for instance, or a delicate panna cotta.

Buckwheat is also sold **as a flour**, a boon for those who can't or prefer not to consume gluten. It produces good pasta, pancakes and crepes, crackers, and some of the best chocolate cookies I've ever had. However, unlike other gluten-free flours, buckwheat is affected by overbeating; take care to stir, pulse, or knead buckwheat only briefly, just until incorporated. Buckwheat flours can be coarse or fine—each yields slightly different results. Get whichever you can find, and just know that the fine, "light" flours yield a more delicate color and crumb.

Lastly, buckwheat makes **a wonderful decaf tea.** Make an infusion by pouring 1 cup of boiling water over 1 tablespoon of toasted buckwheat groats, steep 5 minutes, and strain.

BEETS WITH HORSERADISH CRÈME FRAÎCHE AND TOASTED BUCKWHEAT 216 • **CARAMELIZED CABBAGE FOR MANY OCCASIONS** 226 • **FLUFFY BUCKWHEAT PANCAKES** 162 • **SWEET TOAST** 150 • **WATERMELON AND CUCUMBER SALAD WITH FETA AND SUMAC** 197

CAPERS

Capers have been part of our culinary vocabulary for years now, but when I asked folks which opened, half-full jar in their fridge stared them into shame, capers were often the first thing named. Capers are a no-brainer on lox-capped bagels, in pasta dishes, and, for some, in salsa verde. But they have a much wider range. I think of capers as tiny containers of concentrated salt and acid, laced with a faint but noticeable citrusy flavor. This image opens the door to a lot of dishes (consider how often we use salt and lemon in our cooking). In actuality, capers are the buds of the caper bush, a spiny shrub that flourishes in rocky, wild environments all over the Mediterranean. (Caper berries, by the way, are the fruit the caper plant produces if you don't remove the buds.) Most capers in the US are jarred in a brine, which overwhelms their subtler characteristics and damages their texture. Brined capers just taste salty, and the liquid impedes their ability to ever get crispy (see Crispy Capers, page 348). Capers preserved in salt are different: they retain their nuanced flavors and firm texture.

Before using salt-packed capers, soak them in a small strainer submerged in cool water for 15 to 30 minutes; lift the strainer from the water and transfer the capers to a kitchen towel to dry. From here you can use them as is or fry them in fat until crispy. You can use capers **as a garnish** (crispy or soft), **in a sauce or vinaigrette**, or **blended into a paste**. In whatever final state they take, it is important to remember that capers are pretty intense. Use them not as an ingredient but **as a seasoning**—and even then, sparingly.

CARAWAY

Caraway is underestimated and drastically underused. This warm, sweet, pleasantly pungent seed merits more than a relegation to rye bread.

The caraway seed is integral to many European cuisines, particularly German, Austrian, and Hungarian, but also Dutch, Russian, and Swedish. Though it is practically unknown in southern Europe, caraway is also an important element in North African cuisine, where it is an essential ingredient in harissa, a very spicy chile condiment.

Taste a caraway seed. Chew it well, without trepidation. If you dry-toast it first, even better. For me, the effect is pretty explosive: pungent, warm, sweet, citrusy, a little peppery, with a hint of anise. It's easy to see why it lands well on so many dishes. While caraway is **best suited for savory applications**, the seeds can also be **incorporated into sweet batters and doughs** or **used to flavor liquor and tea.**

Caraway is usually sold as whole seeds. If a recipe calls for ground caraway, toast the seeds in small dry skillet over low heat (just until they are fragrant and lightly colored), then grind the whole seeds using a spice grinder, mortar and pestle, or coffee grinder. Store whole, untoasted caraway seeds in an airtight container in a cool, dark place for up to six months.

CHICKPEA FLOUR

Chickpea flour is a flour in the same way almond "flour" is—it is ground hulled chickpeas. It is a little nutty and a little sweet, but mostly neutral in flavor. What makes it an attractive ingredient is its other attributes: gluten-free, nutritious, and multitalented.

Chickpea flour is often sold as garbanzo bean flour, gram flour, and besan flour. Purchase from a source that you think has turnover—chickpea flour that's been shelved for an eon isn't going to taste great. It's almost twice the price, but you can also find organic sprouted chickpea flour, which may be easier on the digestive tract. Whichever kind you buy, store it in a cool, dark, dry place for up to one year. If you have the space, the fridge or freezer can help increase its shelf life (make sure the bag or container is airtight). But it's best if you just get to using it!

Chickpea flour makes **an incredible batter**—airy and crisp—for deep-fried foods. It is also **a great binder** for things such as falafel, veggie burgers, fritters, and the like. It can be **used to form unique pancakes, crepes, biscuits, flatbreads, panisses, and even tofu**. And, once toasted, it serves **as a surprising, savory, nutty garnish** for salads and noodles. Finally, chickpea flour can be used **as a thickener** for soups, sauces, and gravies. Make a slurry with a little water before stirring into a hot pot.

CHILES

Chiles are the MVP of my larder. To understand why, purchase whole dried chiles and chile flakes from stores with high turnover. The flavor and heat of chiles degrades over time and with exposure to light and air. For this reason, store all chiles and chile flakes in a cool, dry, dark place and (ideally) use within six months of purchase. Keep in mind that the fresher the chile, the hotter it is, so get to know the batch you bought by using them sparingly. Then daringly. These are my favorite varieties:

Aleppo-style pepper is named after the city of its provenance. Most of the pepper now labeled "Aleppo" is actually grown outside of Syria, but, thankfully, a lot of it boasts that perfect combination of fruit and spice for which it has always been known. A fresh batch will be bright red and super moist, mildly hot and deeply flavorful. Use it as you would any dried chile flake, or in place of freshly ground black pepper when finishing a dish.

Chile de arbol are very hot, but more lovable and useful than you may think. I use them regularly but judiciously. I achieve a light touch by using them much as I do a bay leaf, employing them whole to infuse their heat into my cooking and removing them when they've contributed what I wanted them to—sometimes for the duration of a dish's cooking time, sometimes for two minutes, or for, say, twelve. In this way, I get their heat as a background note without overwhelming other flavors. I also use chile de arbol to make Chile Vinegar (page 348) and many homemade spice blends. Every so often I use chile de arbol flakes—when I want a stronger punch of heat. Even then I'm careful. I only use their crushed or powdered form at the end of cooking—never at the start—so that instead of permeating a whole batch of something, they only infuse the places in which they land. Two chile de arbol yield approximate 1 teaspoon coarse chile flakes when ground in a spice grinder. Keep in mind that when you grind your own fresh, you will likely need less than you would of a store-bought, preground chile flake.

Marash (or Maras) pepper hail from Turkey and are relatively chunky and moist. Marash pepper is spicier than Urfa pepper (below), but more mellow than Aleppo-style pepper or chile de arbol the middle road, if you will.

Piment d'Espelette, named after the village of Espelette in France's Nive Valley, are chiles grown in the Basque region of France and Spain. Their flavor offers hints of stone fruit and sea brine, with a nuanced, subtle heat—it is the most mellow red chile I use (hotter than, say, sweet paprika, but less so than most others). Its powdered form—which I use exclusively—is drier than both Aleppo-style pepper and Urfa pepper, and its flakes are smaller, finer, lighter. I choose it when I seek a delicate touch with chile. It's perhaps the easiest substitute for black pepper in most dishes.

Deep-burgundy *Urfa pepper* comes from its namesake town in southeastern Turkey. These peppers are sundried during the day, tightly bundled at night, then dried in the sun again. The process is repeated for one to two weeks, "curing" the

continued

peppers and intensifying their flavor. Echoing its color, Urfa pepper's flavor has notes of smoke, coffee, and raisin; it has a relatively mild, slow-building heat.

I use chiles so often in my kitchen and throughout this book, it would be impractical to list all relevant recipes below. Instead, I've included a selection that exemplifies their use and highlights their unique characteristics.

COCONUT OIL

Unrefined ("virgin") coconut oil is an impressive food. Its sweet, nutty flavor and tropical aroma easily **impart complexity to cooking**. Its relatively high smoke point means **it can handle frying** foods without denaturing. Because it is solid at room temperature, it is **an easy substitute for other fats in pastries** (just reduce the amount by 15 to 20 percent). Perhaps most strikingly, coconut oil is one of the few significant plant sources of lauric acid, also found in human milk, that enhances brain function and boosts the immune system. Coconut oil is a proven antiviral, antibacterial, and antifungal agent; I take teaspoons as medicine with the first signs of a sinus infection, and massage the healing balm into cuts, scrapes, burns, and blemishes.

COCONUT SUGAR

Coconut sugar is made from the nectar produced by coconut blossoms. The sweet liquid is boiled, reduced to a solid, and ground to create a granular substance with a texture and appearance like a slightly drier, lump-free brown sugar. It is primarily produced in Southeast Asia, where it is used in savory cooking and to create a plethora of desserts. Coconut sugar has a mild caramel, relatively earthy, slightly floral flavor. Surprisingly, it tastes nothing like coconut. It is so much more interesting than white granulated cane sugar.

While it is imperative to remember that sugar is sugar, coconut sugar can be viewed as **a healthy alternative to refined sugar**. On the glycemic index (GI), which tracks how foods affect blood glucose levels, coconut sugar has a lower ranking than cane sugar. Foods with low GI values are digested and metabolized at a slower rate, prompting smaller fluctuations in blood glucose and insulin levels, and reducing sugar highs (and crashes) and risk of disease.

When shopping for coconut sugar, you may see it sold as "coconut palm sugar," which is the same thing. But don't confuse it with "palm sugar," which is the sugar of different varieties of palm trees (such as the date palm). Also important to remember, sugar—in all its forms—has a history of exploitation—both of land and people. So I urge you to seek sustainably harvested coconut sugar by looking for fair-trade and organic brands at grocery stores or online. Once opened, coconut sugar should be kept in an airtight container in a cool, dry place, where it will keep indefinitely.

I use coconut sugar in my everyday cooking to **mellow acidic foods** (such as tomatoes) and **to highlight the natural sugars** in others. It can be used 1:1 **in place of cane sugar in many desserts**. It easily dissolves into syrups, and it creams well into both softened butter and eggs. However, it doesn't create quite the same results with desserts that rely solely on cane sugar to achieve their moisture or structure. It also has a lower burning point than cane sugar. So if you start experimenting outside the recipes in this book, start with baked goods that you know are tender and moisture-rich due to fats, eggs, dairy, and purees (quick breads, chewy cookies, yogurt-rich muffins, and so on), and add to things that you don't mind taking on a light-brown hue.

CORIANDER SEED

I find coriander seed to be one of the more captivating and versatile spices out there. I actually think more of our cooking *deserves* it. It is bright, citrusy, slightly grassy, and wonderfully floral. It befriends most other spices and too many ingredients to provide an exhaustive list here.

COCONUT-BRAISED CHICKEN WITH LIME LEAF, PEANUT, AND CRISPY SHALLOTS 268 • CURRY SPICE BLEND 352 • EASY ROAST DUCK LEGS WITH PRESERVED LEMON AND HONEY 278 • HARISSA 342 • MAKRUT LIME GREEN SAUCE 345 • MOLE SPICE BLEND 353 • OLIVE OIL CAKE WITH ALMOND, CITRUS, AND CORIANDER 303 • SUNFLOWER DUKKAH 356

CRÈME FRAÎCHE

Heavy cream is good. Crème fraîche is better. Fermented to the boundary between complex and funky, it is bright, sweet, and interesting, the signature flavor in the classic dishes of Normandy and Alsace. But crème fraîche is no longer reserved for Francophiles. Similar in both flavor and texture to sour cream, Eastern Europe's smetana, and Latin America's crema mexicana, this is a versatile ingredient that offers a combined umami, acidity, and richness that makes as much sense on a taco as it does inside a tarte flambée.

Crème fraîche is simply cultured cream—that is, heavy cream that has been inoculated with good bacteria and left to ferment at room temperature until thick and slightly sour. It is a superior product, made without stabilizers and additives. You can make your own or buy it from a farmers market, cheese shop, or gourmet grocer. When refrigerated in an airtight container, it typically lasts two to three weeks.

Unlike heavy cream, crème fraîche doesn't curdle when heated. With 30 to 40 percent butterfat, it can be whipped until it holds its shape. Strained overnight in a cheesecloth-lined sieve, it becomes as thick as labneh and can be used in its place, yet it isn't as tangy—it is decidedly more decadent, more buttery than bright. Crème fraîche adds another, discernible dimension to our food.

As a seasoning: Finishing a dish with a small spoonful of crème fraîche can have a big impact. Stir some into your simmering oatmeal, polenta, or any other grain porridge, sweet or savory. The same goes with your soon-to-be-scrambled whisked eggs, pot of soup, and spicy daal. Add it to dips. Use it in place of cream as a final element in any sauce (it is especially good with braised poultry, rabbit, and seafood).

As a dressing or sauce: Crème fraîche can also *be* the sauce. Use it like you would heavy cream or a dairy-based dressing. It is an obvious addition to cold deli salads such as potato, egg, and slaw. And it seems natural to fold a heaping spoonful into still-warm pasta, sautéed mushrooms, or braised "creamed" greens like spinach. Thin crème fraîche with a little water and season it with salt to taste. Drizzle this beautiful, stark-white dressing on raw, crunchy leaves, vegetables (raw or cooked), grains, meat, and seafood.

As a condiment: When it comes to rich, creamy condiments, I prefer crème fraîche to sour cream, whipped cream, and—in some cases—mayonnaise. Swipe it across the bread of your next sandwich, salmon-topped bagel, or grilled cheese (pre-grill). Either whipped or flat, crème fraîche can be dolloped onto, underneath, or alongside eggs, blinis, tacos, stews, eggs, potatoes (mashed, roasted, hashed, latke-ed—all the ways), roasted vegetables, poached fruit, pies, and soups.

In baked goods and sweet treats: Like yogurt, buttermilk, kefir, and sour cream, crème fraîche contributes that bright, compelling complexity that can result only from fermentation. It makes cakes tender, light, and rich, and it can slake the sweetness of anything that depends on sugar. Since I rarely have milk or buttermilk in the house, I thin crème fraîche until it is the consistency I need, and I use it instead of these commonly called-for ingredients (think: cornbread, muffins, pancakes, and so forth). It makes a great glaze when whisked with confectioners' sugar, a pinch of fine sea salt, and fresh lemon juice or water. Blitzed with frozen fruit it creates an almost instant ice cream. And, whipped to soft peaks and sweetened to taste, it can even stand alone as a lovely ending to a big meal.

CURRY LEAF

I was blindsided by my love for fresh curry leaves. I first bought the glossy, hunter-green "sweet neem leaf" without knowing anything about them. I just started playing and quickly found a use for them in every meal I made for a few weeks.

The smell and flavor of fresh curry leaf are incredibly complex—I'm not sure I know of an herb that has more to tell. To my senses, the aroma brings to mind lemongrass, soft sheep's milk cheese, damp earth, Thai basil, and cinnamon; when fried in hot oil, they become nutty in the way popcorn can be, but also pleasantly pungent.

Curry leaves are the aromatic leaves of a tree from the citrus fruit family, and they are not related to curry powder; these two different ingredients are not, in any way, a substitute for each other. Curry leaves can be found in Asian markets, some co-ops or natural food stores, and online. They can be frozen in an airtight container for up to three months; no need to defrost before using in most recipes. Dried leaves have practically none of the qualities that make curry leaves a worthy purchase—go fresh or forgo.

Have fun with curry leaves. Unlike a bay leaf, they are tender and subtle enough to eat, but they can also be removed before serving or while eating. Chop curry leaves with a sharp knife or scissors and **blitz them into dressings, sauces, soups, or sugars. Add them to marinades** (start with olives). Use them to **infuse oils, dairy** (consider the cream for your caramel), **teas, stocks, or various simmering pots** that could use subtle notes of citrus and spice: jams, rice puddings (especially one made with coconut milk), soups of all sorts, braised meats and beans, and so on. Lastly—fantastically—throw curry leaves into hot oil for a few minutes and watch them transform into **a captivating, crispy garnish.**

DATE SYRUP

Date syrup is an exciting sweetener because it isn't merely sweet. Let it dissolve on your tongue and it will reveal an array of aromatics: nuts, toffee, wood, flowers. It is viscous but not sticky. It is tart but balanced in itself. To produce date syrup, dates are heated in water before being blended and strained. The resulting liquid is then reduced to a syrup that retains many of the vitamins and minerals found in the date fruit. Date syrup has so much to offer!

You can **pour date syrup in and on things you typically sweeten** with honey or maple syrup: yogurt, muesli, pancakes and waffles, granola, smoothies, milky tea or coffee, cakes, and cocktails (especially one with bourbon, lemon, and bitters). One of the easiest elegant desserts I know is a small bowl of chilled, lightly whipped labneh crowned with date syrup, ghee-fried pine nuts, and flaky sea salt—so good.

But don't always assign it to the last course. Date syrup is a wonderful addition to savory dishes too. Take your bottle of date syrup and souse your soon-to-be-roasted roots, tubers, and pumpkins—it does good things for **high-heat caramelization**. Use a little—along with salt, fat, and acid, of course—to **season marinades, barbecue sauces, wet rubs, and stews. Spike dressings and vinaigrettes**, especially those destined for spinach, chicories, grains, chicken, lamb, pork, and raw or cooked vegetables. Date syrup's flavor, viscous texture, and mahogany hue make it **a lovely garnish** too. Use a few drops to anoint a hummus-like dip, or, if creamy soups are your thing, add—along with olive oil or some browned butter—a few drops of date syrup to finish.

If you don't have date syrup, honey, pomegranate molasses (page 73) or sorghum can sometimes step in—it depends on the dish, and you'll have to taste and make the call intuitively. If you are going to use honey instead, try a dark variety of honey (such as buckwheat), but consider reducing the amount by as much as half—honey is much sweeter.

DRIED LIME

I have a particular affinity for any ingredient that brightens while also offering considerable complexity: pomegranate molasses, sumac, capers, tamarind, and so forth. Exotic and unexpected, dried limes are a part of this special set of playful alternatives to the old standbys of citrus and vinegar.

Dried limes—also known as limu omani, black lime, Persian lime—hail from the Middle East, where they are commonly used to flavor and balance soups, stews, and rich braises of meat. They are typically brined, boiled, and sun-dried, a process that imparts the fruit with a matte, dimply skin and a musk that's at once earthy, sweet, sour, and pleasantly funky. They are sold both "black" and "white" (really a dusty brown); I prefer the black, but either can be used for the recipes in this book.

Dried limes appear in several forms: whole, pierced, halved, skinned, or powdered. Like coffee, the finer the pieces, the more potent the flavor. If you've never used them before, start by brewing a dried-lime half as a tea and get to know what you're working with. Their citrusy, sultry funk is lovable but strong.

To use them whole, prick dried limes a few times with a knife or metal cake tester and **drop them into sauces, soups, braises, savory porridges, simmering grains and beans, and the like.** When it's time to serve, squeeze them gently of their final juices and discard—they've done their job, infusing the hot liquid with their flavor. Unlike fresh citrus juice, which must be added at the end of cooking to lend its effect, the brightening qualities of dried limes endure throughout and beyond cooking times.

Or employ dried limes in powdered form. Since they begin to lose their volatile oils the moment they are pulverized, it's much better to grind your own and store the powder in an airtight container in a cool, dark cupboard for no more than six months. To grind, cut dried limes in half (a serrated knife is helpful), remove any seeds, and pulverize in a clean coffee grinder until fine (2 to 3 limes yields 2 tablespoons powder). **Use the powder as a solo spice or as a bright, bursty note in blends**. It is a particularly good rub for grilled shrimp, chicken, and flank steak, and I often add a pinch to roasting carrots (page 176) and braising greens (such as spinach, kale, collards, etc.).

DRIED SHRIMP

Dried shrimp are a popular seasoning agent in many cuisines, but they remain a head-scratcher to most Americans. This is unfortunate, because they provide a deep, savory flavor and that special salty minerality that only things of the sea can bring. **Use whole, chopped, or ground** across all categories of savory cuisine.

Dried shrimp are available at Asian markets, sometimes in small plastic packages and sometimes in bulk; you can also order them online. They hail primarily from Thailand, China, and Japan, but Louisiana also continues a multigenerational tradition of sun-drying shrimp. Dried shrimp come in a range of sizes and colors. Look for dried shrimp that are relatively large and orange-pink (but without additives), as paling or blanching and browning are indications of age—and loss of flavor. Whatever kind you buy, store them in an airtight container in the freezer until ready to use.

Dried shrimp are often soaked in warm water to reconstitute before using. Some cooks add this soaking water to a dish for extra flavor, but I prefer to discard it and **brew a fresh shrimp broth,** if needed. Although the little creatures have a pleasantly chewy texture, the main way I use dried shrimp is in powdered form, like **a salty, funky spice.** A spoonful or two can be used to jazz up popcorn, pasta, fried rice, omelets, stir-fries, and a number of salads. When added to soups, stews, and sauces, shrimp powder not only brings a subtle depth of flavor—a "meatiness" or umami akin to anchovies and fish sauce—but also serves **to thicken.**

Once you have shrimp powder around and become familiar with it, it may surprise you how often you reach for it. And intrepid eaters won't even know it's there! They'll just comment on the invisible, I-don't-know-what-the-hell-this-is-but-I-like-it quality as they polish the plate.

DULSE

Sea vegetables are astoundingly nutritious and versatile. Their flavor and texture exist somewhere between land and sea, and—like fungi—there is no substitute for their extraordinary character. Dulse is a red seaweed harvested in the cool waters along the Atlantic coast of North America and the shores of Ireland and Norway. Its fronds grow in tidal areas on rocks, shells, and the larger, longer, brown seaweeds. Ruddy-colored dulse tastes faintly smoky and meaty, especially when briefly seared in hot oil. It can be purchased in tangled leaf form or ground into flakes; the former is good **to tear into salads** or **fry until crisp**, and the latter is what you want to **top salads, garnish grain bowls, or make spice blends**. Dulse does not need to be hydrated before use, but it needs to be cut into small pieces, ground, or fried before use—otherwise it is too chewy.

ROASTED WINTER SQUASH WITH PUMPKIN SEED AND DULSE 173 •
SEAWEED GOMASIO 358 • SPICY SEAWEED GOMASIO 358

FENNEL SEED

Perhaps fennel seed has been familiar enough for long enough that it needn't be called out here. But, much like caraway, I think it has more appeal and a broader range than most think. Yes, it **tastes of licorice**, but it is also **grassy, bright, and floral**. It shines as a member of a spicy and/or aromatic chorus. It harmonizes particularly well as a trio, with coriander seed and cumin; but it also pairs well with turmeric, sumac, rosemary, preserved lemon, makrut lime leaf (really all citrus), and any chile. These flavors temper the anise; the fennel, in turn, complements their qualities. As a solo voice, I generally prefer fennel pollen over the seed, but there are exceptions to this (mostly sweeter things, such as cake or granola, but also tea—it is a wonderful digestive aid).

CANDIED SEEDS 351 • CURRY SPICE BLEND 352 • FROZEN YOGURT 316 • MAKRUT LIME GREEN SAUCE 345 • SPICED LAMB CHOPS WITH BLACK VINEGAR AND HONEY 288 • SWEET-AND-SOUR ELIXIR WITH CHAMOMILE AND GINGER 326

FISH SAUCE

Intoxicating and unique, fish sauce offers a distilled flavor of the sea and quintessential umami. I use it often, but sparingly. Its flavor miraculously transforms foods into better versions of themselves.

A staple in Asian cooking, fish sauce **adds a hit of salt, funk, and intrigue** to anything it touches. Don't be deterred by the pungent aroma; used carefully, its intensity dissolves into a dish. This bottle of liquid amber is a surprisingly versatile condiment that will impress you and anyone for whom you cook.

At the store, you'll probably run into a few different varieties of fish sauce. Vietnamese or Vietnamese-style fish sauce often goes by the name nuoc mam. Red Boat 40°N (40 degrees of nitrogen) is made using only fresh anchovies and salt. It is a pleasantly balanced, slow-fermented fish sauce. If you are only going to have one fish sauce on hand, I suggest you choose this one. Thai fish sauce, such as Squid Brand and Golden Boy, is very good but more pungent than the Vietnamese style. *Nettuno Colatura*, an Italian fish sauce, is aged for months in chestnut-wood barrels, which gives it impressive richness. Not surprisingly, Japan produces some exceptionally mellow, clean-tasting fish sauces—sweet, even. Some fish sauces are created from sardines or shrimp. Some fish sauces are aged in whiskey barrels. And some contain additions such as sugar and seaweed. I know chefs who keep many bottles on hand, and I understand why: it is nice to match relatively loud brands with high-volume dishes. For most of us, one bottle will do.

Fish sauce keeps indefinitely. Applied with a judicious hand, it can make food taste incredible without announcing its presence. Used in this way, **it is essentially liquid salt**.

When at the stove wondering what your sauce, soup, or stew needs to make it pop, ladle a little out into a small bowl and stir in a drop of fish sauce. If you like the effect—you're likely to like it—add a proportionate amount to the whole pot. Do the same for vinaigrettes and salad dressings. Fish sauce can sometimes stand in for anchovies, for instance in bagna cauda or salsa verde.

Surprisingly, fish sauce can also be used in desserts. **Think of it as an extract, like vanilla.** Use it to spike caramel sauce, ice cream, or anything with coconut milk. Just be sure to apply it drop by drop, as you would a flower water.

Note: If you want to make the recipes in this book without fish sauce, just use salt and another umami ingredient that works for you—miso, soy sauce, cheese, coconut vinegar, and so on—bearing in mind that 1 teaspoon fine sea salt provides the salinity of approximately 1 tablespoon fish sauce.

BAGNA CAUDA 341 • BETTER BITTER GREENS 222 • BLACK RICE AND ASPARAGUS WITH MIZUNA AND MINT 250 • CARAMELIZED CABBAGE FOR MANY OCCASIONS 226 • COCONUT-BRAISED CHICKEN WITH LIME LEAF, PEANUT, AND CRISPY SHALLOTS 268 • GREEN EGGS 158 • MAYONNAISE VARIATIONS 339 • NAM JIM 345 • POMELO SALAD WITH TOASTED CHICKPEA FLOUR AND CRISPY SHALLOTS 197 • PORK MEATBALLS WITH RICE FLOUR AND FISH SAUCE 273 • RAW MUSTARD GREENS SALAD WITH TAMARIND DRESSING 185

FLOWERS

Flowers are enormously enjoyable and beautiful, and they add a sense of whimsy to food.

While I am fond of a range of edible fresh florals with a wide spectrum of flavors, I stock only a few dried flowers in my larder—and those will be the focus here. Fresh or dried, always seek edible, pesticide-free blossoms from sources you trust. Look for dried flowers in the bulk or spice section of your natural foods store or high-end grocer. Store dried flowers in an airtight container for up to six months.

Dried fennel pollen's sweet, slightly spicy licorice flavor pairs incredibly well with a wide range of foods. Tiny white and yellow *chamomile flowers* have a perfume reminiscent of hot apple pie. *Hibiscus* tastes sour, astringent, and pleasantly floral; the petals are cooling and incredibly high in antioxidants (evidenced by their purplish-red hue) and vitamin C. Grassy, mild *cornflowers* are a lovely garnish—even dried, they bring an almost electric blue to the plate. *Rose* may be the most alluring of them all; it lends its distinctive floral layer to both sweet and savory dishes.

Steep dried flowers—combined with other ingredients such as herbs and teas, or enjoyed as a singular flavor—and serve hot or cold. **Steep petals in warm heavy cream,** then strain; this rose cream can be used for ganache, truffles, panna cotta, and crème brûlée. Dried flowers **steeped in simple syrup** can be strained, then the syrup used to make jams, sorbets (especially good with strawberry, rhubarb, or raspberry), gelatins and kantens, lemonade, cocktails, and poached fruit. **Add them whole**—like nuts and dried fruit—to "jeweled" pilafs of rice or grains, or soak a spoonful and **puree into sauces and condiments,** such as harissa, almond picada, and romesco. Powdered, dried flowers **add an exotic touch to spice blends,** compound sugars and butters, and homemade tortillas and pastas. Use **as a striking garnish** for dips, salads, and sweet treats.

FLOWER WATERS

Rose and orange, the most widely available flower waters, can **add intrigue and balance** to all sorts of dishes. Sadly, they have a bad reputation, earned, I think, by poor products and heavy-handed use in recipes. I use flower waters from small, family-run businesses that still grow, pick, and produce in traditional ways. I store them in dropper bottles or fine-tipped squeeze bottles and use these waters sparingly. Add a few drops to smoothies and milks, vinaigrettes, condiments (like Harissa, page 342), braising meats, rubs (try rose, cilantro, and lime on a whole grilled fish), caramels, vinaigrettes, cocktails, macerated berries, cakes, and so on. Kept in an airtight jar in a dark cupboard, flower waters keep indefinitely.

BEETS WITH FRESH CHEESE AND ROSE 216 • FROZEN YOGURT 316 • OLIVE OIL CAKE WITH ALMOND AND ORANGE 303 • ORANGE SALAD WITH ALMONDS AND ALEPPO-STYLE PEPPER 197 • POMEGRANATE TEA CAKE WITH ALMOND AND ROSE 303 • RASPBERRIES AND CREAM 315 • RHUBARB AND ROSE LASSI 324 • WATERMELON AND CUCUMBER SALAD WITH FETA AND SUMAC 197

GHEE

Ghee is liquid gold—a premium, pure butterfat with a nutty flavor—that I use daily in my kitchen. It is the result of clarification—a fancy term for simmering until separation occurs—that removes all the moisture, milk solids, and impurities from butter. The absence of milk solids and water makes it shelf stable and gives it a relatively high smoke point (465°F), which means that—unlike butter—it can be used for high-temperature cooking: **pan-frying, sautéing and roasting**. I also use it in **baking** (in any recipe that calls for melted butter or melted coconut oil) and as a **warm dressing**. In my experience, ghee is also gentler on the digestive system.

I often make my own ghee, but if I purchase it, Ancient Organics is my preferred brand. Ghee from goat milk butter has also entered the market and can be used in place of cow's milk ghee in any recipe; it lacks the caramel notes of traditional ghee, but it has a robust grassy, slightly gamey flavor of which I'm quite fond. Ghee keeps for up to six months in the refrigerator, or, if you're careful not to contaminate it with food or moisture, covered at room temperature.

JOB'S TEARS

I generally dislike trends, but there is one for which I'm grateful: the current profusion of and enthusiasm for ancient grains. Shoppers all around the country now have access to quinoa, millet, buckwheat, heirloom wheats (such as farro), and barley. While quinoa—with its slightly bitter edge and crunchy, dense texture—took years to gain in popularity, it seems it was just the gateway grain to an enticing array of ancient edibles.

Job's tears are easy to love. Also known as coix seed, Chinese pearl barley, or *hato mugi* in Japanese—they are plump, chewy, relatively sweet, and pleasantly earthy. Each grain looks a bit like a fat, ivory teardrop. Grown across Asia and in parts of Africa, they have been used there in various forms—whole, ground, brewed, strung as prayer beads—for centuries.

Only available hulled, Job's tears are available in natural food stores, Asian markets and herbal stores, and online. They are often sold as tea, **brewed for their various medicinal qualities**. Job's tears are attributed with boosting immunity, reducing inflammation, clearing indigestion, and resolving urinary problems. When I was pregnant with my son, I learned that it is inadvisable to consume Job's tears during pregnancy and menstruation.

Job's tears cook up plump and juicy, and they aren't as sticky as rice. Unlike other grains, they aren't at all bitter, and they are relatively mild in flavor. Elisabeth Prueitt, of San Francisco's renowned Tartine Bakery, describes them as tasting "like a cross between rice and corn and barley." I think this is a perfect description to keep in mind when deciding how to use them in your kitchen.

I prefer to soak Job's tears overnight prior to cooking—this increases their digestibility and decreases their cooking time. Assume they'll take 35 to 45 minutes to soften when held at a simmer.

Like other whole grains, Job's tears **can stand alone** as the base of a salad, the bulk of a stir-fry, the bed of a vegetable-topped bowl, or the backbone of a meal. Their mellow character means they **play supporting roles** well too: add them to grain blends, such as brown rice and millet; stir some into porridges, soups, and stews (especially those that usually feature rice, hominy, or barley); use them instead of nuts **to garnish** everything from leafy greens to ceviche.

JOB'S TEARS "STONEPOT" WITH CRISPY MUSHROOMS AND JAMMY EGGS 247

KEFIR

Kefir is a creamy fermented dairy product that has been consumed for centuries. Recently, modernized versions of kefir have become increasingly popular due to its probiotic content, which can help balance the gut microbiome and confer other health benefits as well.

Like yogurt and buttermilk, plain kefir is a boon to those who need **quick, healthy sustenance**. And it fares well in dishes both sweet and savory. When cooking with kefir, **think of it more as an acid and less as a dairy or fat**—it isn't as creamy as yogurt and crème fraîche. If you want to step away from my recipes and experiment on your own, start by using it in recipes for which you'd usually reach for buttermilk.

If you can't find plain, full-fat kefir, buttermilk (ideally cultured) or plain, full-fat yogurt thinned with water to the consistency of milk will work in all recipes in this book. Water kefirs cannot be substituted in recipes.

KOMBU

Kombu is briny, vegetal, and herbaceous; it tastes like the ocean in the best possible way. It imparts that special flavor we call "umami." And like all sea vegetables, it is uniquely rich in a broad range of minerals and high in protein. It is also a carminative, which helps ease the digestion of fibrous beans and grains. Like the other umami-rich ingredients in this book, kombu—and other seaweeds—has the ability to **accentuate and elevate the flavor of anything it accompanies.**

Kombu looks like a long strip of greenish-black paper brushed with white dust. It curls a bit at the edges and can easily be snapped into two, three, or four pieces, as needed. It is now widely available, and it can be stored in an airtight container at room temperature. When shopping, don't confuse kombu with shio kombu, a value-added product that is made by boiling kombu in soy sauce, mirin, and sugar before being dried and, often, cut into small pieces. This is a product that can be used for garnishing rice dishes or salads, but it is not a substitute for kombu in the recipes in this book.

The easiest way to employ kombu is as you would a bay leaf, dropping it into a simmering pot of anything for 20 or so minutes, then removing it after it has done its job. It serves **as a salt, carminative, thickener, and profound flavoring agent** (a natural MSG, if you will). It also makes a **stellar stock**, and it can be **powdered** and added to spice blends, smoothies, batters, and so on.

Pictured on pages 54–55.

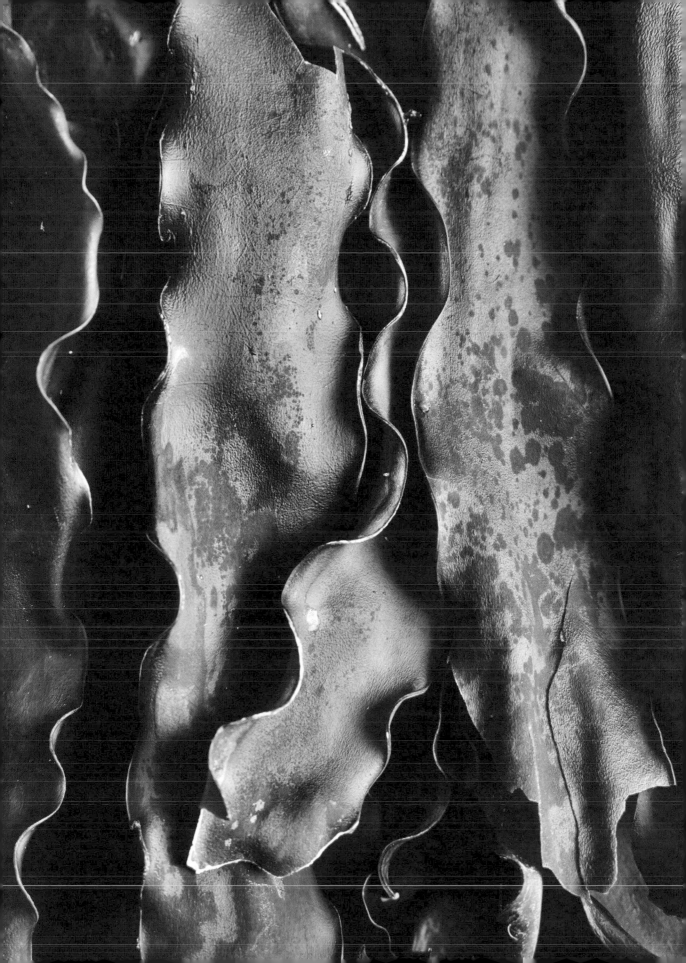

LABNEH

Labneh (or labne) is a fresh, creamy, spreadable yogurt cheese. While eastern Mediterranean in origin, it can travel widely in the kitchen. **Use it as you would yogurt, crème fraîche, and other fresh cheeses** (e.g., ricotta, fromage blanc, etc.). In some instances, it can even stand in for the common cream cheese. See page 336 for directions on making your own.

BEETS WITH FRESH CHEESE AND ROSE 216 • BEETS WITH LABNEH AND CURRY 216 • CARAMELIZED CABBAGE FOR MANY OCCASIONS 226 • FLUFFY BUCKWHEAT PANCAKES 162 • FRIED QUAIL WITH LABNEH AND SPICY SUMAC GOMASIO 275 • HARD-ROASTED WHOLE FISH 256 • MANY WAYS TO SEASON A CHICKEN 264 • MARINATED LABNEH 336 • POACHED EGGS WITH LABNEH AND CHILE 157 • SAVORY CHICKPEA FLOUR PANCAKES 130 • SMASHED PEAS WITH PRESERVED LEMON AND HERB OIL 178 • SPICY ROASTED CARROTS WITH AVOCADO, SPROUTS, AND SUNFLOWER DUKKAH 176 • TOAST SWEET AND SAVORY 150 • WHIPPED LABNEH 335 • YOGURT MAYONNAISE 339

LABNEH: THE TWO-MINUTE MEAL

Whether store-bought or homemade (page 336), labneh is not only an ingredient of many great dishes, it is itself a small meal—a bright and creamy dip that really doesn't need anything more than a drizzle of olive oil and shower of flaky sea salt to satisfy. And if you take a few minutes to give it some extra attention, you'll be rewarded with a substantial snack that seems more like a sumptuous feast. Simply whisk creamy labneh in a mixing or serving bowl with salt to taste (approximately ½ teaspoon fine sea salt for 1 pound labneh) and top it with one of the combinations listed. Serve alongside some raw veg and pita, lavash, or your favorite loaf of bread.

Garlicky Green Hot Sauce (page 345) • Olive oil • Flaky sea salt

Sunflower Dukkah (page 356) • Lemon zest • Olive oil

Sumac-Rose Gomasio (page 357) • Olive oil

Green Za'atar (page 357) • Olive oil

Anchovy Gremolata (page 346) • Olive oil

Blistered Tomatoes with Preserved Lemon (page 201) • Finely chopped cilantro (optional) • Flaky sea salt

Finely diced (⅛-inch) cucumber • Barberries (or currants) • Thinly sliced green onion, minced shallot, or Crispy Shallots (page 350) • Toasted walnuts (or pistachios), finely chopped • Finely chopped mint or parsley (optional) • Dried rose petals, torn or crumbled • Sumac • Olive oil • Flaky sea salt *(Pictured opposite.)*

LARD

Although lard suffered long and hard from a wretched reputation, science redeemed its name. This fine white fat has a neutral flavor and high smoke point, and it is solid but soft at room temperature. The **texture it creates in foods is unmatchable**: pastries are rendered tender and flaky; cookies become mysteriously and pleasantly fluffy; and pan-fried or deep-fried foods are the crispest, most flavorful they can be.

Lard is made by slowly melting down pork fat in a process called "rendering." Lard and leaf lard come from different parts of the body of the pig. Lard is relatively soft, which is why leaf lard—rendered from the firmest fat found exclusively in the loin and kidney area—is generally preferred and fetches a higher price. For pastry doughs, spring for the leaf; for savory cooking, either can be used.

As with olive oil, butter, and really everything, the ingredients and process matter. Purchase lard made from humanely raised hogs and from a producer who doesn't cut the batch with harmful—but cheap and shelf-stable—trans fats. You can buy lard at the supermarket, from your butcher, or online.

MAKRUT LIME LEAF

Makrut (pronounced mah-krut) lime leaf, the leaf of a citrus tree, first captures attention with its shiny, leathery appearance. Investigated further, its abounding, alluring aromatic compounds—distinctly citrus but with a marvelous floral quality that few other familiar fruits possess—convince us to spend more time.

Pictured on pages 62–63.

While named a "lime," makrut lime is actually more closely related to yuzu (page 102). You may see them referred to as kaffir lime leaves, but I recommend avoiding this name, as many consider the term *kaffir* a slur. Makrut lime leaves can be found in Asian markets, farmers markets, and online; as they become more popular, they are starting to show up in grocery stores too. As with curry leaves, dried isn't worth your time or money. Seek out a fresh lot and freeze some for later. They can be frozen in an airtight container for up three months; no need to defrost before using in most recipes. Refrigerated in an airtight container lined with a paper towel or two, they last about two weeks.

Consider using makrut lime leaves anywhere you'd use lemon or lime zest. "One leaf" refers to a single leaf, not an attached duo. For about ½ teaspoon of zest, you'll need about 5 lime leaves; they vary in size, so use your intuition based on your particular lot. Green vegetables, ice cream, poultry, pork, cocktails, seafood, berries, noodles of all kinds—citrus is a widely applied and welcome element, so go a bit on autopilot (while still paying attention) and enjoy the creative impulse. Just take care not to add too much—you want to walk the edge between interesting and intense.

Wash makrut leaves well before using. I dunk mine in a bowl of water and use a kitchen towel to remove water and any clinging dirt. While it isn't an essential step, I usually take the time to bruise the leaves with the flat edge of a knife's blade before use—this helps release the essential oils (which carry the aroma and flavor). The central rib of the leaf is fairly tough, so for dishes in which the leaf is eaten, I recommend removing it before cooking. When shredding, stack and roll three or four leaves lengthwise, then slice as thinly as possible (this is a chiffonade, or "ribbon cut," mentioned often in reference to basil) with a very sharp knife; alternatively, kitchen shears can be used.

Use whole makrut lime leaves to infuse recipes both sweet and savory. Start with something simple: Drop a few torn leaves into a pot of simmering quinoa or rice. You can then discard the leaves and toss the still-warm batch with lime juice or a little vinegar and olive oil or ghee to taste. The makrut lime leaf is gone but the dish has layers of flavor. Much like with bay leaf, add the whole leaf to oils, syrups, cream, puddings, porridges, soups, broths (they're destined for clams and mussels), grains, and even baking sheets or skillets of roasting vegetables or meats (like chile de arbol, the leaf will infuse the fat on the hot pan). When using them in this way, there is no need to remove the stem.

continued

Or chop the leaves (make sure they are completely dry) and grind them in a spice grinder until you have a fine powder. Use it as you might lemon zest, adding a citrusy burst to, say, toasted nuts, grilled vegetables (especially eggplant), falafel batter, chicken rubs, or pasta with seafood.

MIRIN

Mirin is a naturally fermented Japanese rice wine composed of rice, koji, water, and sea salt. Subtly sweet and a little zingy, it **simultaneously accentuates and balances other flavors**. Some mirins are cut with added sweeteners, so read the label before buying. If you can't find it or don't have it, substitute a dry sherry or sweet marsala wine. Dry white wine or rice vinegar will also do, though you'll need to counteract the sourness with about a half teaspoon of sugar for every tablespoon you use.

BIG-BATCH BREAKFAST GREENS 155 •
STEAMED ARTICHOKES WITH KIMIZU 115 • **YUZU PONZU** 342

Miso is more than a soup. Miso is a fermented paste that's made by inoculating cooked and mashed beans (usually soybeans) with shio koji (page 81) that's been cultivated from rice, barley, or other grains and legumes. It's salty, sweet, and earthy and tastes faintly of cheese. It is high in protein, vitamins, minerals, and probiotics. The umami in one small dollop can transform a dish without triggering a "Japanese food" label in the brain. Miso is magical.

Miso is a cultured product that alkalizes the body and aids in digestion and assimilation. It is a complete protein, boasting all eight of the essential amino acids, and it is a rich source of B vitamins. Perhaps because of these health benefits, miso's popularity has soared in recent years. There are now many miso varieties on the American market, such as adzuki bean, barley, chickpea, "red," "yellow," and so on. While it's fun to taste and play with the different bean and grain combinations and aging periods, mellow white miso is the easiest to incorporate throughout your cooking. Made simply with soybeans, salt, water, and a high percentage of koji rice, mellow white miso is fermented for only three months, making it one of the youngest varieties available. Its texture is smooth and supple (whereas barley, for instance, is thick, rough, and sometimes grainy). Use a dollop whenever you want that special sweet, salty, umami hit.

Miso can be stored indefinitely in the refrigerator. It usually needs to be dissolved slightly in about an equal amount of water before being incorporated into a dish; stir the two together in a small bowl to form a smooth paste or slurry.

Use miso **in broths, soups, stews**—really any pot of warm liquid; I include **rice, porridge, polenta, and grains** with that—even a teaspoon will imbue the whole dish with a sweet, umami flavor. If you want to use miso **for its therapeutic properties**, bear in mind that boiling destroys its probiotic nature. And if you want the flavor without any grainy sediment, pass a miso-water slurry through a fine-mesh sieve as you add it to your cooking.

Many recipes—for **dressings, marinades, sauces, spreads, condiments**, and so on—on umami-forward ingredients like fish sauce, anchovies, and dairy. There might be many reasons why we'd prefer a substitute for these, and miso is wonderful choice.

Because it is a live salty ferment (like shio koji), miso can be used **to lightly cure foods**. To cure fish, mix 1 part mirin with 3 parts miso and spread all over lightly salted fish fillets that have been enclosed in two sheets of moistened cheesecloth; marinate 3 days; unwrap the fish and broil until caramelized and cooked through. For more preparations like this, check out Nancy Singleton Hachisu's book, *Preserving the Japanese Way*.

Lastly, miso can be used **in baked goods and other sweet treats.** Depending on which kind you use and how you treat it, miso can provide notes of butterscotch, strawberries (more specifically, strawberries and cream), and, of course, that special salty, nutty, cheesy thing that characterizes it most.

CARAMELIZED CABBAGE FOR MANY OCCASIONS 226 · CHICKEN MISO MEATBALLS 273 · DANDELION AND SWEET PEA SALAD WITH ANCHOVY, CHILE, AND MINT 166 · GREEN BEANS 202 · KOHLRABI SALAD WITH KEFIR AND CARAWAY 186 · MISO BAGNA CAUDA 342 · MISO-MAPLE WALNUTS 137 · MISO SUGAR 358 · OLIVE OIL CAKE WITH APPLES, HAZELNUT, AND MISO SUGAR 303 · RADISHES WITH SPECIAL SAUCE AND HERBS 112 · SPECIAL SAUCE 338 · SWEET TOAST 150

MUSCOVADO

Muscovado is the semirefined (also called "raw") cane sugar of Barbados and Mauritius. Much like regular brown sugar, which is essentially white sugar with some molasses added to it, it is soft and moist with a beautiful caramel hue. However, muscovado's personality has a bit more verve. It boasts dark, smoky, earthy tropical fruit aromas and flavors. And its texture is a bit finer and fluffier. *Light muscovado* is similar in sweetness to commercial dark brown sugar, whereas *dark muscovado* tastes more of molasses (but without a bitter bite).

Muscovado is available online or at gourmet or specialty stores. Store in an airtight container with a tight-fitting lid; if you want to prevent it from clumping or turning hard, add a terracotta sugar saver to the jar.

'NDUJA

'Nduja (pronounced en-DOO-yah or en-DOO-jah, depending on who you ask) is a real cook's cheat. One heaping spoonful of this cured, spreadable salumi lends enough distinction that a dish needs little else. While 'nduja is a specialty of the Calabria region in Italy, where chiles are treasured, a few US companies now produce great versions. Traditionally, this spread was made from cheap, tough cuts and leftover pieces of preserved pork; like all great peasant dishes, the recipe originated from ingenuity and need and resulted in the extraordinary. Many modern producers are preserving family recipes and traditional processes but using heritage pork breeds and other high-quality ingredients.

Pictured on page 340.

Find a good source of 'nduja and then adopt the notion of using meat in a supporting role, **as a flavoring** for other foods. Silky and spreadable, 'nduja is essentially spicy pork butter, and can be used **as a smear** or **as a flavorful fat**.

Because of 'nduja's intensity and loose texture when cooked, it is not a substitute for ground pork. It can, however, be used like its highly flavored, high-fat brethren: chorizo and pancetta. Sauté it as a base for warm dressings, sauces, soups, greens (e.g., kale, collards, cabbage, etc.), eggs, beans, and so on. Make it the foundation of a pasta dish. Spoon some across a platter of roasted pumpkin or crispy potatoes. Stuff a little scoop into wonton wrappers and deep-fry the things; serve with a simple black vinegar dipping sauce (page 18). Shrimp, clams, squid, and octopus are remarkable pairings. Just keep in mind that 'nduja gives off a blast of heat and, unlike chorizo or pancetta, becomes relatively grainy when cooked.

NIGELLA SEED

Nigella—sometimes referred to as black cumin—is an herbaceous plant with delicate periwinkle flowers. It is indigenous to the Mediterranean but grows in many parts of the world. The seeds of the plant are what I'm after: they are tiny and black and proffer a nuttiness and mild onion flavor that I adore. Use them as you would black sesame seeds or other spices of a similar size, texture, and origin (coriander seed, for example)—**in spice blends and condiments, in doughs and batters**, and **as a purposeful garnish** for dishes both raw and cooked. To bring out the most flavor, give the seeds a quick toast in a dry skillet or sizzle them in warm oil or ghee (perhaps with a pinch of chile flakes). Spoon the latter—a quick and versatile sauce—over eggs, daal, labneh, or tzatziki.

BEET BORANI 125 • **HARISSA** 342 •
RAW CARROT SALAD WITH CITRUS AND BLACK SEEDS 189

NORI

Papery, crisp nori is perhaps the most widely known seaweed. **Turn it into chips, crumble on pizza, shower on salads,** and **use as wrappers** for room temperature rice, fish, eggs, and various vegetables. Unlike fellow seaweeds (wakame and kombu, for example), nori sheets don't behave well if overly hydrated. They do, however, gain a lot from a quick toast over an open flame or in a warm oven; if you'd prefer to purchase it already toasted, seek out "yakinori" when shopping.

In **powdered** form, nori can be used to **finish a dish**, much like flaky sea salt. Enlist the feathery, shimmering blackish-green flakes to add instant salinity, umami, nutrition, and color to food. Mix them into blends (nori pairs particularly well with sesame seed, dried chile, flaky salt, fennel seed, and sumac) or sprinkle it directly over softened butter, dips, eggs, salads, rice, noodles, or fish. You can find packages of powdered nori in Japanese stores, natural food stores, and online. To make nori powder, start with toasted nori (see preceding paragraph). Then tear or cut (with sharp scissors; a knife doesn't work well) the sheets into approximately 1- to 2-inch pieces; grind in a coffee grinder or spice mill until they're as fine as you want. Store nori powder as you would whole sheets, in an airtight container in a dry, dark cupboard.

JOB'S TEARS "STONEPOT" WITH CRISPY MUSHROOMS AND JAMMY EGGS 247 • LITTLE GEM SALAD WITH LEMON AND [NORI] 181 • PISTACHIO DIP WITH BURNT ONION AND SEAWEED 124 • POPCORN WITH NORI, CITRUS, AND ROSEMARY 141 • RADISHES WITH YOGURT AND SEAWEED 112 • RICE PORRIDGE WITH ALL THE THINGS 270 • SEAWEED GOMASIO 358 • SEAWEED POWDER 351 • SPICY SEAWEED GOMASIO 358

POMEGRANATE MOLASSES

Pomegranate molasses is one of the great secret ingredients—much as soy sauce was for chefs starting in the 1960s, and fish sauce is in recent years. This luscious, ruby-hued syrup is sweet, fruity, and faintly sour. It can be that thing that makes people ask, "Why is this so delicious?"

Gorgeous, punchy, and full-bodied, there are many uses for pomegranate molasses. First try it **as a finishing touch**; it is viscous and a little sticky but falls freely from the tip of a spoon. Drizzle it directly over a dish that needs the contrast—grilled meats and seafood are classic choices, but creamy dips, caramelized winter squash, hearty grain salads, bitter greens, and crispy cruciferous vegetables are also good candidates. Then use it **in sauces and stews**—start, perhaps, with the romano bean recipe in this book (Slow-Cooked Romano Beans with Tomato and Pomegranate Molasses, page 219), then use a small spoonful to add a clever wink to your standard pasta sauce, beef and tomato stew, or oven-glazed root vegetables. **Stir it into vinaigrettes** (try it on tomatoes instead of balsamic) **and marinades** (perfect for chicken, lamb, and dense, oily fish such as swordfish, tuna, and sardines). **Desserts** are an obvious match. Basically: Anything that suffers from doldrums likely requests a little acid, and that acid could be pomegranate molasses.

When experimenting with pomegranate molasses, keep the following suggestions in mind: It adds a lot of color; this isn't a problem for any of the examples mentioned above, but I'd avoid adding it to white things such as parsnips, artichokes, mushrooms, or potatoes. It really balances brawny, bitter, earthy, and deeply savory things. But if the ingredient in need of acid is lean and already sprightly and sweet—asparagus, peas, avocado, and lobster, to name a few—then reach for a gentler brightening agent such as vinegar or citrus. Lastly, while pomegranate molasses can't stand as the sole sweetener in pastries, it does work well as part of a duo; use it in combination with sugar, and its fruitiness and slight tang will add incredible dimension.

Try to steer clear of brands that use artificial sweeteners or colors—the ingredients on a good bottle will read "pomegranate juice" and nothing else. You can certainly make your own. Pomegranates are in season in the autumn months, and 1 pomegranate yields 1 to 2 tablespoons of molasses. You can juice the pomegranate by hand or with a potato ricer, or you can purchase fresh juice from any number of sources. Use a nonreactive pot that is almost twice as tall as the amount of juice you are using (so it doesn't boil over or spatter the entire area), and simmer over medium heat until it looks syrupy on the back of a spoon. While I keep store-bought molasses in the cupboard, homemade batches reside in the fridge.

PRESERVED LEMONS

With these burnished-yellow, soft, and funky fruits at your disposal, you can add character to almost any dish that desires it. In fact, while the bright punch of fresh lemon juice and the citrus flavor of the raw rind are invaluable, I could argue that the fermentation process renders lemon amenable to even more dishes. During their time in a salt-packed crock, the tartness mellows while the other natural flavors of lemon come forward. Preserved lemons imply citrus but taste and behave entirely different than anything fresh. And they are capable of making a distinctive impact without announcing themselves.

Preserved lemons can be used whole, halved, or finely chopped. Always taste a bite of the rind and consider the intensity of your particular batch and the effect you're after before you use them. Depending on their age, preserved lemons can be mellow or robustly funky. To use **as a topping or accent**, gently rinse and then finely chop or julienne the rind—these tiny cubes or slivers will add bursts of acidity, saltiness, and pungency to dishes both raw and cooked. Think grain dishes and green salads, seafood of all kinds, pastas, eggs, sautéed vegetables, roasted potatoes, fresh cheeses, and even sandwiches. As with chile flakes, adding the chopped rind at the beginning of cooking will permeate the whole dish and thus every bite; when used at the end or off the heat, its flavor is only imparted when the rind itself is eaten. If you're looking for an even greater contribution, drop in the rind of a half or whole preserved lemon at the start of **a soup, stew, or sauce**, or add it to a blender with lemon juice and olive oil for **dressings and marinades.**

Most people will tell you to stay away from the flesh and juice, which pick up a significant amount of salt in the preserving process. While I mostly use the rind and pith, I have found that the flesh and the leftover brine have their place in the kitchen too. A teaspoon of brine makes dressings, purees (e.g., smoky eggplant baba ganoush, cauliflower, labneh, etc.), soups, and sauces more complex. I have wrapped the flesh, along with cilantro stems and fennel fronds, in a cheesecloth bundle and added it to a pot of simmering beans or braising meat.

Preserving lemons (or limes, kumquats—virtually any citrus) is one of the easiest home fermentation projects. Split and salt-packed lemons are pressed deep into a crock or jar. Overnight, the salt extracts lemon juice and the juice dissolves the salt—together they form a brine. While brining for a month or more, the flavor of the lemon shifts. Two months is the minimum time for the skins of most lemons to soften all the way through, but I have left mine fermenting for a year or more, yielding a darker and more intense flavor. Once they've reached their end state, they can be kept for a year in the refrigerator (as long as they are sealed, remain covered in brine, and are extracted using clean utensils or hands). I prefer using Lisbon lemons, but all varieties make a fine product. If you are making your own, just be sure to seek out unwaxed, preferably organic lemons.

PUFFED RICE, QUINOA, AND MILLET

Puffed rice, grains, and seeds—such as quinoa, millet, and amaranth—are intriguing and fun. As they pop between your teeth, they feel and taste like neither seed nor nut. Alone or mixed with spices, they elevate anything they touch by adding a toasty, grassy, pleasantly bitter flavor, a striking appearance, and a fresh, exciting texture. Use them **in a chorus of crunch** (e.g., granola, dukkah, party mix, "power" bars, etc.) or **to contrast soft foods**, such as ceviche, avocado, steamed rice, and caramelized pumpkin. Scatter them across creamy dips and spreads. Pile them onto yogurt or ice cream. Treat them like dry cereal, served cold, or as an instant porridge: add boiling water and/or warm milk to cover and stir with ground flax, a pinch of salt, and a little something sweet (e.g., dried fruit, coconut sugar, date syrup, etc.).

RICE FLOUR

Rice flour's neutral flavor, pale color, and starchy character make it an invaluable ingredient **for gluten-free baking**. I also use it **to thicken** porridges both sweet and savory and to create **batters for fried foods**.

Regular white rice flour is milled from rice with the bran and germ removed; it is available in fine, superfine, or coarse grinds (as is brown, below). I use fine white rice flour exclusively because it is easy to source; it hydrates relatively slowly, so I usually let batters sit before cooking or baking.

Brown rice flour behaves a lot like white rice flour but adds a toasty, nutty flavor and a brown hue to finished dishes. I use it occasionally, often in combination with white, but it definitely needs time to hydrate and can sometimes come off gritty.

Flour made from Japanese sweet, sticky rice is called *mochiko flour*, *sweet rice flour*, or *glutinous rice flour*. While it is gluten-free, it has the effect of mimicking gluten, giving baked goods a pleasantly chewy texture. It can be found in the Asian aisle of most supermarkets and online. Look for Koda Farms Blue Star brand.

SEA SALT

Sea salt is concentrated ocean, crystallized minerals and beneficial trace elements (including iodine), and an animator of all food. We now have access to an array of sea salts from all over the world, and each is unique in its texture, color, and flavor—great for those who don't like the one-note brashness of processed "table" salt. At home I use exclusively fine French grey "Celtic" sea salt that I buy in bulk from a local co-op market; to my palate, it is the best, but I admit it took some practice to adapt to its texture, flavor, and consistency (it is relatively wet and thus clumps a bit). For recipe testing, I used La Baleine fine sea salt because the first restaurant that trained me to taste used it, and it should measure like most fine sea salts on the market. I use the more affordable Diamond Crystal kosher salt for large brining projects, pasta water, and salt baking. And I garnish with flaky salts from Maldon and Jacobsen, as well as various brands of delicately crunchy fleur de sel.

I call for sea salt in virtually every recipe in this book.

SCHMALTZ

Schmaltz—or rendered poultry fat—is a fun word and an ingredient full of potential. Typically associated with chicken (it is also made with duck and goose) and with foods of the Ashkenazi Jewish tradition—matzo balls, chopped liver, and the like—schmaltz is one of the most versatile fats at our disposable. Milder than duck fat but much tastier than lard, chicken fat's flavor can only be described as fried chicken. It gives a savory verve to food.

Schmaltz can be purchased from butchers, local farmers, and specialty grocers; refrigerate in an airtight container for up to three months, or freeze for up to six. You can also render your own using store-bought fat (often sold in the freezer section of butcher shops) or the trimmings from a raw bird. Always save the chicken fat that's the end product of cooking; this won't be as pure as the stuff from the shelf, and it will expire within a week or so, but it is essentially free liquid gold. Simply skim the fat off stock or chicken soup. Or cook a salted chicken on the stove or in an oven, and when it is done, transfer the bird to a cutting board or platter, and assess the situation. If you don't have an ingredient ready to hit the pan—a glut of greens (Baby Bok Choy "Under a Brick," page 220), leftover rice (Fried Rice, page 253), bread to toast, or parboiled potatoes, use a flexible spatula to scrape and squirrel away every last viscous drop. After a night in the fridge, the fat gets spooned off the top of the jus (which is essentially chicken-stock concentrate—use it too) and stored separately. Treasuring this fat is an old and thrifty tradition that I enjoy maintaining. And my cooking is better for it.

Schmaltz has a relatively high smoke point (375°F). **Pan-frying, roasting,** and **sautéing** are obvious ways to use up a crock of the stuff. But you can also use it **in place of butter or lard** in savory batters for things such as quick breads, biscuits, and tamales, or as the base of a **warm vinaigrette.** Pop popcorn, make confit, fry grains, bake beans, spike mashed potatoes. Stir it into soups or savory porridges (congee, risotto, polenta, etc.). It is delicious, even, as a toast topping.

BABY BOK CHOY "UNDER A BRICK" 220 • BLACK VINEGAR CHICKEN 263 • CHICKEN-FAT FRIED RICE 253 • CHICKEN MISO MEATBALLS 273 • MANY WAYS TO SEASON A CHICKEN 264 • SAVORY TOAST 150

SHIO KOJI

Shio koji, or "salt koji," is inoculated rice combined with water and salt that's left to ferment. It is sold in the refrigerated section of Asian supermarkets in three forms: whole (rice porridge–like), pureed, or liquid. All these forms are useful—buy whichever looks good and sounds exciting, making sure the ingredients list includes nothing more than rice koji, salt, and water. You can also make shio koji at home. It's a fun project, but it takes time. Luckily store-bought shio koji tends to be of high quality. If you see the lesser-known and lesser-available ama koji, that works too—it is koji and water fermented without the addition of salt; this allows you to adjust the salt and sweetness to your liking.

If your shio koji isn't already a smooth puree, blitz it in the blender before refrigerating it in an airtight container. Stored this way, the shio koji keeps for up to six months, and it's ready to go whenever you need to steal some personality for the plate. Rub it on meats and seafood, whip it into your eggs, stir it into soups and sauces, add a dollop to salad dressing. Just keep in mind three things. First, as it sits on or in a thing—say, a steak or a vat of hummus—it will alter the texture and flavor of it dramatically. This can be beneficial and beautiful—a chicken that bathes in shio koji for twelve to twenty-four hours cooks up exceptionally juicy, with an enticing bronze glow and a nutty, sweet flavor; its aroma calls to mind the burnt edges of a gratin or baked mac and cheese. Second, it is salty, and you need to reduce the amount of salt you use or omit it altogether. And third, because of the natural sugars in both the rice and the food, browning happens a lot faster than usual. This speedy caramelization does good things to fast-cooking baby brussels sprouts but can lead to a blackened roast chicken if you're not careful. Depending on the dish, you may need to lower the heat or tent or cover, and you definitely need to keep a closer eye on things.

To learn to use shio koji intuitively, look at it **as a liquid seasoning agent** that provides salinity, sweetness, and umami. Begin by stirring a little into still-warm rice or grains (fluffy or porridge-like)—taste and note the difference. Then drop a dash into vinaigrettes to balance their acidity and fat, or make shio koji puree the backbone of a dressing that's both creamy *and* light—without a jar of mayo or buttermilk in sight. Whisk it into wet batters (such as those for tempura, waffles, etc.), soon-to-be scrambled eggs, and even your smoothies (it is live cultures, after all). Play around. Just be sure to adjust your salt use accordingly.

Once you feel confident, start slathering. Use shio koji puree **in place of salt, miso, or soy sauce** in marinades and wet rubs for vegetables, fish, and meat—use just enough to coat (for a 3½-pound chicken, this is about ¼ cup; use the same amount for four 4-ounce fish fillets; eyeball it for vegetables, as you would oil). Vegetables need only a quick toss before hitting the heat; too much time hanging with shio koji will result in pickles (see next paragraph). When allowed to act on meat, it has the effect of dry-aging, breaking down the connective tissue and ridding the meat of moisture. And with fish it creates a slight quick-cure and,

continued

consequently, relatively tender fillets—a boon for those of us who routinely fear overcooking or underseasoning seafood. For all foods, a bath in shio koji results in a rich, sweet, umami-imbued, brown butter–like nuttiness.

Lastly, shio koji can also serve **as a fermentation and pickling medium:** Thinly slice 6 to 8 ounces radishes, cucumbers, turnips, and the like; toss and massage them with a few tablespoons of pureed shio koji, then transfer them to an airtight container. After an overnight sit in the refrigerator, you have pickles—no rinsing necessary.

MANY WAYS TO SEASON A CHICKEN 264 • **RICE PORRIDGE WITH ALL THE THINGS** 270 •
SHIO KOJI-ROASTED BRUSSELS SPROUTS 229

SHISO

Shiso is a member of the mint family. Its flavor is relatively subdued, but menthol is obvious, as are hints of cinnamon and clove. It's a little spicy, pleasantly bitter, and tastes like freshness itself. Baby shiso sprouts (pictured here) are sometimes available, but usually what you'll find are large leaves—either green or purple—with slightly crisp, serrated leaves. Shiso is beautiful. It is accessible. And it can be used in ways no other herb can.

Shiso is cultivated, imported year-round, and increasingly easy to track down—check your nearby Asian grocer. (Korean, Vietnamese, Chinese, and Japanese populations all use shiso or a close relative, such as perilla, sometimes sold as "sesame leaves.") If you are looking for domestically produced shiso, check farmers markets in your area during the summer, and even consider making a request to a few folks or consider growing your own. I've been told that it's a low-maintenance annual that does well in containers or in the ground with lots of light. Use the leaves fresh, as even the most pungent varieties lose much of their aroma when dried. Store a stack of leaves sandwiched between paper towels in an airtight container in the refrigerator until ready to use. If you need to remove dust or dirt from the shiso leaves, rather than submerging them in water, wipe with a slightly damp kitchen towel right before use.

Shiso is typically associated with Japanese salt-pickled plums known as umeboshi (page 95) or the garnish on a sushi plate. But we should consider it whenever we might reach for basil or mint: thinly sliced or coarsely chopped **as an aromatic herb**; **muddled** into cocktails; **brewed** as tea; **steeped** in sugar syrup, cream, or coconut milk for drinks, jams, and all sorts of sweet treats.

Moreover, shiso's size begs for roles that mint can't fill: **as an edible base or wrapper** in place of nori for sashimi and sushi-like preps; like grape leaves for wrapping fish for the grill; or like lettuce leaves in Thai cooking, for gathering larb, meatballs, and the like. It can even be used **as a vegetable**, tempura-ed in a delicate rice flour batter and served with sprinkle of flaky salt and chile.

SUMAC

"The kebab spice" is how sumac was once described to me. Indeed, this burgundy-hued spice is used to season grilled meats and their accompanying salads with its royal color and nuanced tang. But what a small box for such a tremendous spice! Think of sumac, instead, as powdered lemon, only without its searing bite. Truly: **It can be used with practically everything.**

Sumac spice is the ground fried berry from the plant of the same name. I've tried purchasing whole berries and grinding my own, but the hardness of the berries varies between brands and varieties, and some are downright impossible to even chip. I recommend buying ground sumac from a company with high turnover. Also know that, like all ingredients, there is variability and a range of quality. One of my favorite spice companies—Burlap & Barrel—sumac that, instead of being dried and ground, is chopped and preserved in salt—it is coarse, moist, deeply flavorful, and seasoned with a touch of salt (and equitably sourced, to boot). Store ground sumac in a dark, dry place in an airtight container. Use it within approximately six months, which shouldn't be a problem.

TAHINI

Over the past few years, our view of tahini has widened dramatically. It's a great example of a once-exotic ingredient becoming a kitchen staple. Even black tahini is making its way onto shopping lists; made from unhulled black sesame seeds that have been toasted and ground, it is a little more intense than the blond stuff and a bit stickier too. Both products can be used in **dressings, smoothies, soups, sauces, spreads, and desserts**. They can even **replace fat** (such as butter) in some baking and pastry recipes. Keep using tahini in traditional ways—as a sauce, in hummus and other dips, and so forth. But then think of all the places you can imagine peanut butter and put it there too (it might require a bit more salt and/or sweetness). Tahini **adds richness, creates heft,** and **contributes a deeply savory, toasty flavor.**

Tahini should taste fresh; if there is a hint of astringency and sourness— a telltale sign of rancidity—discard that jar. I prefer Soom or Seed + Mill tahini when I need a traditional, all-purpose white sesame paste. I've also made my own, with good results. Store tahini in a cool, dark cupboard in an airtight container. If you don't think you'll see the bottom of the jar within a few months, it's best to stick it in the fridge. Always stir tahini well before using.

TAMARIND

Pictured on page 6.

Tangy, sweet-and-sour tamarind is a tropical fruit that tastes of molasses and dates. In fact, its name (of Persian origin) means "date of India." In the places in which it is grown—primarily Mexico, India, Thailand, Myanmar, and several countries in Africa—it is used as a souring agent, just like lemon is employed in Western cuisine. A relative of peas, it grows in curved, oblong pods that look like overgrown peanuts. Each pod is filled with brown seeds surrounded by fibrous, fruity pulp. As these pods mature, the pulp dehydrates into a delicious sticky paste ("sweet" or "sour" on the package is an indication of how long the fruit was left to ripen). This tangy pulp is what I'm after, but the seeds, flowers, and leaves of the tamarind tree can be used as well.

Most Indian, Middle Eastern, and Mexican grocery stores carry tamarind in various forms. Tamarind pulp contains large seeds that must be removed by hand or strained after a simmer, so value-added convenience products that allow you to bypass this step are everywhere. If convenience is a high priority, purchase tamarind paste. But I recommend you avoid concentrates, as they lack the fruitiness of fresh pulp. If you want to experiment with whole fruit, see the next paragraph for instructions on how to extract the pulp. Otherwise, blocks—"wet" or "dry"; "sweet" or "sour"—are good purchases. For your reference: 2 tablespoons homemade tamarind juice is equivalent to 2½ to 3 tablespoons tamarind paste or 2 teaspoons syrupy concentrate diluted with an equal measure of water.

If using whole fruit: Rinse tamarind pods. Bring 2 quarts water to a boil in a medium pot; add pods. Reduce heat to medium-low and simmer, covered, until just tender and the water is brown, about 15 minutes. Strain water through a fine-mesh sieve into a 3-quart pitcher. Remove and discard skin from each pod. Using your hands, place as much pulp as possible from the softened fruit in a blender, discarding the seeds and fibers. To the blender, add 2 cups of the strained tamarind liquid and a pinch of salt; purée until smooth. Strain purée back through the sieve into an airtight container and refrigerate for up to 1 week.

To seed the pulp from a block: Place it in a heatproof nonreactive bowl and cover with boiling water; cover and let sit for about 1 hour, or until the pulp is hot. Use a potato masher or clean hands to massage and squeeze the block into mush. Strain through a fine-mesh sieve (or a colander lined with cheesecloth) suspended over a large measuring cup or medium bowl, pressing on the pulp to extract as much liquid as possible. Discard the seeds and other solids; refrigerate the tamarind juice in an airtight container for up to 1 week.

Use tamarind as you would lemon, keeping in mind its flavor is darker and sweeter. Perk things up with a few drops or a drizzle: dips, sauces (especially those tomato- or chile-based), beans and lentils, soups, stews, drinks, and dressings—everything benefits from a sour element. Tamarind's sugar content makes it particularly adept at **glazing**; use it to marinate and lacquer roasting vegetables (especially eggplant, summer squash, and pumpkin) and grilled meats or seafood.

CARAMELIZED CABBAGE FOR MANY OCCASIONS 226 · COCONUT-BRAISED CHICKEN WITH LIME LEAF, PEANUT, AND CRISPY SHALLOTS 268 · FRIED RICE WITH CURRY LEAVES AND TAMARIND 253 · RAW MUSTARD GREENS SALAD WITH TAMARIND DRESSING 185 · RED LENTIL HUMMUS 125

TURMERIC

Turmeric has started showing up in some dressy dishes, but underneath all that posh attire it's just an earthy rhizome. Long associated almost exclusively with its role as an essential enhancer to Indian curry, turmeric is now **an all-purpose spice**.

Grate a little fresh turmeric—which looks like a glossier, orange-hued, often skinnier gingerroot—and it will smell like a blend of carrots, sweet citrus, flowers, and ginger. Dried turmeric, on the other hand, lacks a lot of that bloom, putting forward instead a uniquely musky, pleasantly bitter flavor. Both fresh and dried are incredible sources of beta-carotene and curcumin (an antioxidant with anti-inflammatory properties) and are said to strengthen the immune and digestive systems. If turmeric's flavor and health benefits aren't enough, it saturates food with the most brilliant saffron-gold hue.

Turmeric is most commonly sold in a dried and powdered form, usually in the spice section of the grocery store. Fresh turmeric is available from specialty grocers; store and use it as you would fresh ginger (in lieu of peeling, I scrub the thin skin in a bowl of water). There are different varieties of turmeric available. *Alleppey turmeric*, for instance, is darker than *Madras turmeric* and has a deeply earthy flavor; *Pragati turmeric* is an heirloom variety known for its special flavor and especially high curcumin content. Any variety can be used in the recipes in this book—just try to purchase from a place with high turnover, as the unique, nuanced flavors disappear over time. Fresh turmeric is less potent than dried, and you may need to use four to five times as much to get the desired effect. With either form, a brief sauté in a little warm fat does good things for both flavor and nutrition—just don't let it burn.

Like any spice, turmeric can be added to sizzling aromatics, quickly dusted over soon-to-be-cooked meats and vegetables, and incorporated into various spice blends, sauces, and vinaigrettes. Although cooks use turmeric primarily in savory cooking, it bends just as easily toward the sweet side. Try fresh or dried in tonics, drinks, baked goods, ice creams, pastry, breads, and the like.

Fresh or dried and ground, turmeric will stain just about anything. Lemon juice, white vinegar, and bleach can help remove stains from hands, countertops, and dishes, but you must act quickly and will likely need to repeat the cleaning process a few times. Cornstarch and baking soda can help draw oily yellow food stains out of fabric, but again, prompt soaking, dabbing, and laundering are key.

UMEBOSHI

Umeboshi (often shortened to just "ume") are a seasoning agent but also an ancient medicine. They alkalize the blood, eliminate lactic acid, and are antibiotic. They are *the* best cure for a hangover, whether from alcohol or sugar.

To make umeboshi, ume—a plum- and apricot-like stone fruit—are harvested while still tart, covered with salt, weighted, and fermented with shiso leaves (page 84), which give them their vibrant magenta hue. Umeboshi "vinegar" is the leftover brine—the salt and the fruit juice it drew out during the fermentation process.

To purchase umeboshi, check out the selection at your local co-op market or Japanese grocer, if you have one. You can also find many good brands online, and there are a few new American brands hitting the markets too. Not all umeboshi are created equal, so read labels before purchasing. Avoid any that contain red dye, sugar, corn syrup, or sugar substitutes such as aspartame. Refrigerated in an airtight container, they can be stored for several years.

Umeboshi are traditionally eaten with rice, and this is a very good way to enjoy them. In fact, for the first few days after my baby was delivered, I primarily ate rice porridge topped with umeboshi paste, and I'm fairly certain it sped my recovery. When I'm feeling well, I like to use them in less austere applications— bright, sharp, faintly fruity, salty, and soft, they are a very versatile condiment.

Start by pitting and mincing the flesh. Use this mulberry-hued paste **to season your everyday cooking**, reducing some of the salt and vinegar you'd otherwise add.

As a condiment, minced ume can add almost creamy pockets of a unique salty, jaw-tingling acidity to salads, stir-fries, sandwiches and toasts, grains, and rice (see Ume Rice "Salad," page 255). Or a dash can be dissolved **in sauces, soups, stews, and braises**. When whisking up **dressings, brines, and marinades**, keep in mind that a little ume paste or ume vinegar can take the place of salt; decrease or omit the other acid component (lemon, vinegar, etc.) entirely. In fact, ume vinegar can stand in for other fruit and wine vinegars in many scenarios. I'm particularly fond of sousing green onion that's been set aside for finishing a dish; after five to fifteen minutes (while I work on something else), I have a quick pickle—the sharp edges of the onion have dulled, and it tastes remarkable. It's often these small, quick, routine moves that transform our cooking and make it our own.

PLUM AND CUCUMBER SALAD WITH UME AND SHISO 197 • **RICE PORRIDGE WITH ALL THE THINGS** 270 • **SAVORY TOAST** 150 • **UME BUTTER** 343 • **UME DRESSING** 335 • **UME-GLAZED PORK RIBS** 283 • **UME HERB SAUCE** 345 • **UME RICE SALAD** 255 • **UME TONIC** 329

VERJUS

Also known as "verjuice," verjus (vair-ZHOO) is the pressed juice of unripened sour grapes. It has been used for centuries in European and Middle Eastern cooking **as an alternative to light vinegars or lemon juice**. It can be red (made from either purely red grapes or a red-white mix) or white (made from white grapes). While acidic, verjus has an effect that is gentler than that of vinegar. And unlike wine, it is not fermented and therefore nonalcoholic.

When shopping for red or white verjus, know that bottles from different brands will vary greatly in taste (like wines). Once opened, verjus will keep, recorked, in the refrigerator for three to four months.

Use verjus as you would use wine, vinegar, or, in some cases, citrus juice. Whereas fresh citrus juice will only add a kick at the end of cooking, verjus is a mellow, fruity, slightly sour, snappy liquid that will brighten a dish from the start. It can be used for **seasoning, poaching, braising, deglazing, brining, marinating, and dressing**. If you need a vinaigrette with a lot character but a mild acidity (perhaps the salad contains slices of Asian pear, apple, or grapes—all of which contribute a lot of zing), reach for verjus and replace the vinegar or citrus component entirely. It's safest to pair red verjus with red meats and white verjus with poultry and seafood, but there are surely exceptions to this. If you like to make pickles, use white verjus in place of half the vinegar in your favorite recipe. As you'll see in my dessert recipes (see "Sweet Treats," starting on page 295), I believe acid is essential to balancing sugar. Verjus's tartness, subtle sweetness, and mellow character make it a good candidate, and it is especially good with pears, figs, and quince. Lastly, consider verjus's cocktail potential; whether you mix it with spirits or keep it simple with soda water and a touch of simple syrup, this is one bottle you'll want to add to your bar.

WALNUT OIL

Nut oils are my main splurge. They are a luxury—absolutely unnecessary yet so very pleasing. Just a teaspoon transforms a finished dish—balancing, accentuating, elevating. The first restaurant I worked in used them regularly, and I guess I just got hooked. Of all the nut and seed oils, toasted walnut oil is perhaps the most available, affordable, and easy to use. It is at home in salads, of course, and also on fish, meat, vegetables, pasta, porridges, desserts, or a cheese plate. It is delicate and pale in color, with a rich nutty taste.

I've tasted remarkable oils from France—and if you stumble upon those from Jean-Marc Montegottero, consider forking out the cash—but there are also other wonderful producers using traditional methods that sell for less. Many use English walnuts—washed, sorted, dried, and shelled—to make their toasted walnut oil. The kernels are ground and slowly toasted to perfection in cast-iron kettles. The resulting warm paste is pressed, lightly filtered, and bottled.

Don't cook with walnut oil. Rather, use it as you would a fine extra-virgin olive oil. Its rustic, full-bodied flavor makes for remarkable **dressings and vinaigrettes**—blended with olive oil or on its own—and it is particularly well-suited for nutty whole grains like farro and bitter greens such as radicchio, endive, and dandelion. It can also be used **as a finishing element**; scatter a few drops over soups, roasted or grilled vegetables, beans and lentils, pasta, cheese and yogurt, and even ice cream. Basically: Anything that would taste good with toasted walnuts will taste even better with a little walnut oil.

WHEAT (HEIRLOOM)

We are so fortunate that more farms and mills are focusing their efforts on heirloom varieties of wheat. These cultivars have so much more personality than your typical hybridized modern wheat. There's a caramel sweetness, nuttiness, herbaceousness, minerality, and, for some, a smokiness. They're rich. They taste more like grain. And some may find these ancient wheats are easier to digest too. When baking, all-purpose flour is typically one-dimensional in both flavor and texture. I wrest a more complex character by combining it with a whole heirloom wheat flour or replacing it altogether with a combination of rice flour and various ground grains, nuts, and seeds (buckwheat, almond, etc.). Both whole wheat berries and wheat flour keep best when stored in an airtight container in a cool, dry place.

Einkorn, Emmer, Farro, Spelt

These terms all refer to a fairly similar product. They are all nutty, flavorful, nutritional powerhouses. And as flours, because they are lower in protein than more common all-purpose flour, they are softer and result in doughs and batters with a lighter, more tender texture and a warmer, more interesting flavor.

The common ancestor of all wheat is einkorn, which might also be *farro piccolo* (Italian for "little farro"). Spelt is *farro grande* ("big farro"), and emmer is *farro medio* ("medium farro"). Farro, I'm sure you've gathered, is Italian, whereas the other terms are used—sometimes interchangeably—by everyone else. I love these grains simmered whole; they are almost impossible to overcook—you are aiming for an al dente cushion-like resistance in each berry. All of these wheats can be ground and simmered like corn to make polenta. As flours, they have a nutty, complex flavor that's sweeter and lighter than whole wheat. Substitute farro, spelt, emmer, or einkorn flour for whole wheat flour in any recipe, but combine with all-purpose or bread flour for structure, as their gluten isn't as strong.

White Sonora Wheat

White Sonora is a beautiful, naturally white heritage wheat, one of the oldest in North America. It is available in whole berry form or ground. As a flour, it is prized for its pale golden color, elastic gluten, and mellow but rich flavor. It makes a fine all-purpose flour when combined with hard red spring wheat (you can mix your own or purchase a blend). White Sonora is my preferred grain when making flatbreads, flour tortillas, pitas, and pancakes.

CARAMELIZED CABBAGE FOR MANY OCCASIONS 226 • [WHEAT BERRY] "STONEPOT" WITH CRISPY MUSHROOMS AND JAMMY EGGS 247 • LEMON-TURMERIC COOKIES 306 • MEATBALLS WITH DRIED LIME AND CHILE 273 • RED, WHITE, AND RYE CHOCOLATE CHIP COOKIES 308 • SPICED LAMB MEATBALLS 273 • SUMMER SALAD WITH WHEAT BERRIES, FETA, AND HERBS 245 • WHOLE GRAIN PORRIDGE WITH BONITO AND SHOYU 145

WHEY

Acid whey is the oft-discarded cloudy, watery liquid left behind after straining yogurts and fresh cheeses (labneh, ricotta, etc.). While that description certainly isn't selling it, this by-product is actually a precious ingredient. It has a slightly fizzy quality, a bright acidity, and a mild pungency reminiscent of cheese. Like tamarind and pomegranate molasses, it is an acid with layers of flavor. It can **balance richness, tenderize meats, culture foods and drinks, help breads and baked goods rise** (really: try using it instead of water—all or some—in *any* baking recipe), and **enhance the flavor and nutrition of the cooking medium for numerous foods** (grains, beans, stews, and eggs, to name just four). Whey is full of protein, probiotics, vitamins, and minerals.

When you are ready to experiment, try adding a tablespoon or two to your scrambled eggs, smoothies, and batters both sweet and savory. Use it as a medium (instead of water) for braising brisket or poaching eggs; later, stir a little into the evening's soup, stew, risotto, polenta, braised beans—you get the idea—before tossing what's left into the pot where tomorrow's wheat berries soak (see Summer Salad with Wheat Berries, Feta and Herbs, page 245). It's so satisfying when such a small act has such a big impact! You may soon find yourself seeking excuses to make Labneh (page 336) just to yield more whey.

A POT OF CHICKPEAS 240 • **POACHED EGGS WITH LABNEH AND CHILE** 157 •
SAVORY CHICKPEA FLOUR PANCAKES 130

YOGURT

Though yogurt has long been a popular snack, many home cooks have yet to venture far beyond their prepackaged fruit-on-the-bottoms to explore its full potential.

Like kefir (page 52) and crème fraîche (page 32), yogurt's pleasant sourness is balanced by its fat and natural sugars, and its creaminess creates happy eaters. It's essentially a complete ingredient that needs little to achieve perfection. It needn't be considered a diet food or a clumsy substitute for something richer. Yogurt is full of merit.

Many of my recipes call for plain, full-fat *Greek yogurt*, which is thicker and denser than *regular full-fat yogurt* (I don't even consider the low-fat stuff), making it easier to incorporate into dips, spreads, sauces, and the like. If you have only regular yogurt on hand, you can create Greek yogurt by straining it overnight. The whey that remains is useful too (see Whey, page 99).

When purchasing yogurts for cooking or baking, opt for those that are plain, full-fat, and made without added thickeners or stabilizers. Yogurt doesn't perish as quickly as many other dairy products, and I often ignore expiration dates and rely on my eyes and taste buds instead. If you see mold on the surface of your yogurt (or labneh or whey), discard the entire container. Unlike cheese, the mold on yogurt can't simply be cut away—its relatively high moisture content increases the likelihood that the mold has spread and grown.

Greek yogurt is **a great base for dips, spreads, and sauces**—in fact, yogurt *is* a sauce! (Try tossing 1 cup Greek yogurt with ½ pound al dente pasta and a little pasta water to loosen things up—once seasoned with salt to taste and off the heat, shower with Crispy Shallots (page 350)). Yogurt can be used **in or as dressings, condiments, and marinades, stirred into soups and stews** (off the heat, or it separates), or **incorporated into sweet treats**. In fact, I think yogurt is a baker's beacon. It adds complexity (like a long-fermented sourdough starter would for a bread), an essential tang (you'll notice I use a form of acid in every dessert recipe included), moisture, and the acid required for the swelling and rising of many treats. Baking is the one area in which I use regular yogurt more often than Greek—I actually want the extra moisture it has. I often use yogurt in place of milk, buttermilk, or kefir in recipes; it's a 1:1 ratio, as long as it's thinned with water to mimic the texture of whatever is swapped out.

YUZU

Pictured on page 360.

Because of its mysterious flavor, amazing aroma, and subtle tang, yuzu is a favorite of chefs worldwide. Appearing as a perfectly round, rough-skinned lemon a little larger than a golf ball, yuzu is actually a hybrid of a primitive citrus called ichang papeda and a sour mandarin orange. It originated in China but is most widely cultivated in Japan, where slivers of its rind are used to accent cooked vegetables, mushrooms, fish, and noodles; its zest and juice enhance soy sauces, miso toppings, ponzu sauces, and vinegars.

Yuzu is now grown domestically, primarily in California. Green yuzu is available August through the end of October, and the yellow fruits—sweeter and more aromatic—are available in November and December. I buy a bushel when I spot them and then preserve what I can't use right away. Decide if you want to dry some zest before you cut or juice your yuzu. If so, peel long, wide strips with a Y-peeler, scatter them on a parchment-lined baking sheet, and let them air-dry for a few days. This process can be used with any citrus (seek unwaxed, ideally organic fruit). Dried citrus rind is a warm, aromatic, slightly bitter ingredient that can be added whole (like a bay leaf) to simmering or roasting dishes; pulverized with salt and then used with anything; or added to spice blends, teas, and desserts. Freeze any juice (1 yuzu yields approximately 1 tablespoon juice) you can't use within a few days; in an airtight container, it keeps for up to three months.

Bottled pasteurized juice is also available for purchase, but even the most posh and popular brands lack the aromatic qualities of freshly squeezed. Ditto for freeze-dried rind and yuzu products, such as ponzu and yuzu kosho. I'm not saying to avoid these completely but rather the volatile compounds that make fresh yuzu unparalleled are missing. Some of the brands I tested taste more like soda water than yuzu—a little salty, metallic, slightly bitter. I'd rather reach for freshly squeezed Meyer lemon juice or, depending on the recipe, use a combination of grapefruit, lime, orange, and lemon.

Use yuzu as you would other citrus, keeping in mind that as an acid, it isn't as sharp as lemon or lime; yuzu is clearly sour, but it makes us salivate more than it makes us pucker. Also, its flavor and fragrance—of both its rind and flesh—are more powerful; it has a unique honeysuckle quality I adore.

YUZU KOSHO can be used much like your favorite hot sauce. Made with yuzu peel, green or red chile, and salt, it imbues dishes with a citrusy, floral heat. In addition to vinaigrettes—the easiest employment—**try using it sparingly in marinades, grain and rice dishes, stews, and pasta** (especially with clams!). If you make your own (page 343), it is unlikely to be quite as concentrated as the stuff in the tiny lime green jar from the store; taste either batch before following a recipe or your whims—often a dab will do you.

RECIPES

Snacks, Starters
+ Small Meals

"DEVILED" EGGS ON SHISO

Shiso offers the home cook something other herbs don't: a gorgeous wrapper or bed for some other food. Here, a single leaf is topped with a dollop of mayo, half a boiled egg with a barely-set center, and a dash of Spicy Seaweed Gomasio. Whether you invite friends for dinner or just drinks, they're going to come hungry. Instead of that prototypical platter of classic deviled eggs, pigs in a blanket (which I admit I love), or cheese and crackers, serve these.

Tip—If you need to remove dust or dirt from the shiso leaves, rather than submerging them in water, wipe with a slightly damp kitchen towel; let dry before proceeding.

4 TO 6 SERVINGS

24 large green shiso leaves (see headnote)

¼ cup plus 2 tablespoons plain mayonnaise, store-bought or homemade (page 338)

Six 7½-minute Soft-Centered Eggs (page 144), peeled and quartered lengthwise

2 to 3 teaspoons Spicy Seaweed Gomasio (page 358) or store-bought togarashi

Flaky sea salt

Lay the shiso leaves out on a large, flat platter (or divided among a few), making sure there is at least 1 inch or so of space between them. Fill a piping bag fitted with a no. 12 tip—alternatively, use a teaspoon—and top each shiso leaf with about ¾ teaspoon mayonnaise. Place an egg quarter on top (I like to place it slightly off-center, so eaters are inclined to fold it like a taco; see photo). Finish the eggs with a dusting of the gomasio and a pinch of salt.

CHARRED CUCUMBER AND SHISO QUICK PICKLES

Charring cucumbers may seem like an odd move, but it is a quick way to make the familiar interesting again. They retain their refreshing quality—with additional brightness from the vinegar—but they become a shade darker, more savory in flavor, and almost meaty in texture.

**4 TO 6 SERVINGS
(AS A SIDE DISH)**

1 to 1¼ pounds Persian cucumbers (approximately 5 small)

1 to 2 tablespoons neutral vegetable oil (such as cold-pressed rice bran oil or grapeseed oil)

Fine sea salt

1 tablespoon vinegar (rice wine, white wine, champagne, or red wine)

½ cup (loosely packed) shiso sprouts, or 6–8 shiso leaves cut into 1-inch squares

Halve the cucumbers lengthwise and then again, crosswise. Set a 12- or 14-inch heavy-bottomed skillet, preferably cast iron, over high heat and add the oil. Swirl the oil around the pan until no bald spots remain. Place the cucumbers in the skillet cut side down and char 4 to 5 minutes (you may have to do this in batches so as to not overcrowd your skillet; add more oil between batches if the skillet seems dry). Transfer the cucumbers to a rimmed plate or baking sheet and sprinkle with salt and vinegar. Let cool to room temperature. Taste, and add more salt, if needed. Toss gently and then shower on shiso sprouts or shiso leaves. Stack in small serving bowls.

FIVE WAYS TO DRESS A RADISH

Radishes are my favorite app and snack. And they need only three things to taste excellent: acid, fat, and salt. These elements can come together quite simply: cultured butter and flaky salt are a classic accompaniment to a plate of cleaned and trimmed radishes and a loaf of bread. When I'm in the mood for something slightly more composed, these shaved salad-like preparations are my go-to.

Any type of radish will work in the variations; use one or slice up a mix. If you have access to a variety—red, watermelon, French Breakfast, daikon, black Spanish, etc.—it's fun to pair colors: pink radishes with sumac; green daikon with green za'atar; black radish with Seaweed Gomasio.

4 TO 6 SERVINGS

RADISHES WITH SPECIAL SAUCE AND HERBS

½ pound radishes

Fine sea salt

1 lemon

¼ cup Special Sauce (page 338) or crème fraîche

⅔ cup torn or coarsely chopped dill, chervil, and/or tarragon

1 tablespoon finely chopped chives (optional)

Olive oil, to serve

Flaky sea salt

RADISHES WITH CRÈME FRAÎCHE AND SUMAC-ROSE GOMASIO

½ pound radishes

Fine sea salt

¼ cup crème fraîche

1 tablespoon Sumac-Rose Gomasio (page 357)

Olive oil, to serve

Flaky sea salt

RADISHES WITH YOGURT AND SEAWEED
(Pictured on page 113.)

½ pound radishes

Fine sea salt

1 lemon

¼ cup plain, full-fat Greek yogurt or ¼ cup crème fraîche

⅛ teaspoon Seaweed Powder (page 351) or nori powder, store-bought or homemade (page 71)

Fresh chervil, to serve (optional)

Olive oil, to serve

Flaky sea salt

continued

Five Ways to Dress a Radish,
continued

RADISHES WITH YOGURT AND GREEN ZA'ATAR

½ pound radishes

Fine sea salt

¼ cup plain, full-fat Greek yogurt or
¼ cup crème fraîche

½ teaspoon Green Za'atar (page 357)
or store-bought za'atar

Olive oil, to serve

Flaky sea salt

RADISHES WITH WALNUT OIL

½ pound radishes

Fine sea salt

1 lemon

¼ cup plus 1 tablespoon
Walnut Dressing (page 335)

⅔ cup torn or coarsely chopped
dill, celery leaves, or purslane

Edible flowers (optional)

Flaky sea salt

If you want to peel your radishes, do so—I usually just scrub them with a wet kitchen towel. With a mandoline or a sharp knife, slice the radishes as thin as possible. On your cutting board, sprinkle lightly with fine salt and toss to combine. If using lemon, use a Microplane to grate the zest of approximately half on top; toss once more.

Arrange the radish slices on a platter or divide between (4 to 6) shallow bowls or plates. If using crème fraîche or yogurt, thin with water until it is a drizzable consistency—it should remain thick but fall effortlessly from the tip of an inverted spoon. Spoon dressing (yogurt, crème fraîche, Special Sauce (page 338), or walnut) generously over the sliced radishes. Scatter remaining toppings (gomasio, za'atar, herbs, and so on) evenly across the top. Drizzle with a little more olive oil, if you'd like. Sprinkle with flaky sea salt. Serve immediately. (Radishes release water as they sit in salt.)

STEAMED ARTICHOKES WITH KIMIZU

Kimizu is akin to savory, smoky sabayon (or zabaione/zabaglione)—a sauce traditionally made with wine, egg yolks, and sugar. Kimizu contains dashi and vinegar instead of wine, and mirin acts to sweeten it slightly. I finish my version with fresh lemon juice, which lightens the intensity of the dashi and creates a softer effect than rice vinegar alone. The result is an airy, rich, briny, subtly sweet, and slightly smoky sauce. Here I pair it with steamed artichokes, but it is a fine accompaniment to all seafood (see Crispy-Skinned Fish with Preserved Lemon and Herb Oil, page 258), asparagus, boiled leeks (page 235), radishes, and any grilled vegetables. It does take focus and finesse to get right, so read through the instructions completely before you begin.

4 TO 6 SERVINGS

FOR THE ARTICHOKES

4 large artichokes
(approximately
2½ to 3 pounds)

1 teaspoon fine sea salt

**FOR THE KIMIZU
(MAKES APPROXIMATELY
1½ CUPS)**

4 egg yolks (from medium
or large eggs)

6 tablespoons Dashi
(page 346)

2 teaspoons mirin

1 teaspoon unseasoned
rice vinegar

½ teaspoon fine sea salt

½ teaspoon lemon juice

Bring 1 inch of water to a boil over high heat in a large pot or saucepan. Place a small rack or steaming basket in the bottom of the pot.

Using a serrated knife, cut off the stems of the artichokes so that they sit flat. Cut off the top third of the artichokes. Using kitchen shears, trim the pointed tops from the leaves. Transfer the artichokes to the saucepan and sprinkle with salt; cover and steam over medium-high heat until tender, 30 to 40 minutes, depending on the size of your artichokes.

Meanwhile, make the kimizu. Bring 1 to 2 inches of water to a simmer in a shallow saucepan. Fill a large bowl with cold water and ice and set near the stove. Have a spatula, whisk, and folded kitchen towel (or pot holder) nearby. Grab a stainless steel bowl that rests easily on top of the saucepan without touching the surface of the water. Put the egg yolks in the bowl; whisk in the dashi, mirin, rice vinegar, and salt. Place the bowl over the pan of simmering water, making sure the bottom of the bowl doesn't touch the water (this is a double boiler, and it creates the conditions for gentle heating, thereby preventing the eggs from coagulating too quickly).

Stir continuously with a spatula for 2 to 3 minutes—or until the moment the mixture shows the first signs thickening (it is a subtle shift—the waves created by the spatula will slow slightly). Quickly

continued

return to the whisk, whisking vigorously and continuously. The mixture will begin to froth and expand in the bowl. Make sure the water in the saucepan never gets above a simmer. Continue whisking until the kimizu is thick and ribbony and at least doubled in volume, 3 to 4 minutes more. If at any point your eggs begin to curdle or cook, stop and strain the mixture into another bowl (discard cooked eggs) and return to cooking. If you need to slow things down, halt cooking by submerging the base of the kimizu bowl in the ice bath; continue whisking until the sauce is cool and return to the heat when you're ready.

When frothy and light—and doubled in volume—submerge the base of the kimizu bowl in the ice bath; continue whisking until the sauce is cool. Whisk in the lemon juice. Serve the kimizu immediately or refrigerate for later use (it will lose some but not all its volume): press plastic wrap directly on the surface (this prevents a skin from a forming; you can also skip this step and just skim the skin off the top before serving) and refrigerate for up to 2 days. Temper kimizu at room temperature for 20 to 30 minutes before serving.

Using tongs, transfer the artichokes to plates. Serve with the kimizu alongside for dipping.

FRIED SHISHITOS WITH DANCING BONITO

When tiny shishito peppers are in season, I fry them (or Padróns) almost daily. While they are delicious with nothing more than a shower in salt and lemon zest, bonito's smoky depth stands up strong against the rich, spicy peppers and presents a show at the table: the residual heat makes the crinkly shavings dance.

**APPROXIMATELY
4 SERVINGS**

¼ cup olive oil

1 pound shishito or
Padrón peppers

Fine sea salt

1 small lemon or yuzu

½ cup (loosely packed)
bonito flakes

Preheat oven to 250°F. Line a rimmed baking sheet with parchment paper. Once the oven is hot, heat 2 tablespoons olive oil in a 12- or 14-inch skillet over high heat; tilt and swirl until no bald spots remain. Add half of the peppers; cook, tossing occasionally with tongs, until skins are blistered and flesh is softened, about 3 minutes. It's important not to overcrowd the pan, so work in two skillets, or fry in two batches. If working in two batches, place the still-hot peppers on the baking sheet and transfer to the oven. Repeat the frying process with the remaining peppers, adding more oil, as needed.

Transfer the first batch back to the skillet, season all the peppers with 2 pinches of salt. Use a Microplane to grate the zest of the lemon (or yuzu) on top; gently toss once more. Taste, and add more salt, if needed. Plan to serve in the still-hot skillet, or transfer peppers to a platter or shallow bowl. Shower evenly with the bonito flakes and serve immediately.

CUCUMBERS WITH CRÈME FRAÎCHE AND CRISPY CAPERS

This refreshing dish can be made with any cucumbers, but a mix is ideal. Persian cucumbers are my favorite. Although their name implies import, they are cultivated across the world, and I see them at many local grocery stores and farmers markets. They are thin-skinned and lack almost all bitterness—I never peel or seed them. They are also relatively small and narrow, and they contain less water than other varieties, making them ideal for just about any preparation.

If your cucumbers are relatively skinny and small, consider using a roll cut (also known as an oblique cut) to create two angled sides (see photo). Cucumbers are more visually striking this way. Regardless of how you cut the cucumbers, don't dress them more than 20 minutes before serving—they go from crisp to soggy when held too long.

4 TO 6 SERVINGS

1 cup crème fraîche

2 pounds cucumbers (ideally a mix of varietals such as Persian, lemon, painted serpent, and Mexican sour gherkin)

Fine sea salt

2 trimmed green onions, white and light-green parts, thinly sliced

1 teaspoon lemon juice

1 teaspoon Banyuls vinegar or other red wine vinegar

2 tablespoons olive oil

3 to 4 tablespoons Crispy Capers (page 348)

¼ cup (loosely packed) torn or coarsely chopped fresh dill

Pinch of dill pollen from flowering dill (optional)

Flaky sea salt, to serve

Spoon the crème fraîche into a shallow pool on the base of a serving platter (or divide among salad plates or shallow bowls). Halve the cucumbers lengthwise and slice into ½-inch pieces. Or if you want to try the roll cut, position your knife at a 45-degree angle to the cucumber. Make a diagonal cut at one end, then roll the cuke a quarter to a third of the way toward you. Keeping your knife at the same angle, make another diagonal cut—the piece should now look like owl eyes. Continue rolling and cutting until you reach the end.

If you have found Mexican sour gherkins, keep the smallest ones whole and halve the others lengthwise.

Place all the cucumbers in a large bowl and season generously with fine sea salt. Add the onions, lemon juice, Banyuls, and olive oil; toss to coat. Taste and adjust seasoning.

Add the cucumbers to the top of the crème fraîche, letting the cucumbers tumble from your hands into a fairly even but haphazard layer. Drizzle some of the remaining vinaigrette all over. Just before serving, sprinkle with the capers and dill; dust with the dill pollen (if using) and flaky sea salt. Serve immediately.

DIPS AND SPREADS

Snacking is an essential activity of the modern, busy lifestyle, and dips—as well as the small meals they inspire—come together quickly.

Make one of the following recipes or use the modern larder to put a spin on recipes already in your repertoire. For instance, hummus can be spruced up with a spoonful of brine from preserved lemons, a pinch of powdered dried lime, or a dollop of plain, full-fat Greek yogurt. While it doesn't need more than a drizzle of olive oil, you might also consider garnishing the bowl with Fried Pine Nuts (page 190) or Spicy Sumac Gomasio (page 357). Make this a meal by going beyond the typical pairing of pita and serving the hummus alongside other small plates, such as fruit salad (see The New Fruit Salad, page 196), Charred Cucumber and Shiso Quick Pickles (page 111), and Eggplant Fritters with Chickpea Flour and Date Syrup (page 126).

I think of dips and spreads as basically interchangeable, and any of these dips can serve as a creamy element for a sandwich or as the bed for a side dish or main course; Yogurt with Kale, Fried Shallots, and Crispy Curry Leaves, for instance, can be a bed for grilled smoky lamb chops (reserve crispy toppings for the meat) or a side for a simple roast-chicken-and-rice dinner. I've included a few suggestions for each dip in the chart as well.

4 TO 6 SERVINGS

Pulse ingredients (see recipes on pages 124–25) in a food processor until desired consistency is reached (when making a smooth puree, it is often a good idea to add and pulse dry and cooked ingredients first before adding wet ingredients in a steady stream while the machine is running); then add water, as needed. Depending on the ingredients you're using and your food processor, it may take a few seconds or up to 4 minutes to get something smooth, fluffy, and light. Coarse purees are often done in a few pulses, or they can be made entirely by hand.

Season to taste with salt, acid (lemon, lime, vinegar, and so on), and oil. Scrape into a shallow serving bowl and use the back of a spoon to carve a few swirls into the dip. Garnish with recommended toppings or nothing at all. Dips can be made 3 days ahead; cover and chill. Most are best if brought to room temperature before serving. Serve on toast or crostini, alongside bread, pita, lavash, or crackers, and/or with one of the serving suggestions.

continued

DIP	BLACK LENTIL HUMMUS *(Pictured on page 123.)*	PISTACHIO DIP WITH BURNT ONION AND SEAWEED	YOGURT WITH KALE, FRIED SHALLOT, AND CRISPY CURRY LEAVES
INGREDIENTS	1 cup cooked Black Lentils (page 161), drained if needed ¼ cup tahini 3 cloves black garlic, chopped 2 to 3 tablespoons lemon juice Fine sea salt ¼ cup plus 1 tablespoon olive oil, plus more to serve	6 sheets toasted nori (page 71), cut (with scissors) into 1- to 2-inch pieces 3 green onions, pan-fried until charred and coarsely chopped ¾ cup coarsely chopped fresh mint ¾ cup coarsely chopped cilantro or flat-leaf parsley 1 cup toasted pistachios ¾ cup toasted pumpkin seeds 1 teaspoon Chile Vinegar (page 348, optional) 2 to 3 tablespoons lemon juice Fine sea salt 1 cup olive oil	8 ounces kale, sautéed (leftovers are great) and coarsely chopped into roughly ½-inch pieces ¼ cup Crispy Shallots (page 350), coarsely chopped 3 cups plain, full-fat Greek yogurt 1 tablespoon lime juice Fine sea salt 2 tablespoons Curry Leaf Oil (page 351) 2 tablespoons Shallot Oil (page 350)
CONSISTENCY	Thick and smooth—like hummus	Thick and coarse—pulse until finely chopped and combined	Thick and coarse—stir to combine (no food processor needed)
TOPPING(S) (OPTIONAL)	Seaweed Gomasio (page 358) or toasted black sesame seeds Olive oil	Olive oil Toasted pistachios and/or pumpkin seeds, coarsely chopped Cilantro, whole leaves and tender stems Lemon zest	Crispy Curry Leaves and Curry Leaf Oil (pages 350 & 351) Crispy Shallots (page 350), crumbled Aleppo-style pepper (or other chile flakes)
A FEW SUGGESTIONS FOR SERVING AND PAIRING	Raw radishes, cucumber, carrot, or fennel Roasted pumpkin Sautéed broccoli rabe Feta Eggs Black rice	Raw radishes or cucumber Buckwheat crepes Eggs Fish (fresh, smoked, or tinned) Lamb Sautéed broccoli rabe	Savory Chickpea Flour Pancakes (page 130) Eggs Any simply seasoned meat or seafood Rice, farro

PEA AND YUZU KOSHO DIP	RED LENTIL HUMMUS	BEET BORANI
2 cups shelled fresh peas (approximately 2 pounds of pods) or thawed frozen peas, cooked until tender (3 minutes for fresh; 1 minute for frozen)	2 cups cooked red lentils, drained if needed	2 large or 3 medium beets (approximately 1 pound), cooked and peeled
1 tablespoon yuzu kosho, store-bought or homemade (page 343)	Fine sea salt	1 stalk green garlic (white and light-green parts), finely chopped; or one small clove of garlic, minced
¼ cup coarsely chopped fresh mint	⅓ cup tahini	
	2 teaspoons date syrup	¾ cup plain, full-fat Greek yogurt or sheep's milk yogurt
2 tablespoons thinly sliced chives, plus more to serve	2 to 3 tablespoons tamarind paste (page 90) (or lime juice, or a mix)	½ teaspoon red wine vinegar
Fine sea salt	¼ cup olive oil	1 teaspoon fine sea salt
¼ cup olive oil		¼ cup olive oil
Thick and coarse—pulse until finely chopped and combined	Thick and smooth— like hummus	Thick and smooth— like hummus
Olive oil	Olive oil or Spiced Ghee (page 161)	1 teaspoon toasted caraway, nigella seeds, or poppy seeds
Thinly sliced chive and/or baby mint leaves	Flaky sea salt	Olive oil
Toasted sesame seeds		Fresh dill
Aleppo-style pepper (or other chile flakes)		
Raw radishes	Roasted vegetables, such as pumpkin, carrots, cauliflower	Little Gem lettuce
Little Gem lettuce		Kalamata olives
Feta	Eggs, any way	Eggs
Kalamata olives	Fish (fresh, smoked, or tinned)	Fish (fresh, smoked, or tinned)
Chicken or lamb	Lamb	Lamb, beef, chicken
All seafood	Rice, farro	Rice, farro, quinoa
Rice, farro		

EGGPLANT FRITTERS WITH CHICKPEA FLOUR AND DATE SYRUP

Rarely do I desire to deep-fry at home. But occasionally the mood descends fast and deep, and I generally spring for some sort of fritter—for instance, salted cod and potato fritters with aioli; crispy cardoons with fish sauce, lemon, and chile; or batter-dipped vegetables. But these eggplant fritters are perhaps the easiest, not to mention the most unusual, in my repertoire. You may doubt the pairing of eggplant and date syrup, but I assure you, the deeply savory, slightly bitter vegetable has a true affinity for bright and sticky-sweet things, and date syrup is both. I recommend using the relatively small varieties of eggplant, such as Japanese, Chinese, or (my favorite) Listada, since they are less bitter and don't require pre-salting.

4 TO 6 SERVINGS

Neutral vegetable oil (such as cold-pressed rice bran oil or grapeseed oil) for deep-frying

4 to 6 small to medium eggplants (approximately 1½ pounds, see headnote)

Fine sea salt

½ cup chickpea flour

¼ teaspoon baking soda

¾ cup sparkling water

4 to 6 lemon wedges

¼ cup date syrup or honey

Flaky sea salt

Preheat oven to 250°F. Heat a 1-inch depth of the oil in a large, high-sided saucepan; the wider your pan the faster you'll fry up an entire batch, but the more oil you'll use. Grab a thermometer that can track temperature at least as high as 365°F. Have a spider or slotted spoon ready to go. Whatever dish you will be serving the eggplant on, have that nearby too, along with all ingredients. Line a rimmed baking sheet with parchment and top it with a cooling rack, if you have one (it will help keep the eggplant extra crispy, but it isn't essential). When deep-frying, it is especially important to be prepared before you even light the flame.

Slice the eggplant into ¼-inch-thick rounds and season with fine sea salt on both sides. Meanwhile, in a medium mixing bowl, use a whisk to mix the chickpea flour, baking soda, and ¼ teaspoon fine sea salt; make a well in the center and slowly whisk in ¾ cup sparkling water. Once combined, decide whether or not you need more water—the thinner the batter, the thinner the coating on your eggplant. I like mine on the thicker side for this, but you can go as thin as the consistency of pancake batter.

When the oil reaches 355°F, dip the eggplant in the batter, making sure each slice is lightly covered, tapping the side of the bowl with your hand to release any extra batter, and gently place one piece at a time into the hot oil (use long-handled tongs, if you are uncomfortable using your hands). Continue to batter and gently drop eggplant slices until you have one uncrowded even layer of eggplant in the oil. Fry until golden brown on one side, 1 to 2 minutes, then give it a flip. Use a spider or slotted spoon to transfer the eggplant slices to the rack; immediately shower them lightly in fine sea salt, then keep warm in the oven while you fry the rest, making sure the oil returns to frying temperature between batches. As soon as the last slice is seasoned with fine sea salt, season the slices with a squeeze of lemon and a light drizzle of date syrup. Serve immediately with extra date syrup, lemon slices, and flaky sea salt on the table.

EASY PUMPKIN DUMPLINGS WITH BLACK VINEGAR AND PARMESAN

These dumplings pack sweet, salty, tangy, and umami into a single bite. Piney rosemary is a new but amiable friend to black vinegar. Along with the richness of ghee and heat of chile de arbol, they heighten and contrast the sweetness of the pumpkin. Simple, good food.

4 TO 6 SERVINGS

FILLING

½ small pumpkin (12 ounces), such as red kuri, Hokkaido, kabocha, or butternut, seeds and strings removed; or 1 cup unsweetened canned pumpkin puree

1 egg yolk (from a medium or large egg), lightly beaten (reserve white for dumpling below)

¼ teaspoon fine sea salt

DUMPLINGS

36 round or square wonton wrappers

1 egg white

¼ cup plus 1 tablespoon ghee

Scant ¼ cup (loosely packed) rosemary or sage leaves

1 chile de arbol, thinly sliced

Flaky sea salt

1 teaspoon black vinegar (such as Chinkiang)

4 ounces Parmigiano-Reggiano

To make the filling, preheat oven to 400°F. Place the pumpkin directly on a baking sheet, cut side down, and roast until tender when pierced with the tip of a knife, 30 to 45 minutes. When the pumpkin is cool enough to handle, scrape the flesh from the peel, transfer to a food processor, and process until smooth. Transfer 1 cup pumpkin puree to a bowl; save the rest for soup, pie, or savory porridge. Add the egg yolk and fine sea salt. Cover the filling and refrigerate until ready to use (can be made 3 days in advance).

Bring a large pot of salted water to a boil. Arrange 18 wonton wrappers on a work surface or baking sheet lined with parchment or wax paper. Brush all edges lightly with egg white. Place 1 heaping teaspoon pumpkin filling in the center of each (be careful not to overfill or the filling can escape while they cook). Top each with another wrapper, lining up the corners as you work and gently pressing edges to seal completely.

Boil the dumplings in salted water until just tender, 3 to 4 minutes. Meanwhile, in a 10- or 12-inch skillet or sauté pan, melt the ghee with the rosemary leaves and half of the chile de arbol over medium heat. Once the rosemary starts to crisp, remove the pan from the heat until the dumplings are ready for their transfer.

Use a spider to transfer the dumplings from the boiling water directly to the rosemary-and-chile-infused ghee. Add 2 tablespoons dumpling cooking liquid and the vinegar; *gently* toss to coat.

Place 1 ravioli in a small bowl and taste. Adjust the whole batch to suit your palate: add flaky sea salt, vinegar, and/or sliced chile. Right before serving, use a Microplane to shower each serving with cheese.

SAVORY CHICKPEA FLOUR PANCAKES

Pictured on pages 132–133.

Flatter than a fritter, denser than your typical flapjack, and deeply savory, these exceptionally good and filling pancakes are made with ease from the pantry. If you're looking to pack more vegetables into your (or your kids') snack, you can add almost anything, as long as it is tender—a great use for leftovers or fridge-cleans—and I've included some ideas here. These sturdy pancakes love toppings, and there is a list of those here as well.

Tips—If you want to make these without dairy, omit the whey and use unsweetened almond milk, oat milk, coconut milk—or even water. Just add 1 tablespoon of fresh lemon or lime juice to the mix, since they need an acid component. Also, I generally try to avoid plastic wrap. If you plan to refrigerate the batter overnight (which I recommend as both the texture and flavor improve), mix the wet ingredients in a round, 2-quart food storage container with an airtight lid instead of the typical mixing bowl.

MAKES 6 TO 8 PANCAKES (3½- TO 4-INCH DIAMETER)

¾ cup chickpea flour

¼ teaspoon baking powder

½ teaspoon fine sea salt

¼ teaspoon ground turmeric (optional)

1 large egg

¼ cup olive oil, divided

¼ cup whey or 2 tablespoons plain, full-fat Greek yogurt plus 2 tablespoons water (see tips for dairy alternative)

¼ cup thinly sliced green onion, white and light-green parts (optional)

1 cup finely chopped tender (raw or cooked) vegetables, such as raw spinach, fresh herbs (and/or herb stems), grated zucchini (bundled in cloth and squeezed of most water) Caramelized Cabbage for Many Occasions (page 226), and/or roasted pumpkin (page 128), (all optional)

¼ cup water

OPTIONAL TOPPINGS

1 cup labneh, store-bought or homemade (page 336); fromage blanc; plain, full-fat Greek yogurt; or crème fraîche

Poached, fried, or 6½-minute Soft-Centered Eggs (page 144)

Smoked salmon or trout

Thinly sliced green onion, white and light-green parts

Preserved lemon, julienned

Lemon or lime wedges

Sprouts

¼ cup fresh dill, cilantro (whole leaves and tender stems), herb blossoms, or mint

Aleppo-style pepper (or similar) or ground sumac

Olive oil

Flaky sea salt

In a medium mixing bowl, or food storage container (see headnote), whisk together the chickpea flour, baking powder, ½ teaspoon fine sea salt, and ground turmeric (if using) until combined. Make a well in the center; add the egg and whisk it to break up the yolk. 1 tablespoon olive oil, and ¼ cup whey; add this mixture to the chickpea flour mixture and whisk to combine. Switch to a spatula or wooden spoon and stir in the green onion and chopped vegetables, if using. Add ¼ cup water (or more whey, if you'd like), slowly, as needed, to achieve the consistency of pancake batter: thick and moist, but not runny. Let the batter sit for at least 20 minutes, or, ideally, refrigerate in an airtight container overnight, or up to 48 hours (no need to bring to room temperature before proceeding).

Heat approximately 1½ tablespoons olive oil or ghee in a 10- or 14-inch heavy-bottomed skillet, preferably cast iron, over medium-high heat. Swirl the pan to distribute the fat; there shouldn't be any bald spots—if there are, add more fat. Use a ¼ measuring cup to drop the batter into the pan, leaving about 1 inch of space between each pancake as you go. Cook until the bottoms are lightly browned and bubbles form on top, 2 to 3 minutes. Use a spatula to carefully flip the pancakes over and cook until browned and cooked through, 2 to 3 minutes longer. Transfer to a plate or keep warm in a 200°F oven. Repeat with another 1½ tablespoons oil and remaining batter. Serve pancakes warm or at room temperature, with whichever toppings you'd like.

Tips—Cool any leftover cooked pancakes and store in an airtight container; refrigerate for up to 4 days or freeze for up to 3 months. Defrost in the refrigerator overnight, if needed, then reheat in a hot skillet slicked with ghee or oil until edges are crisp and pancakes are warmed through.

SHAVED FENNEL WITH LEMON AND BOTTARGA

Pictured on page 106.

This is one the simplest recipes in the book, because an ingredient such as bottarga begs for simplicity. Fennel and seafood are a classic combination, and for good reason: the floral, citrusy, and anise-like flavor of fennel is the perfect partner for briny bottarga. Seek out fennel that is firm, small, and slender. It will be more flavorful and less fibrous than the big bulbs.

4 TO 6 SERVINGS

2 teaspoons lemon juice

Fine sea salt

2 tablespoons olive oil

4 small or 2 large fennel (approximately 1½ pounds with stalks and fronds attached), stalks and outermost layer discarded, tender fronds reserved, root end trimmed

1 lemon

⅓ cup (loosely packed) finely grated (on a Microplane) bottarga (mullet or salmon), or more to taste

Combine the lemon juice and a pinch of salt in a small mixing bowl; whisk in the olive oil. Coarsely chop a handful of tender fennel fronds; set aside. Cut the fennel bulbs in half lengthwise and thinly slice on a mandoline (if you have one; if not, use a sharp knife). Place the sliced fennel, a pinch of salt, and all but a good pinch of the fronds in a medium mixing bowl; use a Microplane to grate the zest of half the lemon on top. Add half the lemon dressing and gently toss. Taste and add more dressing until the slices are just coated—fennel is easily weighed down, and you want this salad light and springy. Add all but a few tablespoons of the bottarga and toss gently once more. Transfer to a platter or divide among plates or shallow bowls; top with the reserved fronds. Sprinkle the remaining bottarga on top. Serve immediately.

I use a Japanese mandoline anytime I call for something "thinly sliced" (⅛- to 1/16-inch thick) or when preparing planks for a matchstick cut. It isn't necessary—you can always use a sharp knife—but using a mandoline makes for precise and efficient slicing.

CRISPY CHICKPEA FRITTERS

I love panisses—the deep-fried chickpea snacks that hail from Provence—but they involve a good amount of work, a few pans, and time to wait. These little chickpea fritters, on the other hand, require only a single bowl and skillet and take about 10 minutes from start to finish. Inspired by *tortillitas de camarones*, a seafood snack from Spain, they are fast, crispy, deeply savory, and visually striking. And they are a perfect thing to whip up for a spontaneous gathering of a few or many.

If shrimp powder isn't your thing, just omit it—both in the batter and topping. They'll lose umami but won't seem wanting. And you can always riff on the recipe further, based on what's in your pantry; add ¼ teaspoon of ground turmeric to the batter, perhaps, or adorn plain fritters with Aleppo-style pepper or Green Za'atar (page 357).

MAKES APPROXIMATELY 24 SMALL FRITTERS, 6 TO 8 SERVINGS

½ cup chickpea flour

½ teaspoon fine sea salt

½ teaspoon baking soda

1 tablespoon Dried Shrimp Powder (page 352)

1 cup sparkling water

Olive oil for frying

TO SERVE

Zest of 2 lemons (use a Microplane for best results)

6 lemon wedges

Chile Vinegar (page 348, optional)

Dried Shrimp Powder (page 352)

¼ cup finely chopped chives (optional)

Flaky sea salt

Preheat oven to 250°F and line a baking sheet with parchment paper and 2 paper towels; have a slotted spatula nearby (I use a fish spatula). In a medium mixing bowl, whisk together the chickpea flour, fine sea salt, baking soda, and dried shrimp powder. While whisking, add the sparkling water, smoothing out lumps with your fingertips, as needed.

Heat a 12- or 14-inch heavy-bottomed skillet over medium-high heat and pour in enough olive oil to coat the bottom of the pan by a ½ inch. When the oil is hot, move swiftly: drop a heaped tablespoon of the mixture into the pan and immediately use the spoon to swirl the batter out as thinly as possible—as you do this, use your spoon to make little holes (the batter should appear lacey). Depending on the size of your pan, repeat 2 or 3 more times, 1 heaping tablespoon for each fritter, to make a batch. Flip the first and check the others— if they are a golden brown, flip them too (2 to 3 minutes per side).

Transfer the fritters to the lined baking sheet and keep warm in the oven while you repeat the process with the remaining batter. Between batches, stir batter, use a paper towel to remove any bits of batter from the skillet, and make sure there is a ½ inch of hot (but not smoking) olive oil coating the bottom of the pan. Serve topped with lemon zest, lemon juice, a few drops of chile vinegar (if you'd like), more dried shrimp powder, chopped chives (if you'd like), and flaky sea salt. Serve warm with lemon wedges on the side.

SKILLET-CHARRED BEANS

Pictured on page 330.

These crispy, creamy-centered beans are as satisfying to eat as french fries but are much easier to make and more unexpected. I usually serve them as a daytime snack or instead of salted or spiced nuts with drinks. But they can also do good things for tacos, hearty salads, pasta, and grains.

Tip—I use dried beans that I'd previously cooked myself (this recipe makes good use of leftovers), and I highly recommend using them over canned—they brown up better and are less likely to get mushy. Any large, meaty bean will do, but I like how the white bean takes on color in the pan.

3 TO 4 SERVINGS, AS A STARTER

¼ cup olive oil, lard, or cold-pressed vegetable oil

1 chile de arbol

Scant 2 cups cooked large white beans (approximately 11 ounces), such as Corona or runner cannellini, drained well and patted dry

¼ teaspoon fine sea salt, plus as needed

OPTIONAL TOPPINGS (CHOOSE ONE)

½ teaspoon fennel pollen

2 tablespoons finely grated bottarga and the zest of ½ lemon (use a Microplane for best results)

1 tablespoon Instant "XO" (page 341)

2 teaspoons Harissa (page 342)

¼ cup (loosely packed) Anchovy Gremolata (page 346)

Set a 12- or 14-inch heavy-bottomed skillet, preferably cast iron, over medium-high heat; once it is hot, add the fat and swirl the skillet to coat the bottom. Add the chile de arbol, beans, and salt. Gently stir to coat the beans in fat and then spread them in a single, uncrowded layer. Let them sear undisturbed for 3 to 5 minutes, or until brown and charred in spots. Flip the beans and cook on the other side for an additional 3 to 4 minutes. The beans should be golden brown, lightly charred, and a bit crunchy on the outside. Off heat, toss with your topping of choice. Taste, and add more salt, if needed. Serve hot or warm.

MISO-MAPLE WALNUTS

Pictured on page 330.

When I want a little something more than my standard walnuts in walnut oil (see sidebar), I make these. They are crunchy, savory, a little sweet, and beautifully caramelized. In short, they are addictive.

1¼ CUPS

1 tablespoon white miso

1 tablespoon ghee,
at room temperature

½ teaspoon maple syrup

⅛ teaspoon fine sea salt

1¼ cups toasted walnut
halves or toasted whole
almonds

Preheat oven to 325°F. Combine the miso, ghee, maple syrup, and salt in a small mixing bowl and stir to create a paste. Add the walnuts and toss until the nuts are well coated. Spread the walnuts on a parchment-lined rimmed baking sheet and bake for 10 to 13 minutes, or until caramelized. Cool to room temperature before serving. Store in an airtight container at room temperature for up to 1 week.

I'm almost embarrassed to call this a recipe, but this is a party trick I have to share: In a small mixing bowl, toss toasted walnut halves with enough walnut oil to coat and season with fine sea salt to taste. Place in a serving bowl (leaving any excess walnut oil behind) or store in an airtight container for up to 5 days (they don't go bad, but they lose their crunch). Serve with drinks or use anywhere you'd use toasted walnuts (e.g., salads, oatmeal, etc.).

PUFFED RICE PARTY MIX

This simple snack is inspired by bhel puri, a savory, spicy snack typically sold via street carts in the western region of India. I've made it a few ways over the years; another favorite version includes pistachios, barberries, thinly sliced green onion, lemon zest, and a pinch of both Aleppo-style pepper and dried mint sizzled in ghee. Have fun making it your own. It makes a great on-the-go, after-school, or bar nosh.

APPROXIMATELY 3¼ CUPS

2 cups unseasoned puffed rice, store-bought or homemade (page 252)

½ cup toasted, salted peanuts or cashews

¾ cup coconut chips

½ serrano chile, thinly sliced

2 tablespoons thinly sliced green onion, white and light-green parts

1 tablespoon Toasted Chickpea Flour (page 351)

1 teaspoon melted virgin coconut oil, ghee, or a combination of the two

Zest of 1 lime (use a Microplane for best results)

¼ teaspoon citric acid powder (optional, but very good)

Fine sea salt

Place all the ingredients in a medium mixing bowl. Mix them together and stir well. Season the mixture with salt, to taste.

This "salad" starts to get a little soggy over time—I recommend serving and consuming within 8 hours of tossing.

POPCORN WITH NORI, CITRUS, AND ROSEMARY

Popcorn is a snack that somehow seems light and indulgent at the same time. It is welcome at any time and for every occasion. Buttered and salted, popcorn is very good. But it is made remarkable when showered with a striking mix of nori, citrus zest, and fresh rosemary. Make more of this seasoning than you need and sprinkle it on fried eggs, cold soba noodles, green salads, grilled vegetables, or Hard-Roasted Whole Fish (page 256).

8 CUPS; 4 TO 6 SERVINGS

½ cup nori powder, store-bought or homemade (page 71)

Zest of 1 orange or yuzu (use a Microplane for best results)

½ chile de arbol, thinly sliced

1 sprig rosemary, leaves finely chopped

¼ teaspoon fine sea salt

8 cups (½ cup kernels) freshly popped popcorn

Place all the ingredients (except the popped popcorn) in a spice grinder and pulse until well combined. Store in an airtight container at room temperature for up to 1 week. Add ¼ cup seasoning to freshly popped popcorn and toss lightly to combine.

Breakfast All Day

SOFT-CENTERED EGGS

My household is never without these. And since "put an egg on it" is practically an American mantra now, I don't think I need to say much to sell the idea of regularly stocking half a dozen with barely set yolks—not quite runny, definitely not firm— for daily snacks and meals, both spontaneous and planned.

Tips—When a recipe calls for "room temperature eggs," just pull your eggs from the refrigerator the night before. In this case you can use cold eggs, but the shells are more likely to crack during cooking and the resulting firmness may differ slightly. If using small or medium eggs, just decrease cooking time by 30 and 15 seconds respectively.

MAKES 8 EGGS

Up to 8 large chicken or duck eggs, at room temperature

Fill a medium mixing bowl with iced water and set aside. Bring a large saucepan of water to a boil over high heat. Using a large spider or slotted spoon, carefully lower the eggs into the boiling water. When the water returns to a boil, cover and turn off the heat (if you are using an electric cooktop, remove the pot from the still-hot surface).

Steep the eggs 6½ minutes for slightly runny center, 7½ minutes for a yolk that is slightly set, or 8½ minutes for the hardest "hard boil" I'm willing to accept. Transfer the eggs to a bowl of ice water and chill until cold. Unpeeled and refrigerated, boiled eggs keep for up to 5 days.

WHOLE GRAIN PORRIDGE WITH BONITO AND SHOYU

Savory porridge is a comfort for me and something I make often. I grew up eating grits, and I have been through many phases in which a hot bowl of congee (rice porridge) was my most coveted meal. And I'm not alone—salty steaming bowls of porridge are eaten daily around the world: atole, champurrado, genfo, grød, groats, jook, kasha, lugaw, okayu, polenta, to name just a few. Many porridges—as well as many popular breakfast soups—contain some version of preserved fish. Not only do they provide an easy way to boost the overall flavor of early-morning cooking, but their warming flavor and nutritional profile also make for a solid start to the day.

I first sampled okaka—a Japanese seasoning that is often associated with rice—over a Japanese breakfast with friends in a tiny Brooklyn restaurant. Even though it is simply dried shaved bonito flakes tossed with soy sauce, the mixture really made an impression on me and has been in regular rotation ever since. My version is made with white shoyu, but you can use regular soy sauce.

3 TO 4 SERVINGS

1 cup multigrain porridge (such as Hayden Flour Mills Farmer's Porridge or Bob's Red Mill 6- or 10-Grain Hot Cereal)

5 cups water or Kombu Stock (page 347)

Fine sea salt

1 cup bonito flakes

1 tablespoon plus 1 teaspoon white shoyu or soy sauce

OPTIONAL TOPPINGS

4 poached eggs, fried eggs, or 6½-minute Soft-Centered Eggs (page 144)

¼ cup thinly sliced green onion, white and light-green parts

Ghee, unsalted butter, or sesame oil

Dry-toast the grains in a medium pot over medium heat, stirring regularly, until they smell nutty and turn a shade darker, 5 to 7 minutes. Slowly add the water (it may spit and spatter a bit) and 2 pinches of salt and bring to a boil, stirring constantly. Reduce heat and simmer, uncovered, over low heat for 25 to 30 minutes, stirring occasionally. If at any point the porridge seems too thick or at risk of scorching, add ¼ cup water. Off heat, add salt to taste. Cover and let the porridge rest for 5 to 10 minutes while you prepare your toppings.

Make the okaka. Put the bonito in a small mixing bowl and gently toss with the shoyu. Divide the porridge among bowls, top with whatever you want, finish with a little pile—a heaping tablespoon or so—of okaka. Serve immediately.

IMPERFECT FRUIT WITH VINEGARED HONEY AND BEE POLLEN (OR WHAT DO WHEN YOUR PEAR IS A LEMON)

My favorite way to serve fruit is on a plate—peak season and perfectly ripe, without embellishment. But sometimes I end up with, well, a lemon—and it needs a little something to make it better than fine. If I'm not in the mood to bake or make jam, I pull this trick: thinly sliced fruit drizzled in honey and accented—balanced, really—with a touch of my favorite vinegar. A sprinkling of bee pollen polishes further and helps to echo the fruity quality of what's beneath. Pears, melons, figs, persimmons, and apricots are all good candidates for this.

2 TO 4 SERVINGS

¼ cup honey

1 tablespoon Banyuls vinegar

⅛ teaspoon fine sea salt

2 firm but ripe pears (any variety), cored and halved lengthwise; or 1 small ripe melon, peeled, halved, seeded, and cut into quarters

Approximately 2 teaspoons bee pollen

In a small bowl, whisk together the honey, vinegar, and salt. Place the fruit flat side down on a cutting board and thinly slice. Transfer fruit to a serving platter (which could easily be your cutting board) or divide among plates; top each piece with a heaping spoonful of the vinegared honey and sprinkle with bee pollen.

STEWED PRUNES
WITH CARAWAY

Caraway gives these sweet, sticky prunes an unexpected but welcome savory note. Serve these on sweet porridge (wheat, oats, rice, etc.) with a splash of kefir or crème fraîche or as a topping for buckwheat crepes, waffles, ice cream or frozen yogurt (page 316). Or chop them coarsely and fold the fruit into batter for scones, muffins, coffee cake (and other fruit-swirled cakes and quick breads), or (in place of raisins) oatmeal cookies.

3 CUPS

1 teaspoon caraway

3 cups pitted prunes (approximately 14 ounces)

½ cup honey

½ cup water

⅛ teaspoon fine sea salt

½ teaspoon lemon juice

Toast the caraway in a 9- or 10-inch dry skillet for 1 to 2 minutes, or until they release their aroma and start to pop. Let them cool to room temperature, then coarsely crush the seeds in a spice grinder or mortar. Bring all the ingredients except the lemon juice to a boil in medium saucepan over medium-high heat; reduce heat to low and simmer, uncovered, for 17 to 20 minutes. Turn off heat and add ½ teaspoon lemon juice, or more to taste. Use at once or store in an airtight container for up to 3 weeks. (They taste even better after sitting overnight.)

TOAST SWEET AND SAVORY

Fancy and surprisingly expensive, toast is on just about every menu at every restaurant, café, and food-truck lot in America. Luckily—with the aid of the modern larder and some premade foundations and finishes (page 333)—unique and hearty open-faced sandwiches are easy to make and enjoy at home.

I like thick slices of most breads, though for sprouted or Danish-style rye I opt for a thinner slice. I'm also a fan of oiling or buttering the toast before it cools; it soaks up the fat and softens a bit. Even better, I sometimes pan-fry the bread in hot ghee, olive oil, or schmaltz, over medium heat, for 2 to 3 minutes per side. And regardless of the topping, I always top with flaky sea salt.

SWEET

- Unsalted butter or ghee + labneh, store-bought or homemade (page 336) + honeycomb + bee pollen + (for more texture) toasted buckwheat (page 21), sliced almonds, or sesame seeds

- Unsalted butter or ghee + labneh, store-bought or homemade (page 336) + Dates in Date Syrup (page 296) + Sweet Hazelnut Dukkah (page 356)

- Unsalted butter or ghee + Miso Sugar (page 358)—heavily or lightly broiled until caramelized, or not *(Pictured on page 151.)*

- Unsalted butter or ghee + roasted strawberries or strawberry jam + Sumac-Rose Gomasio (page 357)

SAVORY

Vegetarian

- Olive oil, butter, or ghee + any dip on page 122

- Olive oil + avocado + Green Za'atar (page 357) or Seaweed Powder (page 351) + (more) olive oil

continued

- Ghee or olive oil + coarsely chopped Caramelized Cabbage for Many Occasions (page 226) + Aleppo-style pepper or Green Za'atar (page 357)

- Ghee or olive oil + thinly sliced avocado wedges + Yuzu Kosho Dressing (page 335) + thinly sliced chives + chervil or cilantro, whole leaves and tender stems

- Ghee or olive oil + labneh, store-bought or homemade (page 336) or other fresh cheese + chile flakes + Crispy Curry Leaves (page 350) *(Pictured on page 35.)*

- Olive oil + sliced feta or labneh, store-bought or homemade (page 336) + Blistered Tomatoes (page 201)

- Olive oil + sliced tomato + Miso Bagna Cauda (page 342) + arugula

- Ghee or lard + smashed roasted pumpkin (page 128) + toasted and cracked caraway + pumpkin seed oil or olive oil *(Pictured on page 153.)*

- Ghee + Yogurt Mayonnaise (page 339) + thickly sliced or halved 6½-minute Soft-Centered Egg (page 144) + Crispy Capers (page 348) + dill or tarragon

Fish & Meat

- Schmaltz + Green Za'atar (page 357)

- Lard (or drippings from a pork roast) + sliced white onion + piment d'Espelette

- Olive oil + 'nduja + thinly sliced tomato + fresh herbs + shavings of ricotta salata

- Olive oil, butter, or ghee + labneh, store-bought or homemade (page 336) + smoked salmon + julienned preserved lemon + fresh dill + thinly sliced chives + lemon juice + olive oil

- Ume Butter (page 343) + oil-packed sardines, drained + thinly sliced chives

- Unsalted butter, ghee, or olive oil + thickly sliced or halved 6½-minute Soft-Centered Egg (page 144) + oil-packed anchovies or Anchovy Gremolata (page 346)

- Unsalted butter or ghee + shaved radishes + lemon zest and juice + Furikake (page 358), Dried Shrimp Powder (page 352), or grated bottarga

BIG-BATCH BREAKFAST GREENS

It is obvious that cooking greens in a searing-hot pan licked with lard, garlic, chile, and/or fish sauce is a good way to go. But sometimes I want a cleaner preparation, either because I feel bloated in the brain or belly, or because I'm serving something rich and seek a side that balances it. *Then* this is a good way to go. Here I blanch and marinate, a method that also facilitates big-batch cooking on a Sunday afternoon, perfect for those who want to grab greens on the go Monday through Friday. Moreover, the greens retain more of their integrity over the course of days, compared with those that have been sautéed or roasted.

I keep of vat of these dashi-infused greens and use them—along with 6½-minute Soft-Centered Eggs (page 144)—to adorn steaming bowls of rice, savory porridge, or—when the weather is warm—cold soba noodles. Heartier than toast, longer lasting than baked goods or granola—savory, veg-topped grain bowls are the weekday breakfast you've been looking for.

4 TO 6 SERVINGS

1½ pounds kale, Spigarello, spinach, bok choy, Swiss chard, or turnip or beet greens, washed well

1 tablespoon mirin

¼ cup white shoyu or 3 tablespoons soy sauce, plus more to taste

1 sprig rosemary

1 cup Dashi (page 346) or Kombu Stock (page 347)

Prepare an ice bath in a large mixing bowl. In a large pot of salted boiling water, cook the greens until tender, 1 to 2 minutes, depending on the type. Immediately transfer to the prepared ice bath to cool.

Meanwhile, in a small saucepan, bring the mirin, white shoyu, and rosemary sprig to a simmer over medium-high heat, then remove from heat. Combine the soy mixture with the dashi. Taste, then add more dashi if a more mellow flavor is desired. Let cool completely; discard the rosemary.

Drain the greens. Using your hands, squeeze out as much water from the greens as possible, then transfer to a container, pour the dashi marinade on top, and toss to coat. Let the greens marinate for at least 30 minutes. The greens can be stored in the marinade—in an airtight container in the refrigerator—for up to 5 days.

To serve, place a pile of the greens on rice, porridge, or noodles. (Japanese cooks often place them in a neat line, or compressed into a cylinder shape, but loosely mounding them works fine.) Drizzle some of the dashi marinade on top.

BAKED OMELET WITH YOGURT AND FRESH TURMERIC

This round omelet—reminiscent of a frittata, but much lighter—is delicious for brunch, lunch, or dinner. Make it a biggish meal by serving it with bread, lavash, toast, or steamed rice; or daal, pickles, and a green salad. It is best eaten warm from the oven while the omelet is still custardy in the center. That said, I've cut leftover cold omelet into triangles and made a sandwich with a thick smear of Labneh (page 336) or Yogurt Mayonnaise (page 339), a few tomato slices, a thin layer of cilantro leaves, and almost-too-much serrano chile, and it was pretty sublime.

3 TO 4 SERVINGS

8 medium or large eggs

¼ cup plain yogurt, preferably full-fat Greek or sheep's milk, plus more to serve

½ teaspoon fine sea salt

1½ tablespoons ghee

2 teaspoons finely grated fresh ginger (use a Microplane for best results)

2 teaspoons finely grated fresh turmeric (use a Microplane for best results)

1 garlic clove, finely grated (optional)

1 teaspoon cumin seeds, toasted and ground with a mortar and pestle or spice grinder

½ cup cilantro, whole leaves and tender stems

Thinly sliced green onion, white and light-green parts, to serve (optional)

Thinly sliced green chile (such as serrano), to serve (optional)

Flaky sea salt

Preheat oven to 400°F. Whisk the eggs with the yogurt and sea salt until just combined; set aside. Heat the ghee in a large ovenproof frying pan over medium-high heat and add the ginger, turmeric, garlic, and cumin. Sauté for 1 to 2 minutes; don't let the cumin burn or garlic brown.

Adjust the heat to low, add the eggs, and stir until they just start to scramble, 1 to 2 minutes. Transfer to the oven and bake, uncovered, until just set, 4 to 5 minutes; or cooked to your liking (I like them soft and wet in the center). Dollop with yogurt (or serve a bowl alongside) and shower with cilantro, green onion (if using), a few sliced chiles (if using), and flaky sea salt. Serve at once.

POACHED EGGS WITH LABNEH AND CHILE

While the praises of acid are now sung by many a home cook and hearty eater, it remains an oft-overlooked element to perfectly prepared eggs. Which is shocking, really, considering the obvious richness of the things. When I fry eggs for a typical breakfast of toast and such, I finish them in the skillet with a few drops of Banyuls vinegar. But there are many other exciting ways to balance eggs with acid and vice versa: tomatillos (see Green Eggs, page 158), tomatoes, yogurt. This recipe does it twice; by poaching the eggs in whey and serving them atop tangy labneh.

2 TO 4 SERVINGS

1½ cups labneh, store-bought or homemade (page 336)

Fine sea salt

1 teaspoon olive oil, plus more to serve

½–1 cup whey, store-bought or homemade (from making labneh)

4 medium or large eggs

1 teaspoon Aleppo-style pepper, Marash pepper, Urfa pepper, or piment d'Espelette chile flakes

Flaky sea salt

Thinly sliced chives and/or finely chopped dill, for serving

Toast, bread, pita, or lavash, to serve

Stir the labneh with a pinch of salt and a teaspoon or so of olive oil. Divide between 2 (or 4, if you're one-egg people) plates or shallow bowls—I spoon into the center in a mound and then use the back of the spoon to spread it into a thick swirl—and set aside.

In a medium saucepan, bring about 3 quarts of salted water to a boil. Reduce heat to medium and add the whey; using a slotted spoon, swirl the water to create a whirlpool. Crack 1 egg at a time into a bowl, slide the egg into the center of the whirling water, and poach until the egg white is firm but the yolk is still runny, 2 to 3 minutes. Using a slotted spoon, transfer the eggs to a clean kitchen towel to drain slightly; divide between plates. Top with the chile flakes, a drizzle of olive oil, some flaky sea salt, and the chives and/or dill. Serve immediately.

GREEN EGGS

This hearty egg dish is inspired by two of my favorite morning meals: chilaquiles verde and shakshuka. It's based on a bright, thick sauce of tomatillos, green aromatics, and fish sauce. Even though the tomatillos are slightly sour and bear a citrusy aroma, I opt for even more acid in the form of crème fraîche. I also like mine on the spicy side, but you can easily adjust the heat according to your preferences.

Tips—Tomatillos show up in markets in mid-June through October. Select specimens that have an intact husk and firm, evenly colored fruit. Store them in the refrigerator in an airtight container lined with paper towel and they will last for more than 1 week. Remove the husk and rinse the slightly sticky skin before using.

3 TO 4 SERVINGS

1 pound tomatillos
(10–12 medium, see Tips)

2 cups (loosely packed) cilantro, whole leaves and tender stems

1 cup (loosely packed) flat-leaf parsley

6 green onions, white and light-green parts, sliced

1½ teaspoons yuzu kosho, store-bought or homemade (page 343) or ½ teaspoon lime zest (use a Microplane for best results) plus 1 teaspoon minced serrano chile

1 teaspoon fish sauce (optional)

¼ cup olive oil

¼ teaspoon fine sea salt

6 medium or large eggs

1 lemon or lime (optional)

TO SERVE (OPTIONAL)

Crème fraîche

Cilantro, whole leaves and tender stems

Thinly sliced white or green onion, white and pale-green parts

Yuzu kosho, store-bought or homemade (page 343); sliced serrano chile; or your favorite hot sauce

Shaved radish

Avocado, quartered or sliced

Tortillas, pita, or bread

Bring a large pot of salted water to a boil. Blanch the tomatillos until soft but still whole, about 5 minutes. Remove from heat and drain; place the tomatillos in a blender with the cilantro, parsley, green onions, yuzu kosho, fish sauce (if using), olive oil, and salt. Puree until smooth, adding water as needed to achieve a sauce the consistency of tomato puree. This pureed tomatillo mixture can be prepared up to 3 days in advance; cover and refrigerate until ready to use.

Transfer the sauce to a large sauté pan with a tight-fitting lid (you'll need it later) and bring to a boil over high heat. Lower the heat and simmer, uncovered, for about 8 minutes, or until the sauce is slightly reduced (it will spit and spatter when thick). Turn off the heat, taste the sauce, and adjust the seasoning as needed; more salt is always worth considering, and depending on the acidity of your tomatillos, a little lemon or lime juice may be needed. If you'd like more heat, slice another chile and serve it on the table.

Use a spoon to make a well near the perimeter of the pan and break an egg directly into it. Spoon a little sauce over edges of the egg white to partially submerge and contain it, leaving the yolk exposed. Repeat with the remaining 5 eggs, working around the pan and toward the center as you go. Season each egg with a little salt. Cover the pan, reduce heat to the lowest setting, and cook until the egg whites are barely set and the yolks are still runny, 4 to 5 minutes. (Keep in mind that they'll continue to cook off the heat.)

Garnish the skillet (or each serving) with a spoonful of crème fraîche and a scattering herbs, radish slices, and sliced onions, if desired. Serve immediately alongside more yuzu kosho (or chile or hot sauce), avocado, and tortillas, pita, or bread.

BAKED EGGS WITH LENTILS, SPINACH, AND SPICED GHEE

Before my son was born, I was pleased to spend hours shopping, menu sketching, and cooking. If a recipe required a big pile of finely chopped greens—pilaf, say, or a savory pie (see Lamb and Lamb's-Quarter Pie, page 285), saag paneer, or kuku—I'd turn on whatever music suited my mood, crack the window, and happily work away. Now, as I try to satiate an insatiable and high-chair-bound one-year-old by feeding him blueberries between household chores, a pile of anything makes me shudder. But while the laundry can wait, food is a necessity. And I crave leafy green things.

Once, during a particularly desperate-seeming day, I sautéed spinach as a side but didn't have time to get a main on the stove. I instinctively reached for the scissors, a day-old batch of lentils, and a jar of spiced ghee. I ended up with this—a delicious one-pot dinner. It is easy, substantial, and lovely to boot.

2 TO 4 SERVINGS

3 tablespoons ghee

4 green onions, white and light-green parts, thinly sliced

Fine sea salt

12 to 14 ounces fresh spinach

1 cup cooked Black Lentils, drained if needed (recipe follows)

1 teaspoon Banyuls or other red wine vinegar

4 medium or large eggs

Flaky sea salt (optional)

⅓ cup plain, full-fat Greek yogurt (optional)

1 teaspoon lemon juice

2 tablespoons Spiced Ghee (recipe follows)

Scant ¼ cup coarsely chopped fresh dill, cilantro, or mint

Preheat oven to 300°F. Melt the ghee in a 10- or 12-inch sauté pan or deep, heavy-bottomed skillet over medium heat. Add the green onions and a pinch of salt; lower heat slightly. Cook until soft, about 6 minutes. Add the spinach, a splash (a tablespoon) of water, and another pinch of salt; cover and cook 2 to 3 minutes. Uncover, stir, increase heat to medium-high, and cook, turning frequently, until all greens are soft and wilted and most of the liquid has evaporated, 6 to 8 minutes more. Off heat, tilt the pan so that all the spinach slides to one side; grab your kitchen shears and, submerging the tip under the cooked greens, just scissor, scissor, scissor until it is a coarsely chopped. (Alternatively, transfer the spinach to a cutting board and chop with a knife.) Add the lentils, vinegar, and another pinch of salt; stir to combine. Return pan to medium heat.

Make 4 deep indentations in the spinach mixture. Carefully break 1 egg into each hollow, taking care to keep yolks intact; give each egg a sprinkling of fine or flaky sea salt, if using. Transfer the pan to the oven and bake, uncovered, until the egg whites are just set, 11 to 15 minutes. To serve, top with dollops of yogurt, if you'd like; drizzle with lemon juice and spiced ghee, and garnish with a generous scattering of herbs. Serve immediately.

SPICED GHEE

¼ cup ghee or virgin
coconut oil

1 teaspoon Curry Spice
Blend (page 352)

This spiced ghee is very versatile. Use it instead of olive oil to finish
dishes (keeping in mind that if the food is too cold, it'll make the
ghee seize and harden): drizzle it over roasted carrots, cabbage
(page 223), or beets (page 213); anoint a warm pumpkin soup or
room temperature dip (page 122); spread it on a chicken sandwich;
or serve it as a sauce for chicken or fish. If you'd prefer to just use
a single spice, mustard seeds, black cardamom, or chile de arbol,
work in place of the spice blend.

Heat the ghee and spices in a small saucepan over medium heat until
fragrant, about 3 minutes. Off heat, steep, uncovered, for 4 to 5
minutes. Use warm. Refrigerate in an airtight container for up to
2 weeks; warm over low heat before using.

BLACK LENTILS

2 TO 2½ CUPS

1 cup black beluga
(or Le Puy or Castelluccio)
lentils, picked over
and rinsed

2 cups water

Fine sea salt

2 tablespoons olive oil

1 teaspoon Banyuls
vinegar or other red wine
vinegar

Put the lentils in a medium saucepan with the water, a pinch of salt,
and the olive oil. Bring to a simmer over medium heat, then lower
the heat to low and cook—uncovered—at a very gentle simmer,
stirring occasionally, until the water is absorbed and the lentils are
just tender, 22 to 25 minutes. You'll know they are done when they
are no longer gritty but still have some texture (you don't want
them mealy). Off heat, let the lentils cool slightly before stirring and
seasoning with Banyuls vinegar and more salt to taste. Refrigerate in
an airtight container for up to 3 days.

FLUFFY BUCKWHEAT PANCAKES

Pictured on page 142.

Don't be deterred by the relatively long ingredient list. These are quick and satisfying pancakes to make. I dare say they're doable on a weekday, especially if you mix the dry ingredients the day—or even a month—before. The buckwheat flour, rice flour, and flaxseed give them a wholesome heartiness that can help carry you through whatever your morning may bring. Plus, the combination of maple, vanilla, and earthy, pleasantly bitter buckwheat pairs extraordinarily well with the flavor of coffee. I like these straight from the skillet topped with a thick schmear of Labneh (page 336), a drizzle of maple, and a sprinkling of both flaky sea salt and soba cha (page 21), which mirrors the flavor of the pancake and adds the nuance of crunch.

Tips—To make this nondairy, you can substitute almond or coconut yogurt for the Greek yogurt and coconut oil or a neutral vegetable oil (such as cold-pressed rice bran oil or grapeseed oil) for the ghee. Also, I generally try to avoid plastic wrap. If you plan to refrigerate the batter overnight, mix the wet ingredients in a round, 2-quart food storage container with an airtight lid instead of the typical mixing bowl. Cool any leftover pancakes and store in an airtight container; refrigerate for up to 4 days or freeze for up to 3 months. Defrost in the refrigerator overnight, if needed, then reheat in a hot skillet slicked with ghee or oil until edges are crisp and pancakes are warmed through.

Make these autumnal Fluffy Buckwheat Pancakes with Apples and Cinnamon by adding ¼ teaspoon cinnamon to the dry ingredients and 1 packed cup coarsely grated tart apple to the wet. Proceed with the recipe as written.

**MAKES 8 PANCAKES
(3½- TO 4-INCH
DIAMETER)**

90 grams (¾ cup)
buckwheat flour

40 grams (¼ cup) white
rice flour

2 tablespoons ground
flaxseed (flaxseed meal)

1 teaspoon baking powder

½ teaspoon baking soda

Slightly rounded
¼ teaspoon fine sea salt

3 tablespoons plain,
full-fat Greek yogurt
or 2 tablespoons plain,
full-fat kefir

1 large egg

2 tablespoons maple syrup
or date syrup, plus more
to serve

½ teaspoon vanilla extract

28 grams (2 tablespoons)
ghee or 30 grams (2 tablespoons) unsalted butter,
melted and warm, plus
more for the skillet

1 cup warm water

In a small mixing bowl, whisk the flours, flaxseed, baking powder, baking soda, and sea salt. In a medium mixing bowl or food storage container (see headnote), whisk the yogurt, egg, maple syrup, vanilla, melted ghee, and warm water.

Overmixing the buckwheat flour creates a dense pancake, so add the dry ingredients into the wet in about 3 equal portions, using a flexible spatula to gently fold and stir each portion until almost fully incorporated. After the third addition, fold the batter until just combined (it will be lumpy, and that's fine). The batter can be used right away or refrigerated in an airtight container overnight (no need to bring it to room temperature before proceeding).

Heat a 10- or 14-inch heavy-bottomed skillet, preferably cast iron, or griddle over medium heat until hot and coat the surface well with ghee. Drop a scant ¼ cup of batter onto the skillet for each pancake, leaving about 2 inches between each. Cook for about 2 to 3 minutes, or until a few bubbles form at the edges and on the surface. Flip the pancakes and cook until lightly browned on the bottom and cooked through in the center, 1 to 2 minutes more. Transfer to a plate or keep warm in a 200°F oven. Repeat with any remaining batter, adding more ghee to the skillet between each batch. Serve hot or warm.

Salads + Sides

DANDELION AND SWEET PEA SALAD WITH ANCHOVY, CHILE, AND MINT

Spring produce tends to be a little too dainty and sweet for my taste. But when it is tossed with something bitter or pungent, salty and spicy, I get excited. This is one of my favorite salads. I like to serve it alongside a slow-roasted lamb shoulder or Hard-Roasted Whole Fish (page 256) with bread or lavash or as a vegetarian lunch, with a steaming-hot bowl of farro and maybe a few 6½-minute Soft-Centered Eggs (page 144) on the side. If you're using leftover bagna cauda, revive it with a little lemon zest and lemon juice right before adding it to the salad.

4 SERVINGS

4 ounces dandelion greens or arugula, trimmed, leaves cut or torn into 2-inch pieces

8 ounces sugar snap peas, strings removed, halved lengthwise

1 small fennel bulb (approximately 3 ounces), halved lengthwise and thinly sliced crosswise (use a mandoline for best results)

Fine sea salt

¼ cup warm Bagna Cauda (page 341, see Miso Bagna Cauda for a vegetarian option)

2 handfuls pea shoots (approximately 2 ounces)

Scant 1 cup (loosely packed) mint, large leaves torn

2 to 3 tablespoons thinly sliced chives (optional)

Lemon zest (use a Microplane for best results) and lemon juice

Toss the dandelion greens, sugar snap peas, and fennel in a medium serving bowl with a pinch of salt. Right before serving, add the warm bagna cauda and toss once more. Add the pea shoots, mint, and chives (if using) and toss to combine. Taste, then add salt, lemon zest, lemon juice, and more bagna cauda, to taste, until you're not sure if you're willing to share.

GHEE-ROASTED PARSNIPS

Ghee really brings out the sweet, nutty flavor of parsnips. And because it has a higher smoke point than butter, it can withstand the heat of an oven set to roasting temperatures.

If you've never enjoyed roasted parsnips before, try this method. Together, a relatively low roasting temperature (most recipes ask for between 425°F and 450°F) and ample ghee create caramelized, moist, perfectly crisp, and tender roots.

Tips—When possible, seek out small or medium parsnips for this dish; the larger they are, the tougher the core and pithier the flesh. Can't find parsnips of any size? Try this with similarly textured vegetables, such as turnips, rutabagas, and even radish (oven times will vary based on size and water content).

4 TO 6 SERVINGS

⅓ cup ghee

1 tablespoon olive oil

2 pounds parsnips, peeled, cut into 3- to 5-inch lengths, halved, or quartered if large

4 branches of thyme (optional)

Fine sea salt

Preheat oven to 400°F. Line a rimmed baking sheet with parchment paper. Place ghee and olive oil onto the prepared pan and slide it into the oven for 2 to 3 minutes, or until most of the ghee has melted.

Carefully (the pan will be hot) toss parsnips, thyme (if using), and warm fat; season generously with salt and toss once more. Spread parsnips into one even layer. Roast parsnips, tossing once or twice, until tender and properly brown (deep golden all over and dark brown in spots), 45 to 55 minutes. Serve immediately, if you'd like. Or let the roots cool to room temperature and toss them into a White Winter Salad (page 168). Ghee-Roasted Parsnips can be refrigerated overnight and reheated in a 300°F oven for 15 minutes.

WHITE WINTER SALAD

I concocted this salad while perusing a small midwestern grocery store in the dead of winter. Unable to arm up with my California cronies—fresh herbs, citrus, heirloom chicories—I imagined an elegant salad of all white roots. Parsnips were available, as were endives, fennel, cider vinegar, and walnut oil. To my surprise, the result was a dish I've returned to again and again, with only a few minor adjustments to the original.

Although composed of fairly humble ingredients, this salad is extraordinary. The all-white palette is stunning, the comforting sweetness of caramelized parsnips is balanced by the bite of raw turnip and the bitter edge of endive, and the range of textures—creamy roasted root, crunchy walnut, feathery fennel, crisp and juicy endive—forbids restraint. You can easily make this a main course by adding slices of poached, steamed, or roasted chicken breast.

APPROXIMATELY 6 SERVINGS

1 small shallot, finely chopped

1 tablespoon lemon juice

1 teaspoon apple cider vinegar or sherry vinegar

Fine sea salt

½ teaspoon Dijon mustard (optional)

3 tablespoons olive oil

1 tablespoon walnut oil

5 large Belgian endives (approximately 1¼ pounds)

1 large or 2 small fennel bulbs (approximately 6 ounces), halved lengthwise and sliced ⅛-inch thick crosswise (use a mandoline for best results)

4 small white (hakurei) turnips (approximately 4 ounces), sliced ⅛-inch thick

1 small or ¼ large daikon, sliced ⅛-inch thick

Ghee-Roasted Parsnips (page 167), at room temperature

1 cup coarsely chopped toasted walnut halves

In a large mixing bowl, whisk together the shallot, lemon juice, apple cider vinegar, and a pinch of salt and set aside for 5 minutes or so. Whisk in the Dijon (if using), olive oil, and walnut oil.

Cut an inch off the bottom of each endive and discard. Gently peel back the leaves, continuing to trim the root as you go, until you get to the core (with tightly bunched leaves attached); cut each core in half lengthwise. Add the endive leaves and cores, fennel, turnips, daikon, and a pinch of salt to the bowl of vinaigrette and toss gently to coat. On a large serving platter, layer the roasted parsnips with the endive salad and toasted walnuts. Complete this layering process until the ingredients are all incorporated. Serve at once.

SPROUT SALAD WITH 'NDUJA AND MINT

I am a big fan of hearty salads with warm vinaigrettes: frisée with lardons, panzanella with schmaltz-fried croutons, bitter greens with bagna cauda (see Dandelion and Sweet Pea Salad, page 166). This salad—a bowl of perky, intensely flavorful green things coated in a bright, spicy, umami-rich 'nduja dressing—may be the epitome of its kind. Serve as a side to a simple main, or as the meal itself, alongside tortillas or rice.

4 TO 6 SERVINGS

SALAD

8 ounces mixed shoots and sprouts (such as pea, alfalfa, mung bean, sunflower, buckwheat, etc.)

2 generous handfuls watercress, arugula, or purslane (approximately 2 ounces)

4 ounces sugar snap peas (approximately 1¼ cups), thinly sliced on the diagonal

3 cups (loosely packed) mint and/or cilantro, whole leaves and tender stems

VINAIGRETTE

¼ cup plus 1 tablespoon olive oil, divided

5 ounces 'nduja

2 green onions, white and light-green parts, thinly sliced

3 tablespoons lime juice

Fine sea salt

In a large serving bowl, gently toss the shoots and sprouts, watercress, sugar snap peas, herbs, and a pinch of salt. Set aside (if you're not planning to eat for a bit, refrigerate) while you prepare the warm dressing.

In a 10- or 12-inch skillet over medium-high heat, combine 1 tablespoon olive oil and the 'nduja and fry for 4 to 5 minutes, or until caramelized and crispy. Off heat, use a slotted spoon to transfer the 'nduja to a plate lined with paper towels. Add the green onions to the pan with the hot fat; then add the remaining olive oil, the lime juice, and a pinch of salt. Steal a few of the greens from the serving bowl and dip them in the dressing; add more lime juice or salt, if needed.

When ready to serve, add the dressing (including the crispy bits of 'nduja) to the serving bowl and toss gently (I recommend using your hands) to combine; taste again, and add more salt, if needed.

ROASTED WINTER SQUASH WITH PUMPKIN SEED AND DULSE

This salad is a centerpiece. It is substantial—requiring both a knife and a fork—and delicious on its own or as a contrasting side to a simple main. Or invite your friends over and serve it as I sometimes do—Ottolenghi style—as part of a spread of other vegetarian dips, salads, and sides.

Rich caramelized kabocha and smoky dulse (a type of seaweed) were made for each other. But they need a fresh element to balance their intensity. The list of greens is just a template—let the market be your guide, buying whatever looks fresh and intriguing. Use a dozen variations or just use two—as long as you have something sweet, something peppery, and little to no lettuce, it will work.

4 TO 6 SERVINGS

1 kabocha squash (approximately 3 pounds), stemmed, peeled, seeded

Fine sea salt

2 chile de arbol

Few sprigs rosemary or marjoram (optional)

2 tablespoons olive oil, plus more for roasting

Scant ¼ cup toasted pumpkin seeds

1 heaping tablespoon (loosely packed) dulse flakes

½ teaspoon Chile Vinegar (page 348) or red wine vinegar, divided

1 teaspoon pumpkin seed oil or olive oil

2 teaspoons lemon juice

2 handfuls tender greens (approximately 2 ounces), ideally a mix of sweet and spicy varieties (such as pea shoots, fava leaves, mizuna, arugula, frisée, and/or mâche)

⅓ cup (loosely packed) edible flower petals (optional)

Preheat oven to 450°F. Line 2 rimmed baking sheets with parchment paper. Cut the pumpkin into about 1½-inch wedges and divide between the 2 pans. Toss each batch with 2 pinches of salt, 1 chile de arbol, a rosemary or marjoram sprig or two (if using), and olive oil to coat (approximately 3 tablespoons per baking sheet). On each pan, spread the wedges in a single, sparse layer. Roast 40 to 45 minutes, or until tender and caramelized, turning the pieces halfway through (use a spatula, as tongs break up the flesh) to ensure even browning.

Meanwhile, chop the toasted pumpkin seeds and dulse with a small pinch of salt until you have a mix of crumbs and shards (or use a spice grinder—but don't grind it too fine). Throw this mix into a small bowl and toss with ¼ teaspoon vinegar and 1 teaspoon pumpkin seed oil. In another small bowl, stir together the lemon juice with a pinch of salt and 2 tablespoons olive oil. Set both bowls aside.

Once the pumpkin is ready, drizzle a little chile vinegar all over (this is easiest if you have your vinegar

continued

Roasted Winter Squash with
Pumpkin Seed and Dulse,
continued

in a fine-tipped squeeze bottle, but a small spoon works too). Let the pumpkin cool slightly; discard the chile and herb sprigs.

Scatter half of the greens on a large, flat platter or divide among plates; drizzle half the lemon dressing evenly over the top. Place the pumpkin on top, then another scattering of greens and the pumpkin-seed-and-dulse mixture. Drizzle the remaining lemon dressing all over, and top with edible flower petals, if you'd like.

ENDIVE SALAD WITH
WALNUT AND ANCHOVY

This is my riff on the brilliant salad from New York's Estela restaurant. My version uses anchoïade, a rough-pounded paste from the South of France. Anchoïade typically uses a lot of garlic, but on this salad I prefer it without. Together, anchovy and walnut create enough tension and texture to make endive crave-worthy. Make extra and use it as a spread for crostini, as an accompaniment for lamb and roasted red peppers, or, once thinned with a bit more olive oil, as a sauce for pasta and a dressing for chicories.

**APPROXIMATELY
4 SERVINGS**

2 ounces oil-packed
anchovy fillets

1 cup coarsely chopped
toasted walnut halves

1 tablespoon plus
1½ teaspoons lemon juice

3 tablespoons olive oil

3 tablespoons walnut oil

Fine sea salt

3 to 4 large endives
(approximately 1 pound;
any variety)

Zest of 1 lemon
(use a Microplane for
best results)

Coarsely chop the anchovies and mix them in a small mixing bowl with the walnuts, 1½ teaspoons lemon juice, 1 tablespoon olive oil, and 1 tablespoon walnut oil. Taste and add salt, if needed.

In a small prep bowl, mix the remaining 1 tablespoon lemon juice with a pinch of salt; stir in the remaining 2 tablespoons olive oil and 2 tablespoons walnut oil.

Cut an inch off the bottom of each endive and discard. Gently peel back the leaves, continuing to trim the root as you go, until you get to the core (with tightly bunched leaves attached); cut each core in half lengthwise. Spoon the anchoïade onto the base of a large platter or divide between shallow salad bowls; spread it out into a somewhat even layer. Top with the endive leaves and cores to cover completely (I try to copy Estela's artful line cooks, overlapping the leaves just slightly, in concentric circles); season the endive leaves lightly with salt, shower with lemon zest, and spoon the dressing on top, making sure to get a little in the cup of each leaf. Serve immediately.

SPICY ROASTED CARROTS WITH AVOCADO, SPROUTS, AND SUNFLOWER DUKKAH

Carrots, avocado, and sprouts may sound too standard to deserve your attention, but I assure you, this salad satisfies. It's really the dukkah that does the trick—bright, spicy, salty, and a little sweet—it gives this salad a complex, savory depth.

4 TO 6 SERVINGS

3 pounds small carrots

2 whole chile de arbol

Fine sea salt

2 teaspoons honey

Olive oil

½ lemon, halved

3 ripe but firm large avocados

¼ cup Sunflower Dukkah (page 356) or toasted sunflower seeds

3 to 4 ounces sunflower sprouts, halved crosswise if long

1 cup (loosely packed) cilantro, whole leaves and tender stems and/or flowers

1 serrano chile, very thinly sliced (optional)

Flaky sea salt

Chile Vinegar (page 348, optional)

Crème fraîche; plain, full-fat Greek yogurt; or labneh, store-bought or homemade (page 336), for serving (optional)

Preheat oven to 425°F. Line 2 baking sheets with parchment. Divide the carrots between the pans. Toss each batch with 1 torn chile de arbol, a pinch of fine sea salt, 1 teaspoon honey, and enough olive oil to coat every carrot. I toss everything right on the pan, using my hands to distribute the wet ingredients evenly. Spread the carrots in an even layer, making sure there is space for water to evaporate quickly (½ inch or so in between each one). Roast for about 25 minutes, turning once or twice, or until sticky and caramelized. Season each batch with a squeeze of lemon. Cool slightly.

Cut the avocados in half lengthwise and remove the pits. Slice in half lengthwise once more, peel each quarter, keeping the quarters intact, if possible. Season the avocado—directly on the cutting board—with a squeeze of lemon and 2 pinches of fine sea salt. On one serving platter or divided among 4 to 6 plates, layer the components in loose layers: avocado, carrot, a pinch of dukkah, sunflower sprouts, cilantro leaves, a few slices of serrano chile (if using), and a scattering of flaky sea salt; repeat the layering once more. Dot the chile vinegar (if using) or more lemon juice over the top, drizzle lightly with olive oil, and sprinkle with flaky sea salt. Serve straight away with a bowl of crème fraîche, yogurt or labneh alongside, if you'd like.

SMASHED PEAS WITH PRESERVED LEMON AND HERB OIL

This versatile dish can swing as a side or a sauce. Sweet, slightly starchy peas are briefly and partially blitzed, creating a contrast of textures. Serve this as a vegetarian main, next to a pot of polenta or basmati rice, or as a side for any meat or fish.

4 SERVINGS

Fine sea salt

2½ cups peas (approximately 13 ounces), fresh or frozen

1 to 2 teaspoons lemon juice

¼ cup Preserved Lemon and Herb Oil (page 347), divided

½ cup (loosely packed) torn or coarsely chopped fresh herbs (flat-leaf parsley, dill, green sorrel, mint, and/or finely chopped chives)

1 cup labneh, store-bought or homemade (page 336); ricotta; or fromage blanc, for serving (optional)

Bring a large pot of water to a rolling boil; add a handful of salt. Prepare an ice bath. Boil the peas for 1 minute, at which point the peas should be intensely green. Using a large spider, slotted spoon, or colander, drain and ice the peas. Let stand for 2 to 3 minutes, then drain the peas once more. Scoop about ½ cup peas into a food processor and puree, stopping and scraping down the bowl as needed. Add the remaining peas into the processor with 1 teaspoon lemon juice, then pulse a few times—your aim is an uneven texture, with some peas whole and some split. Fold 2 tablespoons herb oil into the peas. Taste and adjust for seasoning, adding more salt or lemon juice, as needed.

If using labneh (or other fresh cheese), mound it in the middle of a large serving platter (or divide among dinner plates); use the back of a spoon to spread into a thick bed. Spoon the peas on and around the cheese. Dress with another 2 tablespoons herb oil. Strew the reserved herbs across everything. Serve immediately, offering more herb oil at the table, if you'd like.

NOT JUST A SIDE SALAD

The antidote to a wilted, easily forgotten side salad is Little Gem lettuce, a darling varietal with sturdy romaine-like leaves, a sweet flavor, and a refreshing, juicy bite. The small, crisp leaves hold dressings and toppings well and beg to be eaten by hand (which makes eating more fun).

4 TO 6 SERVINGS

LITTLE GEM SALAD WITH YUZU KOSHO, AVOCADO, RADISH, AND HERBS

4 to 6 heads Little Gem lettuce (approximately 1½ pounds) or any small, crisp lettuce (such as baby romaine)

Fine sea salt

¼ cup Yuzu Kosho Dressing (page 335)

1 medium watermelon radish or 3 small radishes, thinly sliced (use a mandoline for best results)

2 large avocados, cut lengthwise into eight wedges, peeled, and seasoned with fine sea salt

1½ cups (loosely packed) torn or coarsely chopped fresh herbs (a mix of tarragon, chervil, flat-leaf parsley, cilantro, and/or dill)

2 tablespoons thinly sliced chives

LITTLE GEM SALAD WITH PARM AND CRISPY CAPERS

4 to 6 heads Little Gem lettuce (approximately 1½ pounds) or any small, crisp lettuce (such as baby romaine)

Fine sea salt

¼ cup Basic Lemon Dressing (page 335), Basic Banyuls Dressing (page 335), or Preserved Lemon Dressing (page 335)

3 ounces Parmigiano-Reggiano or similar cheese, shaved

¼ cup Crispy Capers (page 348)

continued

LITTLE GEM SALAD WITH CRÈME FRAÎCHE AND CRISPY SHALLOTS

4 to 6 heads Little Gem lettuce
(approximately 1½ pounds) or
any small, crisp lettuce
(such as baby romaine)

Fine sea salt

¼ cup Crème Fraîche Dressing
(page 335)

½ cup Crispy Shallots
(page 350)

1½ cups (loosely packed) torn or
coarsely chopped fresh herbs
(tarragon, chervil, flat-leaf parsley,
cilantro, and/or dill) (optional)

LITTLE GEM SALAD WITH LEMON AND BOTTARGA

(Pictured here.)

4 to 6 heads Little Gem lettuce
(approximately 1½ pounds)
or any small, crisp lettuce
(such as baby romaine)

Fine sea salt

¼ cup Basic Lemon Dressing
(page 335)

Zest of 1 lemon (use a Microplane
for best results)

¼ cup (as grated; do not pack)
freshly grated bottarga (use a Microplane
for best results), Dried Shrimp Powder
(page 352), Seaweed Powder (page 351),
or nori powder (store-bought or
homemade, page 71)

2 green onions, white and
light-green parts, sliced thinly
on the diagonal

For any of these recipe variations, follow these directions: Cut an inch off the bottom of each Little Gem head and discard. Gently peel back the leaves, continuing to trim the root as you go, until you get to the core (with tightly bunched leaves attached); cut each core in half lengthwise. Gently wash the leaves and dry well.

Place the Little Gem leaves and cores in a large mixing bowl and season with 1 to 2 pinches of salt. Drizzle about 3 tablespoons of the vinaigrette or dressing over the leaves and gently toss, adding more as needed, until every leaf is dressed. Arrange the leaves on a large serving platter—"cup" side up—and top with half of the remaining ingredients. Repeat layering once more. Serve immediately.

WHOLE ROASTED CAULIFLOWER
WITH TURMERIC GHEE

A few years ago, raw kale salad won the nation's belly. Then baby kale leaves were turned into "chips," scoring food awards and the most coveted spots on supermarket shelves. I'm not sure if this was before or after the crispy brussels sprouts craze. Now cauliflower is in. These trends have made me realize that people want to eat cruciferous vegetables, but they need to be told how to make them the best—or at least intriguing—versions of themselves.

Whole roasted cauliflower is stunningly beautiful, hearty, and elemental. And since cauliflower is so versatile, once you learn the technique, you can adapt the flavors to suit your every whim. Try omitting the turmeric, yogurt, and lime and drenching the roast—once it's out of the oven—in Bagna Cauda (page 341), Anchovy Gremolata (page 346), or Green Za'atar (page 357) instead.

4 SERVINGS

1 medium head or
2 small heads cauliflower
(approximately 2¼ pounds)

3 tablespoons ghee

1 chile de arbol, torn in half

1 tablespoon ground
turmeric

Fine sea salt

1 cup plain, full-fat Greek
yogurt, Labneh (page 336),
or 4 lime wedges, to serve

Preheat oven to 375°F. Trim the base of the cauliflower slightly (so it will sit upright); if your head has leaves, leave them on—they're delicious. Place an ovenproof dish with high sides—ideally one just large enough to hold the cauliflower—over medium heat. Add the ghee and chile de arbol, and let the spice infuse the warm fat for 2 to 3 minutes. Turn off the heat and stir in the turmeric. Have a spoon nearby. Using gloves if you don't want yellow-stained hands, spread the ghee mixture all over the cauliflower; use the spoon to drizzle some of the ghee between the crevices. Season the entire head generously with salt. Nestle the cauliflower, stem side down, in the now ghee-coated dish. Roast the cauliflower, uncovered, for 40 to 45 minutes, or until caramelized and tender—when you pierce it with a skewer it should offer little to no resistance. If it still seems a bit firm, return the cauliflower to the oven, reduce the temperature to 350°F, and continue to check every 5 minutes until it is cooked and caramelized. If it is browning too much (you want caramelization but not a black dinner), tent it with foil. Discard the chile and any turmeric ghee left in the pan. Serve with yogurt, labneh, or lime.

RAW MUSTARD GREENS SALAD
WITH TAMARIND DRESSING

This is a very simple but surprising salad. Sweet, tangy tamarind is the perfect foil for mustard greens' kick, and together they're the perfect contrast to heavier or fattier dishes. If you'd like to make it more substantial, this bowl of mustard greens welcomes steak, pork loin, and even fish or shrimp.

4 TO 6 SERVINGS

2 teaspoons lemon juice

1 teaspoon fish sauce

½ teaspoon tamarind paste (page 90)

Fine sea salt

¼ cup olive oil

10 ounces small, young, frilly mustard greens (purple mustard greens pictured)

1 green onion, white part only, trimmed and thinly sliced

In a small mixing bowl, whisk together the lemon juice, fish sauce, and tamarind paste with a pinch of salt. Add the olive oil and whisk to combine. Put the mustard greens, the green onion, and a pinch of salt in a large mixing bowl; toss gently to combine. Add three-quarters of the dressing, tossing gently, and adding a bit more dressing slowly, until the greens are coated—don't add so much that they're weighed down. Taste and adjust as needed; refrigerate any leftover dressing in an airtight container for up to 5 days. This salad is best served straight away.

KOHLRABI SALAD WITH KEFIR AND CARAWAY

You may initially doubt the combination of mayonnaise, kefir, miso, and caraway, but proceed confidently: this sauce—and salad—are addictively good.

Alien-like with its bright-purple skin, circumferential ridges, and antennae-like leaves, kohlrabi has a flavor reminiscent of sweet earth and mild mustard. Unlike its leafy relatives in the cabbage family, kohlrabi's texture is somewhere between starchy potato and water chestnut (firm, crisp, and juicy), making it perfect for shaving and serving raw, caramelizing in a hot oven, stir-frying until tender, or simmering into a silky soup.

Tips—You can find kohlrabi at farmers markets, co-ops, and Asian grocers from November through April. They range greatly in size, so if they're destined for a puree, purchase the larger ones, which make peeling and chopping a breeze. Otherwise, opt for smaller specimens, whose insides are less likely to be pithy or fibrous. The different colors of the kohlrabi varieties are only skin deep; the flesh's white hue and delicate flavor remain the same.

**APPROXIMATELY
4 SERVINGS**

¼ cup plus 1 tablespoon Special Sauce (page 338)

¼ teaspoon ground caraway

1 tablespoon finely chopped chives, plus more to serve

2 tablespoons finely chopped fresh dill, plus more to serve

1 medium kohlrabi (approximately ¾ pound once trimmed of greens), peeled and cut into thin matchsticks (use a mandoline for best results)

Fine sea salt

In a medium mixing bowl, whisk together all the ingredients except the kohlrabi; let sit 10 minutes to let flavors meld. Add the kohlrabi and toss to combine. Taste and add more caraway or salt, if you'd like. Top with more chopped dill and chives.

RAW CARROT SALAD WITH CITRUS AND BLACK SEEDS

A trio of acids and nutty, pleasantly pungent seeds enhance and balance the sweetness of carrots. This recipe makes twice as many toasted black seeds as you need, so either double the carrots or use the seeds to garnish other dishes. I use the seeds on top of red beets, Black Lentils (page 161) (with yogurt and olive oil), black rice salads, and charred, grilled vegetables. And leftover salad makes a great topping for sandwiches (think: Black Lentil Hummus, page 124, canned sardines and butter, labneh and sprouts, or pulled lamb and mint).

4 TO 6 SERVINGS

1 tablespoon black sesame seeds

1 teaspoon poppy seeds

1 teaspoon nigella seeds

1 tablespoon lemon juice

1 teaspoon orange juice

1 teaspoon Banyuls vinegar

Fine sea salt

⅓ cup olive oil

1 pound jumbo carrots, cut into thin matchsticks (use a mandoline for best results)

Preheat oven to 350°F. Toast all the seeds on a rimmed baking sheet for 5 minutes. Alternatively, toast them over a medium heat in a 9- or 10-inch dry skillet, tossing occasionally until they smell nutty and start to make popping noises, 3 to 5 minutes.

In a medium mixing bowl, whisk the lemon juice, orange juice, and vinegar with a pinch of salt, then whisk in the oil. Add the carrots, toss, and let sit at least 30 minutes (and up to 1 hour). Toss with about 1 tablespoon toasted seeds just before serving. Taste and add more acid or olive oil, as needed.

HEARTY CAULIFLOWER AND RADICCHIO SALAD WITH FRIED PINE NUTS, BARBERRIES, AND SUMAC

This is one of the salads I eat straight from the mixing bowl, all four servings, all for me. I think winter salads are their own art form, and my framework includes four elements: bitter or peppery greens (chicories, arugula, dandelion, etc.), creaminess (could be cheese, large white beans, a tahini dressing, or cooked vegetables such as roasted pumpkin), crunch (chopped nuts, toasted sesame or buckwheat, crispy capers, or fried breadcrumbs), and something tangy to lift everything up (citrus, pomegranate, vinegar, etc.). This salad has all of that, and—striped and splattered with different hues of white and magenta—it is striking too.

Seek out Treviso or the lesser-known Lusia radicchio. These beautiful, variegated chicory varieties are relatives of the more-familiar Chioggia radicchio. Lusia has a light-green base with red speckles and all the boldly bittersweet flavor of its chicory family relatives. If you can't find barberries, use dried currants instead.

Tips—If you're not that into chicories, just omit them and nix the dressing; shower the roasted cauliflower in the pickled red onion, barberries, pine nuts, and sumac and serve it as a side for two to three people. Dig chicories, but looking to make this into a main course? Add chickpeas (page 240), or, instead of cauliflower, use leftover roast chicken—sliced, chopped or pulled into bite-sized pieces.

4 TO 6 SERVINGS

½ small red onion, very thinly sliced

1 teaspoon Banyuls vinegar or other red wine vinegar

Fine sea salt

2 medium heads cauliflower (approximately 4½ pounds), cored and cut or broken into small (approximately 1 to 1½ inches) florets

½ cup plus 3 tablespoons olive oil, divided

2 medium or 4 small heads radicchio (12 to 14 ounces) (such as Lusia, Chioggia, and/or Castelfranco), leaves separated, large leaves torn into 3-inch pieces

2 tablespoons barberries

1½ teaspoons ground sumac, divided

FRIED PINE NUTS

1½ tablespoons olive oil or ghee

⅓ cup pine nuts

Fine sea salt

Preheat oven to 450°F. Toss the onion and vinegar in a large bowl; season with salt. The onion will pickle slightly while you prepare the rest of the ingredients.

Line 2 rimmed baking sheets with parchment and divide the cauliflower florets between them. Toss each pan of cauliflower with ¼ cup olive oil and season with salt. Arrange the cauliflower so a flat side is facing down and roast until dark brown and crisp on bottom, 15 to 20 minutes. Remove from oven and turn the pieces over. Roast until the other side is dark brown and crisp, 10 to 15 minutes. Let cool slightly.

Meanwhile, fry the pine nuts. In a 9- or 10-inch skillet, heat olive oil over medium heat. Add the pine nuts and fry for 2 to 3 minutes, giving the skillet a

continued

shake a few times, or until golden brown. Tip them onto a cutting board (if you leave them in the skillet with the hot fat, they'll continue to brown), toss them with a pinch of salt, and let them cool. Coarsely chop them; I find it prevents them from all ending up on the bottom of the mixing bowl.

In a large mixing bowl, toss the radicchio with the cauliflower, onion, the onion's vinegar, and a pinch of salt. Add 3 tablespoons olive oil, most of the barberries, half the sumac, and most of the pine nuts and toss to coat. Transfer the salad to a platter or shallow bowl and top with reserved barberries, sumac, and pine nuts. This salad holds better than most, but I recommend serving within an hour of tossing.

CELERY ROOT SALAD WITH YOGURT, CAPERS, AND TARRAGON

This is a lighter, brighter version of the Parisian bistro classic remoulade—a platter of crisp, raw celery root tossed in a creamy dressing that's punctuated by briny capers and wisps of tarragon. Celery root, also referred to as celeriac, is a kind of celery (there are many wonderful varieties of this common biennial) prized for its enlarged root versus its stalks or leaves. You will spot it intermittently throughout the fall and winter. Purchase small, heavy roots; the larger, lighter ones can be pithy inside. Store celery root with the skin on, in the refrigerator, for up to 1 week. Peel and discard the skin (and any nooks holding dirt) before using it. If you find celery root with the leaves still attached, use the slightly bitter greens in soups, stews, or stock. To peel it, lop off the root and opposite end with a chef's knife, stand the round root on a flat end, then take the knife and cut downward, working around the outside, to slice off the tough skin.

Tips—Celery root discolors a bit once exposed to air, so it's ideal to make the dressing before cutting. (Some will tell you to drop your cut veg into acidulated lemon water as you work, but I find the clinging water droplets dilute the finished salad.)

4 TO 6 SERVINGS

½ teaspoon lemon juice

Fine sea salt

½ cup Yogurt Mayonnaise (page 339)

1 celery root (1 to 1½ pounds), cut into thin matchsticks (use a mandoline for best results)

2 tablespoons salt-packed capers, soaked for 15 to 30 minutes in cool water, rinsed, drained, and very coarsely chopped (so coarse that most are just halved)

¼ cup (loosely packed) coarsely chopped fresh tarragon

3 tablespoons thinly sliced chives

In a medium mixing bowl, stir together the lemon juice with about ½ teaspoon salt. Whisk or stir in the yogurt mayonnaise. As you cut the celery root, occasionally scoop up the pile from your workspace and toss it with the dressing. Let the celery root soften for roughly 30 minutes (and up to 2 hours) before mixing in the capers, tarragon, and chives. Toss again, taste, and add more lemon juice or salt, if needed.

SUMMER SQUASH SALAD WITH DRIED SHRIMP AND CRISPY SHALLOTS

Inspired by som tum, a green papaya salad eaten throughout Southeast Asia, this is one of the most complex and unusual salads I make. I think of it as a "condiment salad," one you likely don't eat by the bowlful but that serves as a much-needed complement to relatively mild dishes—things such as rice, noodles, steamed or roasted fish, shrimp, tofu, tempeh, pork chops, and so on.

The ingredient list may seem long for a salad, but you can save time by planning ahead: the shallots can be fried days in advance (and used for other dishes too), and the dried shrimp powder can be made months in advance. If you don't have dried shrimp powder on hand and don't want to make it, add 2 teaspoons fish sauce instead, but decrease the salt slightly, adding more to taste as you go.

4 TO 6 SERVINGS

1 pound small yellow summer squash, cut into thin matchsticks (use a mandoline for best results)

½ teaspoon fine sea salt

1 to 2 serrano or Fresno chiles, stemmed and thinly sliced

2 teaspoons lime juice

½ teaspoon coconut sugar

2 tablespoons Shallot Oil (page 350)

1 cup Crispy Shallots (page 350)

¼ cup coarsely chopped toasted peanuts

1½ cups (loosely packed) fresh Thai basil or mint leaves (large leaves torn in half)

2 tablespoons Dried Shrimp Powder (page 352)

1 lime, cut into quarters

Place the squash in a large colander and gently toss with the salt to coat. Let the squash drain over a sink or bowl for 20 to 30 minutes.

In a medium mixing bowl, combine about three-quarters of the chile with the lime juice, coconut sugar, shallot oil, and 2 pinches of salt. Give the squash a few vigorous shakes in the colander to remove any standing water (this will also bruise the squash slightly and enable it to absorb more flavor); add to the dressing and toss to combine. Add three-quarters of the following: crispy shallots, peanuts, basil, and dried shrimp powder. Toss to combine and taste. If you want more heat, add more sliced chile; if it needs salt, acid, or shallot oil, add sparingly before tossing and tasting again. Transfer to a serving dish; garnish with the remaining shallots, peanuts, basil, and dried shrimp powder; serve immediately (or the crispy shallots will go soggy) with lime wedges on the side.

THE NEW FRUIT SALAD

There are many reasons to be enthusiastic about a fruit salad. When made well, it has the potential to delight more than anything else you make. Fruit salad makes sense at any time of day and for practically any occasion. And it provides a unique opportunity to enjoy relatively extreme contrast; the texture, juiciness, and sweetness of fruit is unmatched, and these qualities make it a perfect partner for countless crispy, salty, tart, frilly, and creamy ingredients. When thinking about the possibilities, I was overwhelmed with options—there should be an entire book dedicated to the modern fruit salad!

Tips—It is important to taste your fruit before proceeding with a recipe. (Always be tasting!) Even the same variety of a fruit can vary widely in sweetness, tartness, and texture. So you must nibble and contemplate and adjust components accordingly. Cut your fruit in a way that makes sense to eat and is pleasing to the eye; I've noted my preferences (I often opt for thin slices or irregular, sculptural cuts), but, of course, you can go your own way with good results. Slicing fennel, onion, apples, and so forth on a mandoline makes the job easy and efficient. Use a Y-peeler or Microplane for cheese. Keep components chilled and separate until the last minute; then, instead of tossing, layer and compose, following the order of the chart on the facing page. Otherwise, fruit will leach juice and everything will become a dreadfully soggy texture and uniform in flavor.

4 TO 6 SERVINGS

	WATERMELON AND CUCUMBER SALAD WITH FETA AND SUMAC *(Pictured on page vi.)*	PLUM AND CUCUMBER SALAD WITH UME AND SHISO	KOHLRABI, PERSIMMON, AND WALNUT SALAD	POMELO SALAD WITH TOASTED CHICKPEA FLOUR AND CRISPY SHALLOTS *(Pictured on page 199.)*	ORANGE SALAD WITH ALMONDS AND ALEPPO-STYLE PEPPER
FRUIT	¾ to 1 pound (approximately ¾ of a) small peeled and seeded watermelon, cut into irregular 2-inch cubes or sliced ¼-inch thick	¾ to 1 pound (approximately 6) firm-ripe red or black plums, pitted and cut into ½-inch wedges	¾ to 1 pound (approximately 3) Fuyu persimmons, seeded (if needed) and thinly sliced	¾ to 1 pound (approximately 2) pomelos or grapefruits, peel and pith removed, segmented, juice reserved	¾ to 1 pound (approximately 4 medium navel or 5 small blood) oranges, peel and pith removed, sliced crosswise into ¼-inch rounds
ADDTL. FRUIT(S) AND/OR VEGETABLE(S)	3 small Persian cucumbers, thinly sliced ⅓ cup Quick-Pickled Shallots (page 348) or thinly sliced green onion	1 medium cucumber, such as Persian or Painted Serpent, cut into irregular 1-inch cubes or sliced ¼-inch thick	2 small kohlrabi, peeled and thinly sliced	1 medium shallot, peeled and thinly sliced; soaked in ice water for 10 minutes, drained and patted dry	½ white onion, thinly sliced (use a mandoline for best results); soaked in ice water for 10 minutes, drained and patted dry
VINAIGRETTE (3 TABLESPOONS TO ¼ CUP)	Basic Banyuls Dressing (page 335) A few drops of rose water	Ume Dressing (page 335)	Walnut Dressing (page 335)	2 teaspoons reserved pomelo juice 1½ to 2 teaspoons fish sauce 1 tablespoon Shallot Oil (page 350)	Basic Banyuls Dressing (page 335) ½ teaspoon orange flower water
GREENS (APPROX. 1 GENEROUS HANDFUL)	Sprouts (such as buckwheat or sunflower) or tender greens (mâche, watercress, or arugula) Fresh cilantro, whole leaves and tender stems, and/or mint	Shiso, large leaves torn Arugula or mizuna leaves (optional)			
FINISHES	4 ounces feta cheese, sliced ¼-inch thick ¼ to ½ teaspoon sumac Toasted buckwheat groats (page 21), or Fried Pine Nuts (page 190) Flaky sea salt	1 green onion, sliced on a steep diagonal, soused with lemon juice or umeboshi vinegar Flaky sea salt	½ cup coarsely chopped toasted walnuts or walnuts in walnut oil (page 137) 6 ounces Manchego, pecorino sardo, or similar cheese, shaved	¼ to ⅓ cup Crispy Shallots (page 350) ¾ to 1 teaspoon Toasted Chickpea Flour (page 351) Flaky sea salt	¼ cup toasted (ideally Marcona) almonds, chopped Pinch of Aleppo-style pepper, Marash pepper, or piment d'Espelette chile flakes Flaky sea salt

VERJUS-GLAZED SHALLOTS

Glazing vegetables may be out of fashion, but this recipe makes a case for a comeback. Here, shallot's characteristic oniony bite is tamed by the technique, and a glug of fruity verjus renders them remarkable. Nestled up to a deeply flavored main course, these are comforting in their stark simplicity and unctuous texture.

If making this as a side dish, consider doubling it and incorporating leftover shallots in meals throughout the week: top pork chops, toss with sautéed green beans, add to grain salads, or blitz in a blender with olive oil for a light but creamy dressing.

4 TO 6 SERVINGS

1½ pounds shallots (approximately 14 medium)

1 cup Simple Chicken Stock (page 346) or store-bought chicken stock

½ cup white verjus

2 tablespoons ghee or unsalted butter

½ teaspoon fine sea salt

Peel the shallots: trim their roots while making sure to keep the stems intact; make a lengthwise, shallow incision (1–2 skin layers deep) along one side; peel back the skin and pull to remove. Find a deep skillet or saute pan that will fit the shallots in a single layer. Pour over the chicken stock and verjus; add the ghee and season with the salt. Bring to a boil over high heat, reduce to a simmer, and cook the shallots, uncovered, shaking the skillet occasionally, until they're tender, about 10 minutes. Raise the heat to medium and cook the shallots, shaking to turn, until they start to caramelize all over and are coated in a thick syrup. Serve immediately. Any leftover shallots can be refrigerated in an airtight container for up to 4 days.

BLISTERED TOMATOES WITH PRESERVED LEMON

These slightly charred, practically melted tomatoes are made extraordinary by preserved lemon, chile de arbol, and coconut sugar. They are just as happily a simple side or a component to something greater. I usually double the recipe so I can reach for a giant spoonful whenever I'm in need of a quick meal. Toss them with parboiled green beans or pasta. Spoon them on labneh or feta. Use them to turn tinned fish and canned beans into high-impact dishes. They should, at some point, top polenta or another savory porridge. And they are destined to be used as a rich and deeply flavorful braising medium for legumes, meat (such as chicken thighs, meatballs, and lamb shanks), and seafood (see Braised Rock Cod, page 257).

4 TO 6 SERVINGS

1½ pounds cherry tomatoes, stemmed and halved lengthwise

¾ cup olive oil

¼ teaspoon coconut sugar, muscovado, or granulated cane sugar

2 cloves garlic, smashed and peeled

1 chile de arbol or 1 teaspoon Harissa (page 342)

Rind of ¼ preserved lemon, plus 1 tablespoon preserved lemon brine

Fine sea salt

½ teaspoon Banyuls vinegar or other red wine vinegar

Preheat oven to 425°F. In a medium frying pan or other medium ovenproof baking dish (you want the tomatoes in at least two layers, otherwise the braising liquid will evaporate too quickly and burn), toss the tomatoes with the olive oil, coconut sugar, garlic, chile de arbol, preserved lemon (rind and brine), and 2 pinches of salt. Roast the tomatoes for 40 to 50 minutes, or until caramelized in patches—blistered—and slightly shrunken. Remove the chile and lemon rind. Stir in the vinegar; taste and add more salt, if needed. Once cool, the tomatoes can be refrigerated in an airtight container for up to 5 days.

GREEN BEANS

Lean, sweet green beans benefit from contrast, and the modern larder can bring it. Searing the beans until their skin turns blackened and wrinkly in spots exposes a different side of their character, one I really like. I also know that method isn't practical if you don't have the time or patience to cook the beans in several batches. When that's the case for you, just blanch the entire pound in a large pot nearly full of salted boiling water for 2 minutes before using a spider to transfer them to a kitchen towel to drain. From there, you can choose which direction to take based on whatever fixings you've got and on your preferences for heat, acidity, and richness.

> **Tip**—Often, but for this dish especially, people's preference for the amount of dressing varies a lot. So, add to taste.

6 SERVINGS

Read through the options on page 204 before beginning to cook.

Heat a 12- or 14-inch skillet over medium-high heat. Drizzle in just enough olive oil to slick the bottom of the pan; tilt and swirl until no bald spots remain.

Add half the green beans (you don't want to overcrowd the pan) and cook undisturbed, until beginning to blister, about 3 minutes. Toss with tongs and continue to cook, tossing occasionally, until tender and blistered on most sides, about 7 minutes more. Spread the green beans out on a sheet pan or rimmed platter, season with a pinch of fine sea salt, and let cool while you repeat with the remaining green beans.

Once the green beans have cooled to room temperature, pile them on a serving platter. Toss or drizzle and top with whatever you choose, and serve immediately.

continued

SEAR

Olive oil or neutral vegetable oil
(such as cold-pressed rice bran oil or
grapeseed oil) for pan-frying

1 pound green beans,
such as haricots verts or pole beans,
trimmed, washed, and completely dry

Fine sea salt

TOSS   OR   DRIZZLE + TOP

TOSS

Instant "XO" (page 341) or
warm 'nduja dressing (page 171)
+
Cilantro, whole leaves and tender stems

OR

Anchovy Gremolata (page 346) or
any Green Sauce (page 344)
+
Fresh, soft herbs
(one or a few—whatever is in the sauce)
(Pictured here with Nam Jim.)

OR

Blistered Tomatoes with
Preserved Lemon (page 201)

OR

Verjus-Glazed Shallots (page 200)
+
Sliced or coarsely chopped flat-leaf parsley
+
Flaky sea salt

DRIZZLE + TOP

Walnut Dressing (page 335)
+
Coarsely chopped toasted walnuts or
walnuts in walnut oil (page 137)
+
Sliced flat-leaf parsley or tarragon

OR

Tahini Yogurt (page 338) thinned with
water to drizzable consistency
+
Toasted sesame seeds or benne seeds
+
Fresh, soft herbs, such as dill or
cilantro (optional)

OR

Special Sauce (page 338) or
Basic Lemon Dressing (page 335)
+
Crispy Shallots (page 350)
+
Fresh, soft herbs, such as dill,
cilantro, or chervil (optional)

CARAMELIZED ZUCCHINI WITH DATE SYRUP, DILL, AND WALNUTS

I like to honor what's available, and, come midsummer, that's zucchini. Here I coax its underappreciated flavor—mild, tender, sweet, and just the tiniest bit vegetal—by using salt to dehydrate the flesh before searing it in a scalding hot pan. Once caramelized, the still-warm zucchini softens in its own steam until just tender. Then it's added to a big bowl where it soaks up a sweet and sour dressing that is startlingly good.

This makes a stellar side, but I've also eaten it as a light lunch with a big pull of bread. For a little more substance, toss some chickpeas (page 240), farro, or sautéed ground lamb with the zucchini right before serving.

Tip—If you can find small (approximately 4 inches long) zucchini, buy them. Larger zucchini contain a lot more water and are more likely to turn to mush when cooked.

4 TO 6 SERVINGS

1½ pounds zucchini (approximately 16 small), trimmed

1 teaspoon fine sea salt

2 tablespoons olive oil, plus more for pan-frying

6 garlic cloves, smashed and peeled

1 tablespoon lemon juice

1½ teaspoons date syrup

1 tablespoon walnut oil

¼ teaspoon Aleppo-style pepper or Marash pepper

½ cup toasted walnut halves, finely chopped

¼ cup (loosely packed) coarsely chopped fresh dill

Halve the zucchini lengthwise and toss with the salt; place in a strainer set in the sink or over a large bowl and set aside for at least 30 minutes (or refrigerate for up to 12 hours).

Line a baking sheet with parchment. Pat the zucchini dry with a kitchen towel. Place a 10- to 12-inch heavy-bottomed sauté pan over medium-high heat. Drizzle in just enough olive oil to evenly coat the bottom of the pan; tilt and swirl until no bald spots remain. Depending on the size of your pan, you may need to sear the zucchini in batches. Place the zucchini in a single layer—pieces can be close but shouldn't touch—and season with a pinch of salt; add the garlic cloves and sear 6 to 8 minutes.

Meanwhile, in a large mixing bowl, whisk together the lemon juice with a pinch of salt, as well as the date syrup, walnut oil, and 2 tablespoons olive oil.

Carefully turn the zucchini and garlic, lower the heat to medium, cover the pan and steam the zucchini until just tender, 6 to 9 minutes, depending on their size (if thumb-sized, it may only be 1 to 2 minutes). Transfer the zucchini to the baking sheet and

continued

repeat pan-frying process—adding more oil, if needed—with any remaining halves. Transfer the warm, caramelized garlic to a cutting board and chop into a paste—add this to the dressing, ideally while it is still warm. Once the zucchini has cooled slightly, cut into approximately 3- to 4-inch pieces (small zucchini can be left whole); use your hands (not tongs) to gently toss with the dressing and Aleppo-style pepper. Let the zucchini marinate for about 10 minutes. Scatter all but 1 tablespoon or so of the walnuts and chopped dill across the salad; using your hands, transfer the zucchini to a serving platter or divide between plates (the dill and walnuts should get "tossed" and distributed as you do this). Top with reserved dill and walnuts, and another pinch of Aleppo-style pepper. Serve warm or at room temperature.

WHOLE GRILLED FAVA BEANS WITH CHILE, DRIED LIME, AND DILL

Most people will tell you that fava beans have to be taken out of their shell and then individually peeled. This is true for the large, mature beans, which are relatively starchy. This recipe proves there is an exception. It uses the tiniest, most tender favas you can find (any extra energy expended in the shopping process will be regained in the kitchen). The sweet, grassy flavor of the beans is balanced by the smoky lick of the grill, tangy dried lime, and spicy Aleppo-style pepper. In fact, this dish is complex and hearty enough to serve as a vegetarian main, especially if you round out the meal with a bowl of labneh (page 336) or feta and some bread, rice, or farro.

Tips—You can also roast young fava beans in the oven, although the smoky, charred effect is nearly impossible to achieve: spread on a baking sheet in a single layer and roast at 450°F for about 25 minutes, or until tender. As always, the amount of chile heat is up to you; I've provided a range for the Aleppo-style pepper measurement, and I assume you know if you want more or less in each bite.

4 TO 6 SERVINGS

1 to 1½ teaspoons crushed Aleppo-style pepper, Urfa pepper, or Marash pepper

¾ teaspoon dried lime powder (page 38), or more to taste

1 teaspoon fine sea salt

6 tablespoons olive oil, plus more to serve

1 tablespoon water

2 pounds young (relatively short and thin) fresh fava beans, topped and tailed (strings removed from both seams), washed and dried

2 teaspoons lemon juice

½ cup (loosely packed) coarsely chopped fresh dill

Flaky sea salt

Heat a grill to medium-high heat or set up for indirect heat. In a large mixing bowl, combine the Aleppo-style pepper, dried lime powder, fine sea salt, oil, water, and fava beans; toss to coat.

Grill the fava beans until the pods are charred, tender, and begin to open, 2 to 3 minutes per side. Remove the pods from the grill and immediately return them to the mixing bowl along with the lemon juice and dill; give everything a good toss. Add more chile, lime powder, and flaky sea salt, to taste. Serve favas family style, heaped on a shallow platter and drizzled with more olive oil. Encourage others to eat with their hands by eating with yours.

CRISPY SWEET POTATOES WITH TAHINI YOGURT AND SEAWEED GOMASIO

These caramelized potatoes are dense and fluffy on the inside and crisp on the outside; creamy tahini yogurt both enriches and brightens; and spicy seaweed gomasio pulls this dish from the edge of cloying.

Tips—I generally prefer smallish Japanese sweet potatoes—their relatively dry, firm, white flesh remains dense once cooked, unlike orange sweet potatoes, which risk breaking apart during parboiling. If you don't want to make seaweed gomasio, try this dish with store-bought togarashi, toasted sesame seeds, or basic gomasio; the latter two can be mixed with a little Aleppo-style pepper or ground chile de arbol to taste.

**APPROXIMATELY
4 SERVINGS**

2 pounds sweet potatoes
(5 small or 3 medium),
scrubbed

Fine sea salt

1 cup Tahini Yogurt
(page 338)

¼ cup plus 1 tablespoon
olive oil, plus more to serve

½ lemon

3 to 4 tablespoons thinly
sliced green onion, white
and light-green parts
(optional)

1 tablespoon Seaweed
Gomasio (page 358),
Spicy Seaweed Gomasio
(page 358), or store-
bought togarashi

Place the potatoes in a large pot and cover with cold water by 1 to 2 inches. (You start the whole potatoes in cold water so that they cook evenly—from the center out.) Add 2 pinches of salt and bring to a boil over high heat. Reduce the heat to a simmer and cook, uncovered, for 35 to 50 minutes, or until a paring knife inserted meets only slight resistance (at this point, you don't want the potatoes to be completely soft or they will fall apart when smashed.

Meanwhile, preheat oven to 425°F (do not use convection as the skin will quickly burn). Line 2 baking sheets with parchment paper. Thin the tahini yogurt with a few tablespoons of water—you want it the consistency of pancake batter or a creamy soup. Season the dressing with salt to taste.

Drain the potatoes, lay them out on a kitchen towel (to absorb extra moisture). When cool enough to handle, gently press on potatoes with your palm until slightly flattened. If you are using baby sweet potatoes, leave them whole. If large, tear each smashed potato into roughly 4-inch pieces; they will be irregularly shaped and sized, and that is good. The point is to expose its starch without creating mashed potatoes. Divide the potatoes between the two baking sheets and gently toss each batch with 2½ tablespoons olive oil and 2 pinches of salt. Spread them out, leaving 1 or 2 inches around each piece—overcrowding causes steaming and prevents

continued

browning. Roast for 22 to 25 minutes; flip the potatoes and roast for about 15 to 20 minutes more, or until both sides are crispy, caramelized, and—my preference—charred in spots. Squeeze a ¼ lemon over each pan, seasoning each piece with a few drops.

To serve, lay down one layer of crispy potato onto plates or a serving platter or bowl. Drizzle the potatoes with a little tahini yogurt and top with a sprinkling of green onion (if using) and seaweed gomasio. Finish with another layer of potatoes, another drizzle, another sprinkling. Serve warm or at room temperature, with a small bowl of any remaining tahini yogurt on the side.

MARINATED BEETS

Beets are versatile, fridge-stable, iron-rich, and visually striking. They're in regular rotation in my house, and since they take a relatively long time to cook, peel, and cool, I prep a double batch on the weekend and grab handfuls for various meals throughout the week. My technique involves tossing roasted beets in good vinegar, salt, and olive oil as soon as they are peeled and cut; the tender and still-warm beets absorb the dressing, and their sweet, earthy flavor finds its balance. Cooked and seasoned this way—and served with the holy trinity of creamy, crunchy, fresh— these marinated beets can convert even the most adamant of self-proclaimed beet-haters. Devise your own pairings or use my suggestions on page 216—all of which leverage the modern larder.

If your beets still have their greens attached, save them and cook as you would spinach, kale, or bok choy (see Baby Bok Choy "Under a Brick," page 220).

4 TO 6 SERVINGS

2 pounds beets (approximately 6 small), any variety

Fine sea salt

3 tablespoons olive oil, plus more for drizzling

1 tablespoon Banyuls vinegar or other red wine vinegar

Preheat oven to 400°F. Place the beets in a large, deep saucepan or Dutch oven; season with a pinch of salt and drizzle with a little olive oil and a splash of water; cover. Roast beets for 60 to 70 minutes (or less, if you found some small roots), or until easily pierced with the tip of a paring knife. While warm, peel beets by rubbing the skin with a clean cloth towel; it should slide right off. Slice the beets about ¼-inch thick (wedges or rounds, depending on size of beets and what you prefer). While they are still warm, toss with vinegar and salt to taste (2 to 3 pinches). Add 3 tablespoons olive oil and toss once more. Beets can be prepared up to 4 days in advance; refrigerate in an airtight container and, ideally, bring to room temperature before serving.

When ready to serve (see page 216 for pairing suggestions), mound the creamy component in the middle of a large serving platter (or divide among plates or shallow bowls); use the back of a spoon to spread into a thick bed. Arrange the marinated beets in a loose layer on top and drizzle with dressing. Mix dressing ingredients in a small bowl. Strew the remaining ingredients across everything. Serve immediately.

continued

	BEETS WITH HORSERADISH CRÈME FRAÎCHE AND TOASTED BUCKWHEAT *(Pictured on page 214.)*	**BEETS WITH FRESH CHEESE AND ROSE** *(Pictured on page 215.)*	**BEETS WITH LABNEH AND CURRY**
	I love the nose-clearing quality of fresh horseradish. If you don't, just omit it—the combination of crème fraîche, beets, and buckwheat still wins.	Beets pair surprisingly well with floral rose water. Tangy sumac accentuates the flavor of fresh cheese and galvanizes the long-roasted, deeply earthy root.	Marinated beets have a particular affinity for the warm, pungent, citrusy, floral-scented Curry Spice Blend (page 352). Golden beets are especially lovely here, their color echoed by the turmeric. For this recipe, the beets must be at room temperature or else the ghee will turn solid.
BASE	*2 pounds* beets, cooked and marinated, cut into ¾-inch wedges or cubes (see page 214)		
SOMETHING CREAMY	*Approximately 1¼ cups* Horseradish Crème Fraîche (page 337) or crème fraîche	*Approximately 1¼ cups* labneh, store-bought or homemade (page 336); fromage blanc; or ricotta	*Approximately 1¼ cups* labneh, store-bought or homemade (page 336)
DRESSING	*¼ to ⅓ cup* Basic Banyuls Dressing (page 335) or Basic Lemon Dressing (page 335)	*¼ to ⅓ cup* Basic Banyuls Dressing (page 335) *⅟₁₆ teaspoon* rose water	*3 tablespoons* Spiced Ghee (page 161) *1 tablespoon* olive oil *1 teaspoon* lemon juice *1 teaspoon* red wine vinegar
CRUNCHY BITS	*¼ cup* toasted buckwheat (page 21) or soba cha *1 tablespoon* freshly grated horseradish (optional) Flaky sea salt	*1 to 2 tablespoons* Sumac-Rose Gomasio (page 357) Flaky sea salt	*⅓ cup* toasted chopped pistachios or toasted sliced almonds Flaky sea salt
FRESH HERBS	Fresh edible flower petals (optional) or dill	Edible rose petals, red-veined sorrel, dill, or baby beet greens Snipped chives (optional)	Cilantro, whole leaves and tender stems Thinly sliced chives (optional)

GRILLED CORN WITH DRIED SHRIMP BUTTER

When I first made this dish for friends, I worried they would squirm, so I made two batches of corn: one soaked in shrimp butter and chives, one plain-Jane. To my surprise, everyone found the garnish of dried shrimp intriguing and thus inviting, and immediately dug in with enthusiasm. With every kernel of corn soon consumed, they went after the drippings with bread, scooping up every last bit of the mildly pungent, chive-infused, sweet and salty sea-butter. So, while good corn doesn't necessarily *need* anything, there is joy when the very ordinary is suddenly extraordinary, when your friends' faces light up with surprise and delight.

6 SERVINGS

Olive oil, for the grill

6 ears corn, husked

4 tablespoons unsalted butter or ghee

2 teaspoons Dried Shrimp Powder (page 352)

1 teaspoon Chile Vinegar (page 348) or a pinch of piment d'Espelette (optional)

Fine sea salt

3 tablespoons finely sliced chives

Flaky sea salt

½ lemon or lime, for serving

Build a medium-hot bed in a charcoal grill or heat a gas grill to high. Rub the grill grate with oil (I use a kitchen towel and long-handled tongs). Grill the corn, turning occasionally, until lightly charred all over, about 8 minutes. Place corn on a rimmed baking sheet or serving platter.

Or you can boil the corn: Bring a large pot of salted water to a boil. Add the corn, turn off the heat, and let it sit for 3 minutes. Drain and return to the pot, or transfer to a serving platter.

While the corn is cooking, melt the butter in small saucepan or skillet over medium heat. Add the dried shrimp powder, stir to combine, and turn off the heat. Toss the warm corn with the dried shrimp butter, the chile vinegar or piment d'Espelette (if using), and a pinch of fine sea salt. Garnish with the chives and flaky sea salt. Serve immediately with lemon or lime wedges.

SLOW-COOKED ROMANO BEANS WITH TOMATO AND POMEGRANATE MOLASSES

I have a particular affinity for dishes that straddle seasons and help me transition from one to the next. Come early October, I've tired of raw tomato salads but still can't resist buying the things. I'm craving something more warming and complex than the typical summer dish but I'm not quite ready for roasted pumpkin or braised beef. So I make this. *This* is a special dish—ugly, but good; humble, yet absolutely intriguing. Given the natural acidity of tomatoes, the pomegranate molasses is better than vinegar or lemon juice; it brightens the dish in a subtle way without being overly sweet.

4 SERVINGS

6 tablespoons olive oil

2 garlic cloves, thinly sliced

Fine sea salt

1 pound red tomatoes, cored and coarsely chopped

2 teaspoons pomegranate molasses

1 pound romano beans, trimmed

2 tablespoons water

1 small or ½ large cinnamon stick

¾ cup flat-leaf parsley leaves

Flaky sea salt

Heat the olive oil in a 10- to 12-inch heavy-bottomed sauté pan over medium heat. Add the garlic and a pinch of fine sea salt and sauté for 1 minute, making sure the garlic doesn't burn. Add the tomatoes, the pomegranate molasses, and 2 pinches of salt. Add the beans and 2 tablespoons water. Once the mixture comes to a simmer, cover the pot, turn the heat down as low as possible, and cook for 15 minutes. Add a pinch of fine sea salt and use tongs to toss and turn the beans—which should have wilted slightly—into the sauce. Return the lid and cook, covered, on low heat for 1 hour, checking on the pan in the last stretch to make sure there is still a good amount liquid (there should be, but add 1 tablespoon water, if needed). Remove the lid and gently nestle in the cinnamon stick. Raise the heat to medium-high, and cook uncovered 15 to 20 minutes more, until the sauce has reduced and thickened. Turn off the heat and stir gently with a wooden spoon or flexible heatproof spatula to incorporate the parsley leaves; discard the cinnamon stick. Cool slightly. Taste; finish with flaky sea salt. Slow-cooked romano beans are best served warm or at room temperature. Refrigerate any leftovers in an airtight container for up to 4 days.

BABY BOK CHOY "UNDER A BRICK"

The idea of weighing down food to facilitate browning and crispy edges is an old one, but it's typically reserved for meat. Here I apply the method to bok choy in order to approximate a fire-heated wok's char and smoky flavor, which is difficult to achieve on most home stoves. The multistep cooking process may seem fussy, but it ensures the bok choy is thoroughly tender while achieving that elusive effect that's reminiscent of a perfect stir-fry.

Tips—This recipe is endlessly adaptable. You can use large heads of bok choy cut crosswise into 3- to 4-inch pieces, or really any leafy veg you'd like—including those iffy greens lingering in the far corner of the fridge. Just keep in mind that cooking times may vary. Reach for any fat—olive oil, bacon fat, coconut oil, rice bran oil, and so on—except butter or delicate nut oils (which would burn). If you don't have chile vinegar but want heat, add a pinch of chile flakes (such as piment d'Espelette) at the end. I use a cast-iron skillet for this, but any heavy-bottomed metal workhorse will do. Just don't use nonstick.

3 TO 4 SERVINGS

1 pound baby bok choy or tatsoi, root ends trimmed (keep heads whole, if you can)

3 tablespoons schmaltz

Fine sea salt

⅓ cup Simple Chicken Stock (page 346) or store-bought chicken stock

Chile Vinegar (page 348) or lemon juice

After washing the bok choy, drain—spin-dry once or twice—but leave a little water clinging to the leaves. Get a 12- to 14-inch sauté pan and find a lid for a smaller pan or pot that will fit flush just inside its rim—this will be your "brick."

Set the sauté pan over medium heat and add the schmaltz. Working in batches, add the bok choy, stirring and folding with tongs to encourage wilting, until all the bok choy fits. Add 2 pinches of salt, toss again, then cover with the "brick" until the greens wilt, about 3 minutes (depending on the size of your bok choy and pan). Use tongs to give things a toss; cook, uncovered, 2 to 3 minutes more, or until most of the liquid and residual steam are gone (you'll know because the sound will shift from simmering to sizzling). Insert a cake tester or paring knife into the thickest part of your bok choy—it should be tender to the core.

Now raise the heat to high and weight with the "brick" once more. Leave the bok choy searing undisturbed for 2 to 3 minutes, or until lightly charred. Plate the bok choy, charred side up. Then add the chicken stock to the still-hot pan; reduce on high heat for 1 minute. Pour this liquid over the bok choy and top the greens with a few drops of chile vinegar or lemon juice. Serve immediately.

BETTER BITTER GREENS

This is a quick and pretty one-pan side dish that's easy to scale up for a crowd and to vary according to whatever bunch of greens you have and love. I'm particularly fond of dandelion greens, which are simultaneously treated as pesky weeds and esteemed as a nutritious ingredient. While these long, slender leaves are certainly bitter, their lovability is obvious when they are simmered with sweet, salty, pungent things, then perked up with a hit of acid—it's all about finding the right balance of tension and harmony. If you can't find dandelion greens, collards, broccoli rabe, and kale make fine substitutes, but all require a longer time in a hot pan.

Like all braised dishes, this dish reheats well, and the flavors will continue to meld if refrigerated overnight; just take care to not overcook, and you may need to add a splash of water or two to get the simmer going again. As always, it is important to taste before serving, adjusting the salt, fat, and acidity as needed—you really need that lemon in the right amount to make the dish come alive, and its sour flavor diminishes after the dish sits or reheats. Want to make a heftier dish, perhaps a main course? Add braised beans (cannellini, chickpea, and Royal Corona would all work particularly well).

4 TO 6 SERVINGS

¼ cup plus 2 tablespoons olive oil

1 chile de arbol

4 stalks green garlic (white and light-green parts) or 3 garlic cloves, thinly sliced

Fine sea salt

1½ pounds dandelion greens or other bitter green (see headnote), leaves trimmed and cut crosswise into thirds

1 teaspoon fish sauce

Pinch of coconut sugar (optional)

¼ cup water

1 teaspoon Banyuls vinegar or other red wine vinegar

1 teaspoon lemon juice

Heat the oil in a 12- to 14-inch heavy-bottomed sauté pan over medium heat. Add the chile de arbol and garlic and a pinch of salt; give the pan a toss and a shake. Once the garlic has softened—about 3 minutes—add the dandelion greens, fish sauce, coconut sugar (if using), and ¼ cup water. Toss with tongs and cover. Simmer the greens for 5 to 7 minutes, turning and tossing in the braising liquid once or twice. Uncover the sauté pan and continue simmering until almost all of the liquid evaporates, about 5 minutes more. Off heat, remove the chile and stir in the vinegar and lemon juice. Take a bite and add more lemon juice, salt, or fish sauce to taste.

GRILLED CABBAGE WITH BLUE CHEESE, HAZELNUTS, AND BEE POLLEN

Make this in the fall, when you're not yet ready to tuck away the grill and cabbage tinged purple by the cold nights has begun appearing at markets. I love the sweet, delicate flavor of bee pollen, and with its faint hints of fruit, it is a perfect match for earthy cabbage and creamy, slightly pungent blue cheese.

I'm aware that directing you to light a grill just for cabbage is probably asking too much. So go ahead and get a steak or whole fish ready too.

4 SERVINGS

1 tablespoon honey

¼ cup lemon juice

Fine sea salt

½ cup virgin olive oil

2 small heads cabbage, ideally Savoy

6 ounces blue cheese, crumbled into large pieces and chilled

½ cup coarsely chopped toasted hazelnuts or walnuts

2 pinches (a heaping tablespoon) of marjoram or thyme leaves

1 tablespoon bee pollen

Flaky sea salt

In a small mixing bowl, whisk together the honey and lemon juice with 2 pinches of fine sea salt; stir in the olive oil. Trim the bases of the cabbage but leave the cores entirely intact; remove any yellowing or wilting outer leaves. Cut each head of cabbage lengthwise into 2-inch "steaks." Lay the cabbage on a parchment-lined baking sheet and brush generously with the lemon-honey dressing on both sides; reserve remaining dressing.

On a grill, prepare a two-zone fire for both high and medium-low heat. Use long tongs to place the marinated cabbage directly over the hot side of grill. If using a gas grill, lower the heat to medium-high (an 8 out of 10). Cook, covered, until well charred on the first side, 4 to 5 minutes. Flip the cabbage and cook until charred on the second side, another 4 to 5 minutes. If necessary, transfer the cabbage to the cooler side of the grill (or lower the heat to low) and continue cooking until mostly tender (a paring knife easily slips through the center of the core) and caramelized, 2 to 3 minutes longer.

Transfer the cabbage to a platter and let cool a few minutes before drizzling with reserved lemon-honey dressing and topping with crumbled blue cheese, chopped hazelnuts, marjoram, bee pollen, and flaky sea salt. Serve immediately.

CARAMELIZED CABBAGE FOR MANY OCCASIONS

Cabbage is a very special vegetable: delicious, hearty, cheap, nutritious, and versatile. What else can you shred, massage, ferment, steam, sauté, stew, stuff, bake, and grill (page 225)? While all of these methods produce good things, something really magical happens to cabbage when it's roasted for long enough at a high temperature. It transforms from raw and crunchy to soft and tender, deeply caramelized, and a little crisp.

At its essence, this is a make-ahead recipe. Roast more cabbage than you need for a single meal and stash some in the fridge. Reach for it when you are too busy or exhausted to cook but can't bear another take-out order. It is an incredible thing to eat, and I guarantee it pairs well with something else you have on hand.

**APPROXIMATELY
12 SERVINGS**

3 medium heads cabbage (approximately 6 pounds)—any variety, any color

½ cup plus 2 tablespoons olive oil or neutral vegetable oil (such as cold-pressed rice bran oil or grapeseed oil), divided

Fine sea salt

Preheat oven to 450°F. Line 2 baking sheets with parchment paper. Trim the very end of the cabbage cores—just an ⅛ inch or so. Cut each cabbage head in half through the core. Cut each half into three or four 1½- to 2-inch wedges, keeping the core intact.

Divide the cabbage wedges between baking sheets. Drizzle each batch with a generous amount of oil (approximately ¼ cup) and 2 pinches fine sea salt. Toss gently, keeping the wedges intact best you can. The cabbage should be completely coated in oil; if you notice dry spots, add more oil (it is better to have a bit too much than too little). Spread wedges out into a single layer, leaving at least a ½-inch or so of space around each piece—overcrowding causes steaming and prevents browning.

Roast cabbage 25 to 35 minutes, or until well caramelized (near charred) and crispy at the edges, flipping the wedges halfway through. How long this takes will depend on your oven, the water content of your cabbage, how tightly you packed your pan, and exactly how large your pieces are. So keep an eye and a nose on it—the goal is cabbage that is burnished brown, tender, a little crisp, sweet, and nutty. Remove the cabbage from the oven and let cool slightly (a few minutes is fine).

Serve hot or warm, composing a dish using one of my suggestions on the facing page or just with a squeeze of lemon and some flaky sea salt. Refrigerate leftover cabbage in an airtight container for up to 4 days. If needed, reheat wedges in a 300°F oven for 15 to 20 minutes, or until warmed through.

- Drizzle with a little lemon juice + olive oil; top with toasted cracked caraway or Aleppo-style pepper + fresh dill

- Drizzle with a little lemon or lime juice + warm Spiced Ghee (page 161)

- Drizzle with a little lemon juice + olive oil; top with toasted buckwheat (soba cha or homemade, page 21); serve alongside a halved 6½-minute Soft-Centered Egg (page 144) or egg yolk

- Top with Nam Jim (page 345)

- Drizzle with Bagna Cauda or Miso Bagna Cauda (pages 341–42); top with toasted breadcrumbs, if you'd like

- Season with a little lemon juice; top with melted ghee or unsalted butter + bonito flakes

- Plate with some crème fraîche + black beans + avocado; top with sliced green chile (or a pinch of ground chile de arbol) + cilantro, whole leaves and tender stems

- Drizzle with Special Sauce (page 338); sprinkle with toasted cracked caraway + thinly sliced radish + fresh dill + thinly sliced chives

- Spread some labneh, store-bought or homemade (page 336), across a plate; top with cabbage + sliced cucumber + thinly sliced green onion + Aleppo-style pepper + olive oil + mint and/or cilantro, whole leaves and tender stems

- Drizzle with sautéed 'nduja or Instant "XO" (page 341); top with thinly sliced cucumber + cilantro, whole leaves and tender stems; serve alongside steamed rice or a simple main

- Spread some yogurt or labneh, store-bought or homemade (page 336), across a plate; top with cabbage + cooked chickpeas (page 240) + Aleppo-style pepper (optional) + Crispy Curry Leaves (page 350)

- Treat like the roasted eggplant on page 237: drizzle with Basic Tahini Sauce or Tahini Yogurt (pages 337 and 338); top with cooked chickpeas (page 240) + sumac + cilantro, whole leaves and tender stems

- Drizzle with a tamarind dressing (page 90); top with Quick-Pickled Shallots (page 348) and/or Crispy Shallots (page 350) + whole or torn basil, mint, and/or cilantro (whole leaves and tender stems) + coarsely chopped salted, toasted peanuts; make this a main by serving it with rice or flatbread and bowl of cooked chickpeas (page 240)

continued

- Season with lime juice and a dash of fish sauce; top with Toasted Chickpea Flour (page 351) + halved Soft-Centered Eggs (7½-minute duck eggs or 6½-minute chicken eggs, page 144) + sliced green chile and/or green onion + cilantro, whole leaves and tender stems

- Nestle wedges (no need to reheat) into simmering Blistered Tomatoes with Preserved Lemon (page 201) or Slow-Cooked White Beans with Tomato and Curry Leaf (page 232); finish either dish with chopped dill or cilantro; serve with a bowl of plain, full-fat Greek yogurt or Yogurt Mayonnaise (page 339)

- Toss wedges with warm farro + coarsely chopped toasted pistachios or Fried Pine Nuts (page 190) + barberries or pomegranate seeds + sumac; dress with lemon juice + olive oil to taste; top with tender herbs such as dill, cilantro (whole leaves and tender stems), parsley, and/or mint; serve with a side of labneh, store-bought or homemade (page 336), or plain, full-fat Greek yogurt

- Coarsely chop wedges; toss with (cold or warm) buckwheat noodles; top with thinly sliced green onion + toasted buckwheat (soba cha or homemade, page 21) or walnuts in walnut oil (page 137)

- Coarsely chop wedges (no need to reheat) and use in fried rice (page 253)

- Coarsely chop wedges (no need to reheat) and stir into batter for Savory Chickpea Flour Pancakes (page 130)

SHIO KOJI-ROASTED BRUSSELS SPROUTS

People generally prefer brussels sprouts brown and crispy. And since I generally prefer an oven affair over a deep-fryer one, I'm often seeking variations in flavor without having to rethink technique. I recently discovered that tossing them in pureed shio koji creates caramelized sprouts with crispy edges, a little char, and a deep, savory character balanced by a hint of sweetness.

4 TO 6 SERVINGS

1 pound brussels sprouts, trimmed and halved through the stem end

3 tablespoons shio koji puree, store bought or homemade (page 81)

¼ cup olive oil, plus more for serving

Fine sea salt

1 small lemon

Flaky sea salt

Finely chopped chives (optional)

Preheat oven to 425°F. Once hot, preheat a rimmed baking sheet for at least 5 minutes. In a medium mixing bowl, toss the brussels sprouts with the shio koji, ¼ cup olive oil, and a small pinch of fine sea salt; really use your hands to coat them well—think of it as a light massage in a quick marinade—doing your best not to separate too many leaves from the heads. Take the hot pan out of the oven and line with parchment; spread brussels sprouts in an even sparse layer. Roast for 15 minutes; flip sprouts, rotate the pan, and roast 9 to 12 minutes more, or until dark brown. Use a Microplane to shower lemon zest all over the sprouts. Sprinkle with flaky sea salt and chives (if using). Serve immediately, topped with a drizzle of olive oil.

Mains

SLOW-COOKED WHITE BEANS WITH TOMATO AND CURRY LEAF

A big bowl of slow-simmered beans is comforting, woolen even, but they needn't be stodgy. This bowl—imbued with the exotic flavors of curry leaf—can simultaneously comfort and inspire.

Make this with any bean you like, but know, in this instance, bigger and meatier are better, and that cooking times between beans vary widely. In the summer, make this with fresh shelling beans or peas, and use fresh tomatoes in place of the canned.

Tips—This is a big batch. But it tastes even better on days two and three, and you can freeze some for up to 3 months (the texture of the beans suffers slightly, but it is still very good). Be sure to leave 8 to 24 hours for soaking the beans.

8 TO 10 SERVINGS

½ cup olive oil

8 whole garlic cloves, lightly smashed and peeled

Fine sea salt

1 handful of cilantro stems, tied with twine (optional)

16 fresh curry leaves

Two 15-ounce jars or cans crushed or whole peeled tomatoes, preferably without basil or other seasonings

1 pound dried white beans (such as Royal Corona, large white lima, or Tarbais), soaked overnight (room temperature is fine) in cool water

2 chile de arbol

One 4-inch piece kombu (optional)

1 teaspoon Banyuls vinegar or other red wine or sherry vinegar, or lime or lemon juice

TO SERVE (CHOOSE ONE OR A FEW)

Yogurt Mayonnaise (page 339), Mayonnaise (page 338), or plain, full-fat Greek yogurt

Crispy Shallots (page 350), coarse fried breadcrumbs, or toasted crusty bread

Cilantro blossoms and/or cilantro, whole leaves and tender stems

Olive oil

Flaky sea salt

Heat the olive oil in a large saucepan over medium-high heat, add the garlic and a pinch of salt, and sauté for 3 to 5 minutes, until the garlic is golden brown. Add the cilantro stems (if using), the curry leaves, and 2 pinches of salt; cook 1 to 2 minutes more (you want the curry leaves to infuse their flavor into the hot fat but you don't want them to burn). Add the tomatoes, the beans, enough water to cover them by 2 inches, and another pinch of salt. Bring to a simmer, then lower heat slightly and cook, uncovered and stirring occasionally, until beans are just tender but not at all mushy (taste a few before making the call)—55 to 75 minutes. If any foam rises to the top, skim off as much as you can (without catching any curry leaves).

In what you think might be the final 15 to 20 minutes of cooking time, add the chile de arbol and kombu (if using). When the beans are tender, remove from heat, discard the chile de arbol, kombu, and bundled cilantro stems. Gently stir in the vinegar. Adjust seasoning to taste and let stand 10 to 15 minutes. Serve hot or warm, topping as you like.

CHARRED LEEKS WITH EGGS, ANCHOVIES, PARSLEY, AND CAPERS

Briny anchovy, rich egg, salty caper, and grassy parsley are perfect contrasts to the sweetness of leeks. Together they create a one-dish meal or a complex side for a simple main. The anchovy is obvious only if you know it is there—otherwise, the dish might call to mind another anchovy-accented dish, say, a niçoise salad. I put this on the table family-style for breakfast, lunch, or dinner, with good bread and butter and a bowl of fresh fruit.

Tips—Take care with each step of this recipe, especially parboiling—you want the leeks just tender. Also, I find the char on leeks really appealing, but the entire broiling step can actually be skipped, and this dish is still plenty flavorful.

3 TO 4 SERVINGS (MAIN COURSE); 4 TO 6 SERVINGS (SIDE)

8 fat leeks (approximately 4 pounds before trimming), white and light-green parts

¼ cup plus 2 tablespoons olive oil, plus more for broiling and serving

Fine sea salt

½ teaspoon Chile Vinegar (page 348) or a pinch of piment d'Espelette (optional)

4 oil-packed anchovy fillets, minced

1½ tablespoons lemon juice

Four 8½-minute Soft-Centered Eggs (page 144), coarsely chopped

½ to ¾ cup sliced flat-leaf parsley leaves

3 tablespoons salt-packed capers, soaked in cool water for 15 to 30 minutes, rinsed, and patted dry

Flaky sea salt

Trim the bulb ends of the leeks and discard the outermost layer. Cut the leeks into 1-inch-thick rounds. Fill a large bowl with water and press in the leeks. Shake the leeks with your hand so they release their dirt; let the dirt settle to the bottom of the bowl, then lift the leeks out and into a strainer. Repeat the process until no dirt remains (usually only twice).

Cook the leeks in a large pot of boiling salted water until *just* tender (they should still be al dente), about 5 minutes. Transfer to a bowl of ice water to stop the cooking. Drain the leeks well, then lay them on a kitchen towel to dry—be gentle as you work; you want the leeks to remain in tight 1-inch rounds, without their layers separating too much. Pat the top of the leeks dry. At this point, leeks can be refrigerated overnight.

Preheat the broiler and move your oven rack close to the heat source. Place the leeks cut side down in one even, uncrowded layer on a rimmed baking sheet or in a 12- or 14-inch ovenproof skillet. (Cast iron works really well, but you will likely have to broil in batches;

continued

just transfer already-charred leeks to a serving platter while you finish with the rest.) Use a fine-tipped squeeze bottle, a brush, or a spoon to coat the leeks lightly in olive oil. Season with fine sea salt. Brown the leeks under the broiler for 5 to 8 minutes per side. The goal is to get them evenly caramelized on both cut sides—slightly charred in spots—and a little crispy around the edges. If you'd like, season each leek with a few drops of chile vinegar (a fine-tipped squeeze bottle speeds this up) or a sprinkle of piment d'Espelette.

Meanwhile whisk together the anchovy with 1½ tablespoons lemon juice and ¼ cup plus 2 tablespoons olive oil. Use a small spatula to transfer the leeks to a platter or divide between plates; spoon three-quarters of the anchovy dressing on and around leeks. Season the chopped eggs with a pinch of salt. Top the leeks with a scattering of egg, parsley, and capers. Drizzle remaining anchovy dressing on top, focusing on getting the parsley dressed. If any area looks dry, drizzle a little more olive oil here and there. Sprinkle with flaky sea salt.

WHOLE ROASTED EGGPLANT WITH TAHINI, CRISPY CHICKPEAS, AND SUMAC

Pictured on pages 238–39.

Eggplant is one of my favorite vegetables—I could fill an entire book with recipes singing its praises, and I don't see why it can't be the star of the show rather than just a supporting act. In this large-format dish, whole eggplants cook until slightly charred on the outside and meltingly tender within. Tahini adds much-needed richness and creaminess, crispy chickpeas add texture (and protein), and lemon and sumac bring brightness. I consider this a lovely vegetarian main course, but it could also serve as a side dish for chicken, lamb, or fish. Any leftovers can be blitzed into a fine eggplant dip in the food processor (add an ice cube for the smoothest result) and refrigerated for up to 3 days.

4 SERVINGS

4 medium eggplants (each approximately 12 ounces)—Listada or similar egg-shaped variety such as Globe

¾ cup olive oil, plus more to serve

Fine sea salt

3 cups cooked chickpeas, homemade (page 240) or canned, drained and patted dry with paper towels

1 tablespoon sumac

½ lemon

2 cups Basic Tahini Sauce (page 337)

½ cup coarsely chopped flat-leaf parsley

Preheat oven to 475°F and line 2 rimmed baking sheets with parchment paper (make sure the parchment fits inside the pan; at this high temperature, any overhang could burn). Peel the eggplants, leaving stems attached; on each, poke the center of the base a few times with a fork or cake tester and divide between the 2 pans. Toss each eggplant with 2 tablespoons olive oil and a pinch of salt, massaging the salt into the flesh a little as you work. Create space between the 2 eggplants on each pan and roast for 40 to 50 minutes, turning the eggplants every 10 to 15 minutes to get even browning on all sides. Remove from oven and set aside.

Meanwhile, heat a 12- to 14-inch sauté pan over medium-high heat and add the remaining ¼ cup olive oil. Once the oil is shimmering, add the chickpeas and a pinch of salt. Pan-fry the chickpeas, stirring occasionally, for 8 to 10 minutes, or until crispy (as they crisp up, a few may pop out of the pan like popcorn). Lower the heat slightly, add the sumac, and cook just 1 minute more. Taste and add more salt, as needed.

Season each eggplant with a squeeze of lemon. Place on warmed plates or in shallow bowls and top the center of the base of each eggplant with a ¼ cup tahini sauce. Top the tahini sauce with a heaping ½ cup sumac-coated, crispy chickpeas. Drizzle a little olive oil around the sides of the eggplant and top the olive oil with a sprinkling of chopped parsley. Serve at once.

A POT OF CHICKPEAS

Some nights, all I want to eat is a bowl of beans and greens. Warm, comforting, and nourishing, brothy legumes deeply satisfy. I always have a cache of cooked beans in the fridge and freezer; most often, they are chickpeas, which I consider the most versatile.

The combination of the bean broth—the resulting liquid from just-cooked beans—and a larder ingredient or two produces amazing flavor from a one-pot, one-hour, humble legume stew. Instead of building the stew from the bottom up—in which I'd start with hot fat plus aromatics such as onions, garlic, and spices, followed by liquid and other ingredients—I just heap a bunch of ingredients into the simmering pot, let them mix and meld with the help of heat, and then serve bowls of the resulting stew with lemon juice, olive oil, and whatever cooked greens and herbs I have on hand.

Tips—While dried beans can last forever, they cook up more quickly and creamier when fresher. Specialty bean companies (such as Rancho Gordo), local farms, co-op food markets, and Mediterranean markets have a relatively fast turnover and are typically your best bet. Also, if you eat a lot of beans, consider investing in a clay bean pot. They increase both flavor and digestibility (as does kombu) and facilitate gentle, even cooking. Be sure to leave 8 to 24 hours for soaking the chickpeas.

4 TO 6 SERVINGS

2 cups dried chickpeas

Whey, for cooking (optional)

3 tablespoons olive oil,
plus more to serve

1 teaspoon fine sea salt,
plus more to serve

1 aromatic bundle tied with twine,
including 1 or more of the following:
herb stems (such as cilantro, parsley,
or thyme), curry leaf, bay leaf, fennel
fronds, green onion, leek, and/or green
garlic (optional)

½ preserved lemon, seeded or
½ fresh lemon, seeded (optional)

One 3- to 4-inch piece kombu

1 chile de arbol (optional)

2 teaspoons lemon juice or vinegar
(I use Banyuls)

Place the chickpeas in a medium Dutch oven or large saucepan and cover with at least 6 cups of cool water. Soak overnight (room temperature is fine).

Drain the chickpeas, rinse once, and return them to their pot. Add fresh water (and some whey, if you'd like) to cover by 4 inches. Set the pot over medium-high heat and bring to a boil. Lower heat and simmer for 2 minutes—skim any scum that rises to the surface.

Add the olive oil, salt, and aromatic bundle (if using). Cook the chickpeas at a gentle simmer, uncovered, for 50 to 90 minutes, or until the chickpeas are still whole but tender and creamy within. Check on them every 30 minutes or so, and add water as needed to keep them covered by 3 to 4 inches (this ensures you have ample bean "broth" and prevents the beans from cooking unevenly).

In the final 30 or so minutes of cooking, add the remaining aromatics: if using a preserved lemon, add it to the pot (both skin and flesh); if using a fresh lemon, use a vegetable peeler to remove the peel and add it to the pot (you can juice the flesh later, to serve). Add the kombu and chile de arbol (if using), and give the stew a gentle stir.

Once the chickpeas are tender, let them cool in their broth for 20 to 30 minutes before discarding the aromatics, kombu, chile, and preserved lemon or lemon peel. Season to taste with lemon juice and more olive oil and salt. If you wish to save the brothy chickpeas for another day, let them cool at room temperature until just warm. Keep them in their lidded pot or transfer both the beans and their broth to an airtight storage container; refrigerate for up to 3 days, or freeze (with a slight loss in texture and flavor) for up to 3 months.

STUFFED POBLANOS WITH QUINOA, PUMPKIN SEED, AND POMEGRANATE MOLASSES

Many stuffed chiles are laden with cheese or heavy sauces. This dish has neither. It is subtly spicy, hearty, warming, and satisfying. Served with a stack of tortillas, I call it dinner.

Tips—Poblanos' large cavity makes them good stuffers, but they range in heat—if you can, inquire or taste before buying to ensure you get a mild lot. Make sure both grains and beans are not overcooked; you want the contrast in texture between the cooked peppers and the filling. You can use white quinoa instead of black, and walnuts and walnut oil instead of pumpkin seeds and pumpkin seed oil.

3 TO 4 SERVINGS (MAIN COURSE); 6 TO 9 SERVINGS (STARTER OR MEZE)

PEPPERS AND STUFFING

9 medium fresh poblanos or other stuffing chile, such as Anaheim or Hungarian

1¼ cups cooked black quinoa

¾ cup cooked Black Lentils (page 161) or other small bean of your choosing, drained if needed

1 teaspoon Mole Spice Blend (page 353) or 1 teaspoon freshly ground toasted cumin plus ¼ teaspoon ground chile de arbol

¼ cup toasted pumpkin seeds, finely chopped

¼ cup finely chopped cilantro

1 teaspoon Banyuls vinegar or other red wine vinegar

1 teaspoon pomegranate molasses

3 tablespoons olive oil, plus more for cooking

1 teaspoon pumpkin seed oil or olive oil

Fine sea salt

1¼ cups vegetable stock, Simple Chicken Stock (page 346), Kombu Stock (page 347), or water

TO SERVE

1 teaspoon Banyuls vinegar or other red wine vinegar

1 teaspoon pomegranate molasses

3 tablespoons olive oil

1 teaspoon pumpkin seed oil

Fine sea salt

1 cup crème fraîche

TOPPINGS AND SIDES (CHOOSE ONE OR MANY)

Cilantro, whole leaves and tender stems, torn or cut into 1- to 2-inch pieces

Fresh pomegranate seeds

Puffed quinoa

Thinly sliced white or red onion, perked in ice water for a few minutes

Thinly sliced serrano chile

Tortilla chips, warmed tortillas, or steamed long-grain rice

Sliced or mashed avocado

Quartered radishes

Preheat oven to 400°F. (I like to use gloves for this next step, as my hands get super irritated by the seeds of fresh chiles—up to you.) Lay the peppers on your work surface, flattest side down. For each pepper, trim the tip of the stem (leaving a ½-inch nub), then cut an opening, 12 inches wide lengthwise, in the side of the pepper (leaving the head and stem on). Use your fingers to dislodge the white pith and seeds (it's okay if there are few seeds left). In a medium bowl, mix all the stuffing ingredients except the stock with 3 pinches (about ¾ teaspoon) of salt—taste and add more salt or oil. It should be seasoned enough to eat on its own.

Using a high-sided ovenproof pan that's just wide enough to accommodate the peppers snuggly in an even layer, stuff the peppers fully, but don't overstuff—you don't want quinoa spilling out as they cook. Arrange them in the pan side by side as you go. Place the pan over medium-high heat, add the stock around the peppers, and bring to a boil; immediately reduce to a simmer and cook 15 minutes. Drizzle the peppers with olive oil (enough to coat them lightly) and transfer to the oven—still uncovered—for another 40 to 45 minutes, or until the peppers are cooked through and brown on top. Rest for 5 to 10 minutes.

Meanwhile, in a small bowl, stir together the vinegar, pomegranate molasses, olive oil, and pumpkin seed oil with a pinch of salt. Plate the peppers and drizzle with the pomegranate vinaigrette. Serve warm or at room temperature with crème fraîche, and whichever optional toppings and sides you'd like.

Without toppings, stuffed peppers can be made 2 days ahead. Transfer to an airtight container and chill. Reheat in a 350°F oven, covered, until heated through, about 20 minutes.

SUMMER SALAD WITH WHEAT BERRIES, FETA, AND HERBS

I think grain salads should be everybody's go-to when the going gets tough. They are gorgeous, healthy, and satisfying one-dish meals that hold relatively well at room temperature (great for make-ahead dinners or to take to a friend's place).

This grain salad features soft, golden White Sonora wheat berries; their mild flavor and chewy texture is a great canvas for whatever vegetables and fruits you happen to have on hand. Here they're paired with summer vegetables and herbs, rich and salty feta (chewy grains beg for a creamy element; avocado could easily stand in), and bright, juicy fruits.

Tips—If you don't have White Sonora wheat berries, farro, freekeh, or even white quinoa can be used. I recommend dry-toasting all grains and soaking them overnight; this advance prep doesn't take much time, but it does decrease cooking time and increase flavor, nutrition, and digestibility. To make this salad nondairy, you can substitute 1 large firm, ripe avocado (cut into a 1-inch dice) for the feta.

6 SERVINGS

FOR THE HEIRLOOM WHEAT

1 cup White Sonora wheat berries or farro

Fine sea salt

1 teaspoon Banyuls or sherry vinegar

2 tablespoons olive oil

FOR THE SALAD

1 teaspoon Banyuls or sherry vinegar

Fine sea salt

2 tablespoons olive oil

½ firm ripe melon (such as cantaloupe or Charentais), cut into 1-inch pieces

5 small tomatoes (any variety) or tomatillos (approximately 7 ounces), husks removed, washed well, and cut into approximately ¾-inch wedges

1 small Persian or Armenian cucumber, cut into approximately ¾-inch pieces

8 Padrón peppers, thinly sliced

3 generous handfuls summer greens (approximately 3 ounces), one or a mix: arugula, sunflower sprouts, purslane, mâche, and/or watercress

¼ cup thinly sliced chives or thinly sliced green onion, white and light-green parts

3 cups (loosely packed) torn or coarsely chopped fresh herbs (such as basil, dill, tarragon, flat-leaf parsley, mint, shiso, and/or cilantro)

6 to 8 ounces feta cheese, thinly sliced or crumbled

Flaky sea salt

continued

In a medium pot over medium-high heat, dry-toast the wheat berries for 3 to 5 minutes, or until a shade darker. Let cool to room temperature. Cover with cool water and soak overnight (leaving them at room temperature is fine).

Drain the wheat berries. Fill the same pot three-quarters full with water and bring to a boil over high heat. Add a generous pinch of salt and return the wheat berries. Lower heat and simmer 35 to 60 minutes; different wheat berries will need more or less time—taste and decide when yours are tender, and add more water if the pot gets dry. Drain and return to the pot. Off heat, toss the still-warm grains with 1 teaspoon vinegar, another pinch of salt, and 2 tablespoons olive oil. Taste and adjust seasoning. Let wheat berries cool to room temperature while you finish prepping everything else.

In a large mixing bowl, whisk together 1 teaspoon vinegar, 2 pinches of salt, and 2 tablespoons olive oil. Using your hands, gently toss the melon, vegetables, and cooled wheat berries in the vinaigrette with the greens and half the herbs. Taste and add more salt, acid, or oil, as needed. Turn out the salad on a wide serving platter and top with feta and remaining herbs. The salad—without melon, herbs, and cheese—can be cooked and dressed up to 2 days in advance; let come to room temperature before adding the reserved ingredients and serving.

JOB'S TEARS "STONEPOT" WITH CRISPY MUSHROOMS AND JAMMY EGGS

I have a soft spot for sizzling-hot stone bowls filled to the brim with rice, vegetables, meat, and an assortment of fermented things. Also known as bibimbap, Korean stonepots are one of my top cravings. My homemade version often includes Job's tears, a gluten-free grain native to Southeast Asia that I think greatly benefits from the technique. The slight char tempers their bright, grassy notes and adds character to their plump, chewy texture. With crispy and earthy maitake, rich duck eggs, and a kick from two forms of chile de arbol, Job's tears become stick-to-your-ribs, can't-stop-eating, feel-good fare.

This dish is endlessly adaptable. It is hearty enough as a main as is, but you could certainly incorporate diced tofu or thinly sliced meat, frying and seasoning it separately, then adding it to the bowl along with the mushrooms. You can use any variety of mushroom, but you'll need to keep an eye on the oven, as cooking times will vary. The Job's tears and eggs can be cooked up to 3 days in advance

2 TO 3 SERVINGS

CRISPY MAITAKE

1¼ pounds maitake, or similar mushroom

2 to 3 tablespoons neutral vegetable oil (such as cold-pressed rice bran oil or grapeseed oil)

Fine sea salt

STONEPOT

6 tablespoons neutral vegetable oil (such as cold-pressed rice bran oil or grapeseed oil), lard, or duck fat

One 2-inch piece fresh ginger, scrubbed and cut into thin matchsticks (use a mandoline for best results)

6 green onions, white and light-green parts, thinly sliced, divided

Fine sea salt

3 cups cooked Job's tears, farro, or barley (from 1½ cups uncooked; follow instructions on package)

½ cup Caramelized Cabbage for Many Occasions (page 226), plain fermented cabbage (optional)

3 to 4 Soft-Centered Eggs (page 144, 7½-minute duck eggs or 6½-minute chicken eggs)

Flaky sea salt

⅓ cup thinly sliced radish (optional)

½ cup radish sprouts, halved lengthwise, if long (optional)

1 tablespoon Spicy Seaweed Gomasio (page 358) or toasted sesame seeds

2 teaspoons Chile Vinegar (page 348) or rice wine vinegar

1 to 2 tablespoons toasted sesame oil

1 sheet toasted nori, torn into 3-inch pieces (optional)

continued

Preheat oven to 425°F. Arrange the maitake on a rimmed baking sheet in a single layer—if there are big "heads," pull them apart. Drizzle with the oil, season generously with salt, and toss to coat. Roast for 20 to 30 minutes, until tender, deeply golden, and crispy in spots.

Meanwhile, heat a 9- or 10-inch heavy-bottomed skillet, preferably cast iron, directly on the stovetop over high heat until extremely hot (a few drops of water splashed on the side should sizzle and dissipate immediately).

Add the oil and swirl the pan to the coat the bottom. Add the ginger, a little over half the green onion, and a pinch of salt; cook for 1 to 2 minutes, until the ginger turns a light golden brown. Add the crispy mushrooms and cooked Job's tears; season with a pinch of salt. Mix once, spread the mixture in an even layer across the pan, then leave undisturbed for 3 to 5 minutes, or until the bottom of the mix is toasted and a little crunchy. Remove from heat and stir in the cabbage, if using.

Halve or quarter the eggs and season each with flaky sea salt. Scatter the cut eggs across the stonepot. Top with the radishes and radish sprouts (if using), reserved green onion, and gomasio. Drizzle everything evenly with the vinegar and sesame oil. Top with torn toasted nori, if you'd like. Serve immediately. (I put the skillets on trivets on the table and let everyone help themselves.)

BLACK RICE AND ASPARAGUS WITH MIZUNA AND MINT

I originally wrote this recipe for *Sunset* magazine's April 2018 issue, and it has been a part of my spring repertoire ever since. The nuttiness of the black rice perfectly complements asparagus, and the spicy mizuna plays well with sweet mint. A gutsy tahini-and-fish-sauce dressing creates a delicious tension that makes this dish unexpectedly satisfying.

Tips—Black rice is a whole grain that has its bran layers—and therefore its nutrients—intact and receives its uniquely colored robe from anthocyanin, a powerful antioxidant. There are several varieties available in the US, typically sold under the following names: Forbidden Rice, Japonica rice, black sticky rice; Nerone rice; riso nero. I recommend purchasing black rice from a store or site with high turnover, as rice will go rancid if stored improperly or for too long. I recommend soaking it overnight before cooking, so be sure to leave 8 to 24 hours for this step. Black rice can be cooked up to 2 days in advance; refrigerate in an airtight container and bring to room temperature before using.

4 TO 6 SERVINGS

Fine sea salt

⅓ cup medium-grain black rice, soaked overnight (room temperature is fine) in cool water, then drained

1 bunch medium to fat asparagus spears (approximately 1 pound), trimmed, and peeled if skin is tough

4 green onions, white and light-green parts

2 tablespoons black sesame seeds

1 tablespoon fish sauce

Zest of 1 lemon (use a Microplane for best results)

2 tablespoons lemon juice

1 teaspoon mild honey

2 tablespoons tahini

3 tablespoons olive oil

3 generous handfuls mizuna, arugula, baby mustard greens, or baby tatsoi (approximately 3 ounces), cut into 3-inch pieces if large

1 cup (loosely packed) fresh mint, leaves torn if large

½ to ¾ teaspoon Aleppo-style pepper or Marash pepper

Flaky sea salt

2 to 3 tablespoons Puffed Black Rice (recipe follows, optional)

Line a rimmed baking sheet with parchment paper. Bring a medium pot of water to a boil over high heat; add salt until it tastes like the sea. Add the black rice and simmer until almost-but-not-quite tender, 5 to 6 minutes (it will continue cooking as it cools). Drain, then immediately spread out the rice on a rimmed baking sheet to cool it quickly (because this is a salad, it is important that the rice grains remain fluffy and separate).

Meanwhile, bring another medium pot of water to a boil over high heat and add salt generously. Fill a large bowl with ice water and place near the stove. Slice the asparagus into 3- to 4-inch lengths, then thinly slice lengthwise. Cook asparagus until crisp-tender, 30 seconds, then, using a slotted spoon or spider, immediately transfer to the ice bath.

Slice the green onions into 3-inch lengths, then thinly slice lengthwise. Add to the bowl of asparagus, with more ice if needed. Let sit until the green onions crisp and curl, about 6 minutes. Drain the vegetables well, spread on a kitchen towel, and pat dry. The blanched and dried asparagus and crisped green onion can be prepared up to 2 hours in advance, chill until ready to use.

Heat a medium (not nonstick) frying pan over medium heat. Add the sesame seeds and dry toast until just fragrant, about 3 minutes, shaking the pan every now and then. Pour onto a plate to cool.

In a large bowl, whisk together the fish sauce, lemon zest and juice, honey, tahini, and olive oil with 2 teaspoons warm water. Season to taste with fine sea salt. Add the cooled black rice, the asparagus, the green onion, three-fourths of the mizuna, half of the mint, the toasted sesame seeds, and the chile flakes. Add 2 large pinches of fine sea salt and toss gently to combine. Pull out several asparagus spears and set aside for topping, if you like.

Spread the salad on a large serving platter and top with the remaining mizuna, mint, sesame seeds, and chile flakes, plus a sprinkle of flaky sea salt and the puffed black rice (if using).

continued

PUFFED BLACK RICE

2 CUPS

2 cups neutral vegetable oil (such as cold-pressed rice bran oil or grapeseed oil)

½ cup raw long-grain Chinese black rice (or Forbidden Rice)

Fine sea salt

This recipe makes more than you need for the salad above, but if stored properly, it stays crisp for up to 5 days. It is a striking topping that adds a pop of crunch and a salty nuttiness to my morning oats, roasted root vegetables, and all kinds of salads.

In a medium saucepan, heat the oil over medium-high heat until it reaches 375°F on a deep-fry thermometer (or test by dropping a couple of rice grains into oil; they should sizzle immediately and quickly rise to surface).

Line a baking sheet with 2 layers of paper towels and set aside. Add the black rice to the hot oil (it will bubble a bit but will quickly subside). Fry until the rice is crispy and beginning to puff (you can see a bit of white inside most of the grains), 30 to 45 seconds. With a long-handled fine-mesh strainer, transfer the rice to paper towels. Season with a pinch of salt and let cool completely. Cool the oil, drain through a fine-mesh strainer, and store airtight for another day, another crispy rice craving.

Make ahead up to 5 days; store in an airtight container at room temperature.

FRIED RICE

My fried rice is composed primarily of leftovers, but it is rarely boring or drab. In fact, I think fried rice creates a perfect opportunity to be creative, resourceful, and skillful in the kitchen. These versions use the larder to make new a tried-and-true thing. Fry ingredients in order of listing.

2 TO 4 SERVINGS

FRIED RICE WITH CURRY LEAVES AND TAMARIND

3 tablespoons ghee or coconut oil

6 curry leaves

1 chile de arbol, torn crosswise (discard before serving, optional)

1 cup coarsely chopped cooked vegetables (such as cauliflower, peas, green beans, winter squash, or zucchini)

2 tablespoons tamarind juice (page 90) or 1 tablespoon lime juice plus 1 tablespoon date syrup

2 cups boiled rice

Salt to taste

Cilantro, whole leaves and tender stems, to serve

CHICKEN-FAT FRIED RICE

2 tablespoons schmaltz

1 chile de arbol, torn crosswise (discard before serving, optional)

2 garlic cloves or green onions, thinly sliced

Scant 1 teaspoon grated fresh ginger

½ cup Caramelized Cabbage for Many Occasions (page 226), coarsely chopped

2 tablespoons water

2 cups boiled rice

Salt to taste

Chile Vinegar (page 348) or lemon juice, to taste

Cilantro, whole leaves and tender stems; celery leaves; thinly sliced green onion; or thinly sliced cucumber, to serve

CURRIED FRIED RICE WITH CHICKPEAS AND CABBAGE

3 tablespoons ghee

2 green onions, thinly sliced

1 heaping teaspoon Curry Spice Blend (page 352)

½ cup Caramelized Cabbage for Many Occasions (page 226), coarsely chopped

¾ to 1 cup cooked chickpeas (page 240), drained

2 to 3 tablespoons water

2 cups boiled rice

Salt to taste

Lime or lemon wedges, to serve

Cilantro, whole leaves and tender stems or fresh dill, to serve

SARDINE FRIED RICE

3 tablespoons ghee or olive oil

2 green onions or 1 medium shallot, thinly sliced

Two 3- to 4-ounce cans sardines in olive oil, drained and pulled apart (the tiny bones are all edible)

2 tablespoons water

2 cups boiled rice

Salt to taste

Off heat: Zest of 1 lemon and the juice of ½ lemon; ½ cup coarsely chopped mixed fresh herbs (dill, parsley, cilantro, mint)

Aleppo-style pepper or Marash pepper, to serve

LEMONY FRIED RICE WITH GREENS AND HERBS

3 tablespoons olive oil or ghee

1 to 2 cups coarsely chopped cooked vegetables (kale, cauliflower leaves, cabbage, spinach, chard)

2 to 3 tablespoons water

2 cups boiled rice (I prefer short-grain brown rice)

2 tablespoons barberries or currants

Off heat: a scattering of mixed fresh herbs (mint, cilantro, dill, sorrel)

Sumac or Sumac-Rose Gomasio (page 357), a drizzle of lemon juice, and olive oil, to finish

Yogurt, to serve

UME RICE SALAD

This is a prime example of an elevated everyday dish. While it is definitely better the day it is made, I've doctored up leftovers with an avocado and Soft-Centered Egg (page 144)—their creaminess almost fully recovers the loss in moisture suffered by the refrigerated rice.

Tips—More important than the variety of rice is the cooking time—the rice should not be overcooked; the grains should be firm and separate. The best way to achieve that is to cook the rice as you would pasta, boiling it in lots of water rather than steaming it. You can purchase umeboshi plums already in paste form, but I prefer to just use whole plums: scrape the flesh from the pit, and finely chop to a paste right before using; discard the pit. For 2 teaspoons, you'll need approximately 2½ umeboshi plums, depending on their size.

4 TO 6 SERVINGS

1¾ cups white short-grain rice (such as Kokuho, Calrose, or arborio)

4 quarts water

3 green onions, white and light-green parts, very thinly sliced on the diagonal

2 tablespoons lemon juice

¼ cup plus 1 tablespoon sesame oil, black sesame oil, or olive oil

Fine sea salt

2 teaspoons umeboshi paste (see headnote)

3 generous handfuls mixed herbs and greens (approximately 3 ounces), (mint or shiso, arugula or mizuna, dill or cilantro, pea shoots or fennel fronds), large leaves very coarsely chopped and baby leaves left whole

Flaky sea salt or Shiso Salt (page 352), to finish

Rinse the rice, soak in cold water for 15 to 20 minutes, then drain. In a big pot, bring 4 quarts of lightly salted water to a boil over high heat. Add the rice and boil briskly for 8 to 9 minutes, or until the grains are slightly al dente. Drain the rice in a colander, then return it to the pot, cover it with a kitchen towel and the lid, and steam for 15 to 30 minutes more. (The rice will start to cool, and that is good; too-hot rice will turn the greens and herbs into a sad, wilted mess.)

Meanwhile, combine the green onion and lemon juice with a pinch of salt in a small mixing bowl; let sit for about 10 minutes. Then stir in the sesame oil.

When the rice has cooled considerably (close to room temperature), transfer it to a wide platter, fluff it up with your fingers, and season lightly with fine sea salt. Scatter approximately ¼-teaspoon dollops of ume paste across the top. Pour three-quarters of the lemon-sesame dressing and one-quarter of the greens-and-herb mix over the rice, then fluff with your fingers once more. (You're not tossing; just lightly scrunching, picking up some rice and letting it fall back onto the platter, breaking up the ume paste slightly as you go.) Just before serving, top the rice with remaining greens and herbs. Drizzle with remaining dressing and garnish with flaky sea salt or shiso salt. Taste and correct the seasonings, adding salt, lemon juice, and oil as necessary.

HARD-ROASTED WHOLE FISH

Roasting at a high temperature is a fast and easy way to cook fish. Using a whole fish—like using a whole chicken—prevents drying and increases flavor. (Bones are full of flavor!) Great fish is remarkably good with just salt, acid, and fat, but it is nice to occasionally gild the lily with one of the optional toppings that follow.

2 TO 4 SERVINGS

One 1½- to 2-pound fish (such as snapper or sea bream), cleaned and scaled (your fishmonger can do this for you)

¼ cup olive oil, plus more to serve

Fine sea salt

Half a lemon or yuzu, to serve (optional)

Flaky sea salt, to serve

OPTIONAL TOPPINGS (CHOOSE NONE OR ONE)

Green Za'atar (page 357)

Sumac-Rose Gomasio (page 357)

Green Sauce, especially Nam Jim and Makrut Lime Green Sauce (page 344)

Kimizu (page 115)

Yuzu Kosho Dressing (page 335)

Harissa (page 342)
+ lemon wedges
+ (more) olive oil

Yuzu Ponzu (page 342)
+ thinly sliced green onion

Melted unsalted butter; olive oil; or plain mayonnaise, store-bought or homemade (page 338)
+ lemon wedges
+ Shiso Salt (page 352)

Plain, full-fat Greek yogurt or labneh, store-bought or homemade (page 336)
+ Crispy Curry Leaves (page 350)
+ lime wedges

Julienned preserved lemon rind
+ salt-packed capers (soaked and drained)
+ thinly sliced green or red onion
+ fresh dill
+ lemon wedges
+ (more) olive oil

Preheat oven to 475°F. Place a baking sheet in the oven, and let it preheat too. Cut a piece of parchment for lining the pan and set it next to your stove.

Let the fish sit at room temperature for 15 minutes or so. Pat the fish very dry inside and out. Use a small, sharp knife to score the fish 2 or 3 times on each side. Rub the entire exterior and cavity generously with olive oil. Season the fish inside and out, head to tail, with salt.

Pull the hot baking sheet from the oven and top with the parchment. Place the whole fish in the center of the hot pan and bake for 18 to 22 minutes, or until cooked through (the flesh is slightly firm and the eyes have turned white). Remove the fish from the oven and let it rest for 5 minutes before filleting and serving drizzled with more olive oil. Serve alongside lemon or yuzu (if keeping it simple), bowls of flaky sea salt, and whichever topping you'd like, if any. Serve immediately.

BRAISED ROCK COD WITH BLISTERED TOMATOES AND PRESERVED LEMON

Cooking fish, although quick and simple, can be fraught. If overcooked, it's dry and mealy; undercooked, it's terribly unappealing. If you aren't going to spring for a whole fish and pan-frying is too scary—or maybe you just want to mix things up—braising fillets in sauce is a sure bet. The technique creates really succulent fish, and eaters get a bonus sauce that they can lap up with bread, couscous, or rice. Serve this with a simple herb salad or Cucumbers with Crème Fraîche and Crispy Capers (page 121).

4 SERVINGS

1 to 1¼ pounds rock cod, halibut, striped bass, or other firm white fish, cut into 4 equal pieces

Fine sea salt

2 tablespoons olive oil

1 recipe Blistered Tomatoes with Preserved Lemon (page 201), warm or at room temperature

¼ lemon

Flaky sea salt

Pat the fish dry and salt on both sides. Heat a 12- to 14-inch sauté pan over medium-high heat, and add the olive oil. When oil is shimmering hot, swirl the pan until no bald spots remain then carefully lower in the fish in a single layer. Sear the fish—without disturbing—for 5 to 6 minutes. Add the tomatoes and lower heat until it is a gentle simmer. Cover and braise the fish for 4 minutes more. Turn off the heat and squeeze the juice of ¼ lemon over the top. To serve, transfer the fish to a large shallow serving bowl or divide among rimmed plates—I like to flip the fillets so that the brown, caramelized side is facing up—and spoon the tomatoes on top and around. Top with flaky sea salt, if you'd like. Serve immediately.

CRISPY-SKINNED FISH WITH PRESERVED LEMON AND HERB OIL

Here, briny, sweet fish melds with rich crème fraîche and a citrusy, herbaceous oil for a striking effect. Provided you make the oil in advance, this dish can come together in a flash, offering you a restaurant-worthy meal on a typical Tuesday night.

Tip—Fish spatulas have a great multipurpose design, and I use mine daily. The best are metal (and therefore heatproof), thin (slide easily under things), and slotted (leaving fat and other bits behind as you lift what you need). Some have nearly sharp edges for getting under delicate fish fillets.

4 SERVINGS

Four 5- to 6-ounce skin-on fillets of snapper, branzino, salmon, or trout

¾ cup crème fraîche

1 to 2 teaspoons water

Fine sea salt

1 tablespoon ghee, olive oil, or neutral vegetable oil (such as cold-pressed rice bran oil or grapeseed oil), divided

¼ lemon

⅓ cup Preserved Lemon and Herb Oil (page 347) or good, buttery olive oil

Flaky sea salt

1 handful of fresh, tender herb fronds and/or leaves (such as dill or chervil), to serve

Pat the fish very dry with paper towels and place on a plate, skin side up; chill, uncovered, for 1 hour, and up to 12 hours (this helps dry out the skin and facilitates crisping and browning). If you don't have time for this step, just use paper towels to get the skin as dry as possible before proceeding.

In a small mixing bowl, whisk together the crème fraîche with 1 to 2 teaspoons water and a pinch of salt—you want it to have the consistency of heavy cream. Refrigerate until ready to use.

Season both sides of the fillets with salt. Place a 12- or 14-inch skillet on high heat and add the ghee or oil; swirl and tilt the pan until the bottom is coated. Once the fat is hot and shimmering, add 1 fillet, lowering it into the pan away from you, skin side down. Press gently with a spatula until the fillet no longer wants to curl up and the entire skin side is flush with the skillet, ensuring complete and direct contact. Repeat with the remaining fillets, leaving at least 1-inch of space between each. Cook the fish, gently pressing periodically with a spatula, until the fish is nearly cooked through (it should still be opaque and a bit raw at the thickest part of the fillet), about 3 minutes. Gently turn the fish (working away from you so the oil doesn't splash on you) and finish cooking off heat, about another 1 to 2 minutes. Season each fillet with a few drops of lemon juice.

To serve, spoon a bit of the crème fraîche and herb oil (or olive oil) onto plates and place the fish alongside or on top, skin side up; season the crispy skin with a little flaky sea salt. Scatter a few herbs on top and around. Serve immediately.

SEARED SQUID WITH HARISSA AND PURSLANE

Squid is a sustainable seafood that's versatile and easy to cook, especially if you know a fishmonger who will clean it for you. Harissa really draws out its sweet, subtle appeal and gives the dish a smoky, spicy boost. Purslane is one of my favorite herbs; it is crisp, with a texture similar to a succulent, and its lemony flavor makes it a perfect garnish for seafood.

With a loaf of bread on the table, this is a one-dish dinner. That said, it's even more pleasurable when served with perfectly braised chickpeas (see A Pot of Chickpeas, page 240) and a plate of cool, crunchy vegetables, such as cucumbers or radishes.

HOW TO CLEAN WHOLE SQUID

Cleaning whole squid is fairly straightforward: Have a sharp knife and cutting board by the sink. Work over the sink; put on some gloves, if you'd like. Start by pulling the finned tube away from the tentacles—it should pop off easily—and separate the two parts into piles on your board. As you work, be gentle, taking care to avoid squeezing or puncturing the ink sac. Hold a tube and pull out the transparent quill of cartilage. Now reach a finger inside the tube and pull out the intestines and ink sac (if your finger won't fit, gently squeeze from the bottom up to help dislodge things and create space). Discard all innards. Gently pull or scrape off the dark skin of the tube (this is optional; it is edible). Rinse the tube inside and out with cold running water and set aside on the board. Repeat with the remaining tubes. Working on the board now, slice between the eyes and the tentacles and discard everything but the tentacles. Feel around in the center of the tentacles until you find a hard, pointy thing—pull it out and discard it. Rinse the tentacles under cold running water. Lay all the squid on a clean kitchen towel and pat very dry.

3 SERVINGS

1 pound cleaned squid, bodies and tentacles separated (see sidebar)

Fine sea salt

2 tablespoons Harissa (page 342), plus more to serve

Olive oil, for cooking and serving

4 handfuls tender purslane sprigs and leaves (2 to 3 ounces) or cilantro, whole leaves and tender stems, cut or torn into 1-inch pieces if large

Flaky sea salt

1 lemon, cut in half

½ to ¾ cup plain mayonnaise, store-bought or homemade (page 338), to serve (optional)

continued

Pat the squid completely dry and season with fine sea salt. Place the harissa in a medium mixing bowl and add the squid. Donning gloves if you'd like, use your hands to coat the squid in the paste, massaging a bit as you work. Chill, uncovered, for 30 minutes, or up to 1 hour.

Heat a 12- or 14-inch heavy-bottomed skillet over high heat for 1 minute (it should be scorching hot). Drizzle in just enough olive oil to evenly coat the bottom of the pan; tilt and swirl until no bald spots remain. Immediately, and working in batches to avoid overcrowding the pan (and thus steaming the squid), add half of the squid. Sear the first side until the flesh whitens, tightens, shrinks, and appears lightly charred—30 to 45 seconds for tentacles and 60 to 90 seconds for bodies. Timing will vary, so watch it carefully—squid is tender until the instant it turns rubbery. If at any point the flesh curls, use a fish spatula or slotted spoon to press it down gently. Turn the squid and char the other side. Transfer to a cutting board. Repeat with the remaining squid.

Once all the squid has cooled slightly, slice the bodies in ½-inch-thick rings. Transfer the squid to a platter or shallow serving bowl, tucking purslane in and around the pieces as you go. Drizzle the squid and purslane with olive oil and season with flaky sea salt and a squeeze of lemon juice here and there—toss the remaining lemon on the platter for folks who want more. Serve immediately alongside bowls of harissa and mayonnaise (if you'd like)—condiments for dolloping here and there.

BLACK VINEGAR CHICKEN

I'd keep black vinegar in the house for this dish alone. The chicken drippings, vinegar, and water simmer into a brawny, complex sauce that has a mellow acidity and complex, smoky, fruity flavor.

I find the simplicity of this dish comforting, but you can certainly add another element or two; add thyme sprigs, chile de arbol, sliced garlic, or julienned ginger to the fat for a minute or two before you deglaze with vinegar and water. I like to serve this with steamed white rice and a sharp, sprightly salad (such as watercress dressed lightly in a lemon vinaigrette), but bread or thick slices of toast also do the trick.

Tip—Be sure to leave 24 hours for brining the chicken. Although it may seem odd to bring a chicken to room temperature before cooking, all proteins should have time between cold storage and a hot pan. This tempering facilitates even, efficient, and more predictable cooking.

4 TO 6 SERVINGS

3¼ to 3½ pounds bone-in, skin-on chicken pieces (any combination of legs, thighs or drumsticks, or breasts halved crosswise)

Fine sea salt

3 tablespoons schmaltz or neutral vegetable oil (such as cold-pressed rice bran oil or grapeseed oil)

¼ cup black vinegar (such as Chinkiang)

1 cup water

The night before, pat the chicken dry—both skin and flesh side. Season the chicken generously with salt on both sides. Refrigerate overnight, uncovered—the meat will release water as it sits and the skin will dry out for better crisping and browning when it is cooked.

Pull the chicken from the fridge 20 to 45 minutes before you plan to cook it. Line a rimmed baking sheet with parchment. Heat the schmaltz in a 12- to 14-inch heavy-bottomed sauté pan or large Dutch oven over medium-high heat. Working in batches, add the chicken skin-side down; press down slightly on all pieces so their skin is in maximum contact with the pan. Cook until the skin is golden brown and releases easily from the pot, 8 to 10 minutes. Stoves and pans usually heat unevenly, so if you're able, give your pan (not the meat) a quarter turn every 3 to 4 minutes. Using tongs, turn the chicken to brown on the other side, another 4 to 8 minutes. As the chicken browns, transfer it to the baking sheet. Leave the fat in the pan and add the vinegar and water (still over medium-high heat). Use a wooden spoon or spatula to scrape up any browned bits. Bring to a simmer and return the chicken to the pot, skin-side up. Cover the pot. Reduce heat to medium-low and continue to cook at a gentle simmer until the chicken is cooked through and tender, 20 to 25 minutes.

Remove the chicken from heat and taste the liquid—season with salt to taste. Transfer the chicken to a large serving platter, spooning cooking liquid around. Serve immediately.

MANY WAYS TO SEASON A CHICKEN

If you rely on chicken for many meals during the week, you need a recipe for a memorable bird that practically cooks itself. And for that you have two options. A plain bird is plain easy: Pat a 3½-pound chicken dry and salt generously inside and out; refrigerate, uncovered, overnight. Before you plan to cook, let the chicken hang out at room temperature for at least 30 minutes, and up to 1 hour; roast at 500°F for 50 minutes and wait 10 to 15 more before carving. Serve this with any sauce, starter, side, or salad in this book. This dinner always feels good, and it's doable any night of the week.

If, however, you're like me and—with chicken on the docket many days of the week—you've tired of that dependable-but-homely plain bird, slather the skin with one of the delicious rubs on page 267. Still refrigerate it overnight: this is a dry brine, an important step for flavoring and tenderizing that also helps the rub permeate and adhere. (A third bonus: it divides the prep time!) Then roast lower and slower, so the rub doesn't burn. Always let it (and all meat) rest before carving and serving with the flavorful pan juices. This roast will appear elaborate but it's actually quite easy.

> **Tips**—Be sure to leave 24 hours for brining the chicken. Brines and rubs that contain sugars (even natural ones, such as milk sugar) brown more quickly and deeply than those without. This is a boon for flavor, but it requires a more watchful eye. If you notice the skin darkening too quickly, tent with foil. (I prefer to line my foil with parchment, so it isn't in direct contact with the meat.)

4 TO 6 SERVINGS

continued

One whole chicken (3½ to 4 pounds)

Fine sea salt

CHOOSE ONE:

FOR A DRY RUB: **2 TO 3 TABLESPOONS OLIVE OIL,** **SCHMALTZ, OR GHEE PLUS** **APPROXIMATELY 3 TABLESPOONS DRY MIX**	**FOR A WET RUB:** **⅓ CUP SAUCE, PASTE, OR DRESSING**
1. Curry Spice Blend (page 352) (*Pictured on page 265.*)	1. Shio koji puree, store-bought or homemade (page 81)
2. Mole Spice Blend (page 353)	2. Green Sauce of your choice (page 344)
3. Green Za'atar (page 357) (*Pictured on page 266.*)	3. Harissa (page 342)
	4. Yogurt + 3 tablespoons Spicy Sumac Gomasio (page 357)
	5. Yogurt Mayonnaise (page 339)
	6. Crème fraîche
	7. Labneh, store-bought or homemade (page 336)—slip labneh under the skin
	8. Instant "XO" (page 341)—strain through a fine-mesh strainer, and use the oil as the rub (or else the 'nduja will burn)

The day before you want to cook the chicken, pat it very dry with paper towels—inside and out—and tuck the wing tips under the breast (or cut them off and use them for Simple Chicken Stock, page 346). Unless you are using the shio koji rub, salt generously all over, inside and out. Slather the entire bird in whichever wet or dry rub you prefer. Set on a rimmed pan or plate and refrigerate, uncovered, overnight (12 to 24 hours).

Pull the chicken from the fridge for 30 to 60 minutes before you plan to cook it. Preheat the oven to 325°F and position a rack in the center. Place the chicken on a rimmed baking sheet or a shallow roasting pan. There is no need to tie the legs, but you can, if you want. Roast, uncovered, in the middle of the center rack until the chicken is golden brown and cooked through, 2½ to 3 hours.

Let the chicken rest for 15 to 20 minutes before carving and serving.

COCONUT-BRAISED CHICKEN WITH LIME LEAF, PEANUT, AND CRISPY SHALLOTS

I've made this dish at least twenty times, and it always delights me. Makrut lime leaf brings pep and intrigue; fish sauce adds a mysterious complexity; crispy shallots and ground peanuts add a bit of sweetness. Don't let the length of this ingredient list intimidate you. Once you've gathered everything, this one-dish wonder comes together quickly, cooks itself, and, when it's time to eat, gives back a thousandfold. And if you're one of those people who likes to double batches for things like curry pastes for freezing and future use, you're three-quarters of the way done with this recipe already. This spice paste, if kept covered and refrigerated, can be made 1 month ahead; if kept frozen, for up to 3 months.

Tips—Be sure to leave 24 hours for brining the chicken. The crispy shallots start to sag almost immediately, so wait until the last minute before garnishing the dish. Softening isn't a big problem, though, as they continue to contribute pops of sweetness and umami as you eat. If you're feeling generous, make more than you need and put a little bowl on the table for everyone to help themselves throughout the meal. And while you're at it, also put a bowl on the table for chicken bones; slurping leftover broth is so much easier once the bones are out of the way.

2 TO 4 SERVINGS

2 whole chicken legs or 4 bone-in, skin-on thighs (approximately 1½ pounds)

Fine sea salt

¼ cup toasted peanuts

1 chile de arbol, stemmed

1 teaspoon coriander seeds

¼ teaspoon cumin seeds

⅛ teaspoon ground cinnamon

¼ teaspoon dried ground turmeric or 1 tablespoon finely grated fresh turmeric (use a Microplane for best results)

One 1-inch piece fresh ginger, finely grated (use a Microplane for best results)

1 medium shallot, finely grated or minced (use a Microplane for best results)

One 13.5-ounce can unsweetened, full-fat coconut milk

1 tablespoon coconut oil (optional)

1 teaspoon fish sauce

½ to 1 teaspoon tamarind paste (page 90)

1 teaspoon coconut sugar or other brown sugar

10 fresh makrut lime leaves

1½ pounds Yukon Gold potatoes or similar variety, cut into 1- to 1½-inch pieces

Steamed or boiled rice (jasmine is particularly good), for serving (optional)

1 cup (loosely packed) cilantro, whole leaves and tender stems, for garnish

Lime wedges, for serving

Crispy Shallots (page 350), to serve (optional)

The night before you plan to cook: Pat the chicken dry—both the skin and flesh side. Season chicken generously with salt on both sides. Refrigerate overnight, ideally uncovered—the meat will release water as it sits and the skin will dry out, facilitating better crisping and browning when it is cooked.

Pull the chicken from the fridge 20 to 45 minutes before you plan to cook it. Preheat oven to 300°F. Coarsely grind the peanuts in a spice mill or with a mortar and pestle. Set aside 2 tablespoons for a garnish and keep the rest in the bowl. Combine the chile, coriander, and cumin in a 9- or 10-inch dry skillet and toast over medium heat until fragrant, about 2 minutes. Let cool, then add to the peanuts and grind all finely.

Transfer the toasted and freshly ground spices to a food processor or (my preference) mortar; add the cinnamon, turmeric, ginger, shallot, and a pinch of salt; process to a smooth paste.

In a 10- to 12-inch heavy-bottomed sauté pan or large Dutch oven, heat 1 tablespoon coconut cream (skimmed from the top of the can) or the coconut oil (if using) over medium-high heat until shimmering. Add the spice paste and cook, stirring constantly, for about 2 minutes. Stir in the coconut milk, fish sauce, tamarind paste, sugar, and makrut lime leaves; bring to a boil over high heat. Immediately reduce heat until the liquid is at a lazy simmer. Place the chicken legs in the pot, skin side up; the liquid should come halfway up the sides of the meat and the skin should remain dry. Nestle potatoes in between and around the legs.

Transfer to the oven and braise, uncovered, for 75 to 90 minutes, or until the chicken is brown on top, the meat pulls away from the bone, and the potatoes are tender.

Serve with rice (if desired) and garnish with the cilantro, lime wedges, remaining coarsely ground peanuts, and crispy shallots.

RICE PORRIDGE WITH ALL THE THINGS

Using leftovers from the week's cooking, this loaded creamy rice porridge warms and soothes some bone-deep needs. And while it is certainly food of the humblest sort, I urge you to forget notions of entertaining and invite friends over to help you clean out your fridge by assembling their own bowls. This is a fun, practical, and pleasurable way to feed and be fed.

APPROXIMATELY 4 SERVINGS

1 cup cooked brown or white short-grain rice

4 cups Kombu Stock (page 347), Dashi (page 346), Simple Chicken Stock (page 346), or water

2 slices fresh ginger (each approximately ¼-inch thick)

Fine sea salt

PROTEINS (CHOOSE ONE OR TWO)

1 to 2 cooked chicken thighs or 1 breast, sliced (could be from Black Vinegar Chicken, page 263; or a shio-koji slathered bird, page 264)

2 Ume-Glazed Pork Ribs (page 283), meat pulled

1½ cups diced tofu

½ cup cooked beans (see A Pot of Chickpeas, page 240) drained, warm or at room temperature

3 to 4 (one per person) 6½-minute Soft-Centered Eggs (page 144)

TOPPINGS (CHOOSE ONE OR MORE)

Crispy Shallots (page 350)

Sliced scallions or chives

Toasted peanuts, coarsely chopped

Toasted sesame and/or sunflower seeds

Torn toasted nori, nori powder (store-bought or homemade, page 71), or Spicy Seaweed Gomasio (page 358)

Pickled or fermented vegetables (such as umeboshi plums), minced or cut into bite-sized pieces

Shredded raw cabbage or coarsely chopped cooked greens (such as Baby Bok Choy "Under a Brick," page 220; or Big-Batch Breakfast Greens, page 155)

Roasted or sautéed mushrooms (see Job's Tears "Stonepot" with Crispy Mushrooms and Jammy Eggs, page 247)

Julienned daikon (or other radish)

Cilantro, whole leaves and tender stems, cut or torn into 1- to 2-inch pieces

Chile Vinegar (page 348)

Sesame oil

Place the rice and kombu stock in a medium saucepan over high heat; add the ginger and 2 pinches of salt. Once it comes to a boil, lower the heat to a gentle simmer, cover, and cook, 30 to 40 minutes, or until thickened to the consistency of oatmeal. Ladle the rice porridge into 2 or 3 large warmed bowls and garnish each with a protein(s) of your choice and whatever toppings you desire.

THE MODERN MEATBALL

I always have ground meat in my freezer in case of unexpected company or some other "Oh Shit" moment. It lends itself to the type of scalable and riffable recipes ideal for feeding a hungry crowd with whatever is around in a relatively short amount of time. Meatballs may be the best application for ground meat, and it is time they broke out of their Italian-food-for-a-special-occasion box. The truth is, the world of meatballs is broad and borderless. They are suited to a variety of cooking methods and flavor profiles. Serve any of these meatballs as a one-dish main course. Or, serve them as part of a meze- or snack-like spread, in which the rest of the table is filled out with a salad or two and store-bought lifesavers like feta, pickles, olives, and flatbread.

Tips—I know it isn't always possible to get freshly ground meat, but know that if you can source it, your meatballs will be much airier (and you don't need to worry as much about overcooking them in the name of safety). Before beginning, be sure to flip the page and read through all of the options for cooking and serving. Determine whether you plan to grill, broil, pan-fry, or simmer, as that may affect which meatball recipe and shape you choose. Also: my suggestions are just that; if you've made any sort of meatball before, I'm sure you have ideas too. All toppings and accompaniments are optional. And tomato sauces are always welcome!

MAKES 16 TO 18 MEATBALLS; 4 TO 6 SERVINGS

	CHICKEN MISO MEATBALLS	PORK MEATBALLS WITH RICE FLOUR AND FISH SAUCE	SPICED LAMB MEATBALLS	MEATBALLS WITH DRIED LIME AND CHILE	MOLE-SPICED MEATBALLS
2 POUNDS GROUND MEAT	Chicken	Pork	Lamb	Beef	Beef
BINDER	⅓ cup white miso or 2 tablespoons white rice flour	2 tablespoons white rice flour	¼ cup yogurt, preferably sheep's milk or 2 tablespoons white rice flour	None	¼ cup crème fraîche or plain, full-fat Greek yogurt
SALT AND SEASONING	½ teaspoon fine sea salt 2 tablespoons minced green onion or shallot ⅛ teaspoon ground chile de arbol (optional)	½ teaspoon fine sea salt 2 tablespoons fish sauce 1 teaspoon coconut sugar 2 to 3 tablespoons finely chopped cilantro and/or cilantro, whole leaves and tender stems	1¼ teaspoons fine sea salt 2 teaspoons Curry Spice Blend (page 352) or ¾ teaspoon dried ground turmeric 2 to 3 tablespoons finely chopped cilantro or mint	1¼ teaspoons fine sea salt ½ teaspoon dried lime powder (page 38) ½ teaspoon dried ground turmeric ¼ teaspoon ground cinnamon ¼ teaspoon Aleppo-style pepper or Marash pepper, plus more to serve	1¼ teaspoons fine sea salt 1½ teaspoons Mole Spice Blend (page 353) 2 to 3 tablespoons finely chopped cilantro and/or cilantro, whole leaves and tender stems

STEP ONE: Choose your recipe from the above chart and prepare the meatballs.

In a large bowl, use a fork to break up the ground meat; gently combine with remaining ingredients. Moisten hands with water and roll mixture into 18 balls (1½-inch) or form into 16 oblong sausages (3½- to 4-inch-long cylinder with slightly tapered ends), a good shape for grilling.

Cover and refrigerate, for at least 30 minutes and up to 12 hours, until ready to cook (the colder the mix, the more likely the meatballs keep their shape).

continued

CHICKEN MISO MEATBALLS	PORK MEATBALLS WITH RICE FLOUR AND FISH SAUCE	SPICED LAMB MEATBALLS	MEATBALLS WITH DRIED LIME AND CHILE	MOLE-SPICED MEATBALLS
SIMMER WITH Simple Chicken Stock (page 346)	**SIMMER WITH** Kombu Stock (page 347) **or** **GRILL, BROIL, OR PAN-FRY IN CAST IRON**	**GRILL, BROIL, OR PAN-FRY IN CAST IRON**	**GRILL, BROIL, OR PAN-FRY IN CAST IRON**	**GRILL, BROIL, OR PAN-FRY IN CAST IRON**

STEP TWO: Choose your option for cooking and cook the meatballs.

Simmer: Bring broth (approximately 7 cups) or sauce (approximately 4 cups) to a boil, then lower the heat until it bubbles gently. Season with salt to taste. Lower meatballs into the broth or sauce and cook until they all firm up and turn opaque, 6 to 7 minutes after adding the last one. Serve immediately.

Grill, broil, or pan-fry in a 12- to 14-inch cast iron: Slick the meatballs with olive oil, neutral vegetable oil (such as cold-pressed rice bran oil or grapeseed oil), lard (for pork), or schmaltz (for chicken). Place on a preheated grill. Cook over high heat for 6 to 10 minutes, turning every 2 minutes or so, until deeply browned all over and cooked to your preferred level of doneness. Serve immediately.

CHICKEN MISO MEATBALLS	PORK MEATBALLS WITH RICE FLOUR AND FISH SAUCE	SPICED LAMB MEATBALLS	MEATBALLS WITH DRIED LIME AND CHILE	MOLE-SPICED MEATBALLS
TOP WITH Many tender herbs (such as green shiso, dill, cilantro, parsley, tarragon, and/or chive), thinly sliced or coarsely chopped + Lemon juice and zest + Olive oil		**TOP WITH** Cilantro, whole leaves and tender stems + Pomegranate seeds (optional)	**TOP WITH** Many tender herbs (such as dill, cilantro, parsley, mint), coarsely chopped + Aleppo-style pepper	**TOP WITH** Lime juice + Olive oil + Cilantro, whole leaves and tender stems and/or purslane
	SERVE WITH Cilantro, whole leaves and tender stems +/or ½ cup Nam Jim (page 345) + Steamed rice + Cucumber	**SERVE WITH** Pomegranate molasses +/or Sheep's milk yogurt + Flatbread (such as pita or lavash), farro, freekah, couscous, or rice + Cucumber and/or fresh fruit such as apricots	**SERVE WITH** Yogurt Dressing (page 335) or labneh, store-bought or homemade (page 336) + Flatbread (such as pita or lavash), farro, freekah, couscous, or rice	**SERVE WITH** Crème fraîche + Avocado + Radish and/or jicama + Warmed tortillas or rice + Fresh fruit such as pineapple, mango, or watermelon

STEP THREE: Choose topping(s) and side dishes of your choice and finish the dish, serving immediately.

FRIED QUAIL WITH LABNEH
AND SPICY SUMAC GOMASIO

I hope this quail recipe convinces you to take a break from chicken. The flavor of these small gamey birds is far more interesting, and because of their small bones, they practically command that you put down your fork and use your hands. Serve with rice or bread and a simple salad—bitter and/or peppery greens, such as chicories and arugula, really complement the sweetness of the dish.

Tip—Be sure to leave 24 hours for marinating the quail.

4 SERVINGS

2¾ teaspoons fine sea salt, divided

2 large eggs, lightly beaten

2 tablespoons plain, full-fat Greek yogurt

4 semi-boneless quail (approximately 1½ pounds), halved through the breast and patted dry with paper towels

1 cup chickpea flour

¼ cup potato starch or cornstarch

⅓ cup sweet rice (mochiko) flour

½ teaspoon baking powder

Neutral vegetable oil (such as cold-pressed rice bran oil or grapeseed oil) for frying

TO SERVE

1 cup labneh, store-bought or homemade (page 336)

1 tablespoon Spicy Sumac Gomasio (page 357)

Flaky sea salt

The night before you plan to make the quail: In a large mixing bowl or storage container, whisk together 2 teaspoons fine sea salt, the eggs, and the yogurt; add the quail and toss to combine. Cover and refrigerate overnight.

Pull the quail from the fridge for 30 to 45 minutes before you plan to cook it. Preheat oven to 200°F. In a wide shallow bowl, whisk together the chickpea flour, starch, sweet rice flour, baking powder, and remaining ¾ teaspoon fine sea salt. Line a baking sheet with parchment and top with a cooling rack; if you don't have a rack, top parchment with a layer of paper towels (the rack helps keep the skin crispy while it drains and sits, but the paper towels will at least soak up extra oil).

continued

In a 12- or 14-inch heavy-bottomed skillet or sauté pan, preferably cast iron, heat about 1 inch of oil over high heat until it reaches 360°F. Remove the quail from the egg mixture—letting any excess liquid drip off—and dredge it in the dry coating mixture, shaking off any excess. Using tongs, carefully lower quail pieces one at a time into the oil. You are shallow-frying, so the pieces won't be completely submerged. You will likely need to fry in batches—don't overcrowd the pan. Fry until both sides are crispy and evenly golden brown and the meat is cooked through, about 3 minutes per side. Remove the quail with tongs or a slotted spoon, shaking off excess oil, and drain on the cooling rack or paper towels. If you'd like, hold the finished quail in the low oven until you finish the rest.

Place the labneh on a large serving platter or divide among dinner plates; use the back of a spoon to spread it into a little swirl (see photo). Top the labneh with the fried quail; drizzle a little olive oil around the quail and sprinkle each piece with gomasio and flaky sea salt.

EASY ROAST DUCK LEGS WITH PRESERVED LEMON AND HONEY

This is an impressive dish, reminiscent of duck confit. While steam-roasting brined duck legs may sound ambitious, the active, hands-on time is only about 30 minutes. The dish can be prepared days in advance of serving, and it is nearly impossible to mess up. Once you've made it a few times, you'll always have an extraordinary dinner in your back pocket.

In the spring I like to serve this with bread or flatbread, a grated carrot salad or one of the beet salads on page 216, and a simple green salad. In the fall, couscous or farro piccolo with pomegranate and herbs is the way to go. Any leftover duck, along with its crisped-up skin and a little warm fat, makes a remarkable winter salad. There are endless combinations that work well, but I'm particularly fond of tossing it with frisée, barberries, walnuts in walnut oil (page 137), and Basic Banyuls Dressing (page 335).

Tip—Be sure to leave 24 hours for brining the duck.

8 SERVINGS

8 duck legs (approximately 4 pounds)

Fine sea salt

½ preserved lemon

1½ tablespoons honey

2 tablespoons lemon juice

1 tablespoon toasted coriander seeds, ground

2 teaspoons toasted cumin seeds, ground

¼ teaspoon ground cinnamon

½ cup olive oil

One 2-inch slice fresh ginger

2 garlic cloves, smashed and peeled

Pat the duck dry and place in a heavy-bottomed roasting pan, deep sauté pan, or Dutch oven wide enough to fit the legs snugly in one layer. Prick the duck skin all over with a paring knife or fork; season liberally with salt on both sides and refrigerate overnight.

Preheat oven to 275°F. Pull the duck from the fridge 30 to 60 minutes before you plan to cook. Meanwhile, rinse the preserved lemon under running water to remove the excess salt. Pick out and discard any seeds. Puree the preserved lemon, honey, lemon juice, spices, and olive oil in a blender until smooth. Massage the preserved lemon paste on both sides of the duck legs, and add the ginger and garlic. Re-nestle the legs in the pan in one even layer, skin side up. Cover the pan with a sheet of parchment, and top with a tight-fitting lid or aluminum foil. Braise until the duck is nearly submerged in its fat and the bones wiggle easily in the joint, 2 to 3 hours, depending on the size of the individual legs. (At this point you can refrigerate the duck legs for up to 3 days before serving; rewarm and liquefy the fat before proceeding with the recipe.)

continued

Preheat oven to 475°F. Transfer the duck legs—skin side up—to a rimmed baking sheet (it should be large enough to accommodate the duck legs in one layer, with a ½ inch or so between them). Skim a little duck fat from the top of the braising pan and spoon on top of each duck leg. Roast the legs on the top oven rack until the skin is crackling crisp, 15 to 20 minutes. Rest for 5 minutes before serving.

BRAISED RABBIT WITH VERJUS AND HERBS

Americans are more likely to view rabbits as pets than as food. That's a shame, because rabbit is easy to cook, delicately gamy, and an unexpectedly versatile meat. Here it is gently braised in bright, fruity verjus and seasoned with mild leek, sweet fennel, and fresh herbs.

Tip—Be sure to leave 24 hours for brining the rabbit.

2 TO 3 SERVINGS

One 2- to 3-pound rabbit, cut into 8 pieces

2 teaspoons fine sea salt, plus more as needed

2 medium leeks, well-washed, halved lengthwise and crosswise; or 3 medium shallots, trimmed and cut in half

Tops of 1 to 2 fennel bulbs (both thick stalks and fronds)

2 sprigs rosemary

3 to 4 sprigs thyme

A few parsley stems, if you have them

1 cup white verjus

2 cups Simple Chicken Stock (page 346) or store-bought chicken stock

¼ cup olive oil, plus more to finish

Flaky sea salt

Season the rabbit with 2 teaspoons of fine sea salt and refrigerate overnight, ideally uncovered and in an even layer (so the skin dries out a bit). Let the rabbit sit at room temperature for at least 30 minutes, or up to 1 hour, before proceeding.

Preheat oven to 475°F. In a 12- to 14-inch heavy-bottomed sauté pan or large Dutch oven, use the leeks, fennel bulb tops, and herbs to create a bed for the rabbit; season the vegetables with a pinch of salt. Place the rabbit on top and pour the verjus, chicken stock, and olive oil on top. If the liquid doesn't come halfway up the sides of the meat, add water until it does. Bring to a simmer over medium-high heat. Transfer to the oven, uncovered, for a high-heat blast that will help jump-start the browning process—for 20 minutes. Lower oven temp to 275°F and braise the rabbit, uncovered, for 1½ to 2 hours, or the until the meat begins to pull away from the bone when lightly prodded. Let the rabbit sit in the braising liquid for 20 minutes. At this point, you can cool completely, cover, and refrigerate overnight, or you can proceed.

Preheat oven to 475°F. Place the rabbit on a rimmed baking sheet. Pick out the big pieces of leek and fennel and discard; strain the verjus braising liquid through a fine-mesh sieve and return to the pan. Bring to a boil over high heat and reduce the liquid by about a third. Turn off the heat, return the rabbit to the pan, and place in the oven, uncovered, for 10 to 15 minutes, or until the rabbit is brown and warmed through. Serve the rabbit in a shallow pool of the verjus sauce, drizzle with olive oil, and finish with a pinch of flaky sea salt.

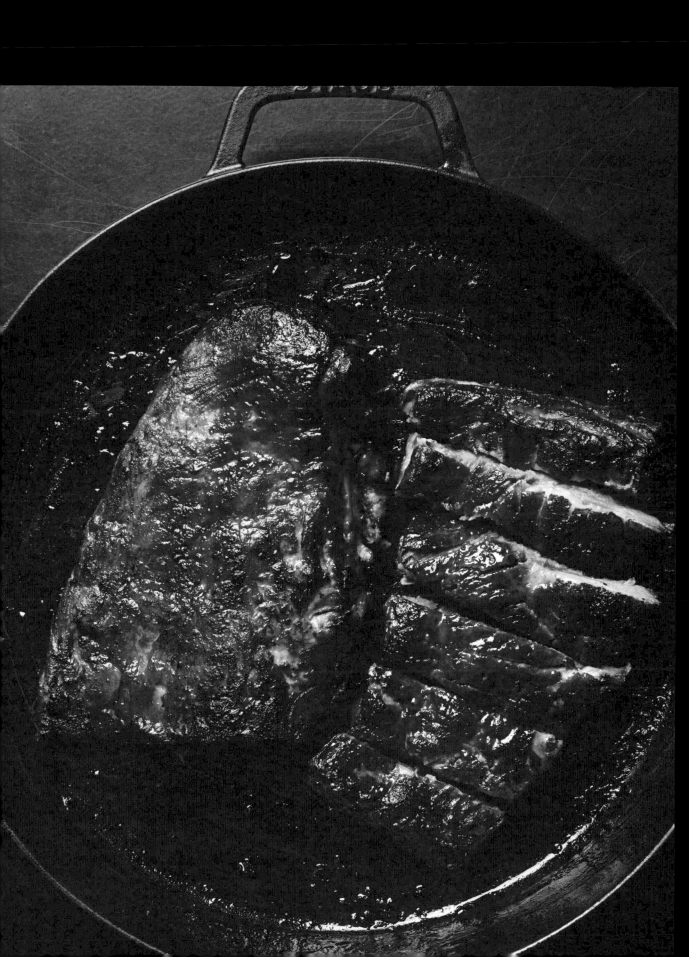

UME-GLAZED PORK RIBS

Though I obviously adore vegetables, I'm definitely a carnivore. And I crave these ribs. They aren't too wet or too dry, too sticky or overly sauced. The meat—as it falls off the bone—is lacquered in a complex sauce in which no one ingredient overpowers another. Moreover, this is the sort of hands-off, minimal-effort meal that gets me excited to cook no matter what shade of difficult my day has turned. Use this recipe as a template for "steam-roasting," a method that turns tough cuts into meltingly tender masterpieces without any messy searing or sauce making.

Serve with a simple starch—steamed white rice or your favorite loaf of bread—and a sprightly mizuna or arugula salad. If you want a few extras on the table, consider Charred Cucumber and Shiso Quick Pickles (page 111), raw cucumber spears, or some good pickles.

Tip—Be sure to leave 24 hours for brining the pork.

4 TO 6 SERVINGS

1 rack St. Louis–style spare ribs (approximately 3 to 3½ pounds), halved crosswise (so they fit in your pan)

Fine sea salt

¼ cup umeboshi plum vinegar

4 cups water or Kombu Stock (page 347)

One 2-inch piece fresh ginger

2 green onions, white and light-green parts

1 tablespoon muscovado or other brown sugar

Lemon juice, as needed

Salt the ribs lightly and refrigerate overnight.

Preheat oven to 285°F. Pull the ribs from the fridge 45 to 60 minutes before you plan to cook. Combine the ribs and remaining ingredients in a wide Dutch oven (I use a Staub 14-inch cast-iron "paella" pan for this) or deep roasting pan; if the kombu stock isn't enough volume so that the bottom three-quarters of the ribs are submerged (this will depend on your ribs and your pan), add water. Seal the pot with a layer of parchment and a tight-fitting lid; if your pan doesn't have a lid, seal the parchment with a double layer of aluminum foil. Braise the ribs for 2½ to 3 hours, or until the meat is tender and a cake tester or the tip of a paring knife inserted into the meat's thickest part encounters little resistance—but not so long that it begins to fall off the bone into the stock. Remove the ribs from the oven and unseal. Ideally you want to cool these ribs in their braising liquid and refrigerate overnight, but if you don't have the time, no worries—just proceed when the ribs are cool enough to handle. Refrigerated in the liquid, these ribs can be braised up to 3 days in advance.

Preheat oven to 500°F. Use a spoon to remove the solidified fat from the surface. (If you didn't refrigerate your ribs, use a liquid fat

continued

Ume-Glazed Pork Ribs,
continued

separator. Reserve lard for another use. Discard the ginger and green onions. Place the ribs flat side up on a parchment-lined rimmed baking sheet in one layer with at least a ½-inch space between the pieces; keep these at room temperature while you make the glaze.

Strain the braising liquid through a fine-mesh sieve and return it to the roasting pan. Bring the liquid to a boil and reduce until it is thick enough to coat the back of a spoon, 13 to 15 minutes. As it begins to thicken, stir it occasionally, and then frequently in the final few minutes, to make sure it doesn't burn on the bottom of the wide pan. Taste and add more sugar and/or umeboshi vinegar, if needed—you want it barely sweet and bright, but not tart. If your glaze is too salty, add lemon juice to taste. If it gets too thick, thin with a few drops of water at a time, until it reaches the right consistency.

Return the ribs to the pan, transfer to the oven, and roast for 5 to 10 minutes, or until they are warmed through and beginning to brown. Brush thickly with the sauce and roast 5 to 10 minutes more, or until caramelized. Let the ribs rest at room temperature for 5 minutes before serving.

LAMB AND LAMB'S-QUARTER PIE

If pastilla and spanakopita produced a child, this would be their girl. And she's a stunner. While this sort of thing is suited to a special occasion, it is easy to prepare and—with its layering and brushing and scattering and layering and brushing and scattering—about as therapeutic as cooking gets. Moreover, the filling can be made up to 3 days in advance—just refrigerate in airtight containers until you're ready to complete the recipe. *And* because it is such a showstopper, you need nothing more than a few accoutrements—perhaps some thickly sliced cucumber or pickled vegetables, a plate of feta, a bowl of fruit—to make it a feast.

This is a recipe that really lets ghee (page 161) shine. It bestows on the otherwise bland dough its nutty, slightly fermented flavor, and it produces a deep golden crust that butter would burn before achieving.

Lamb's-quarter was once highly cultivated but was then replaced by other staple crops such as spinach (which makes a fine substitute). It's available in markets April through September, and you'll know it by its slender, pointed leaves, which are hunter green with a silvery cast. It tastes subtly bitter but balanced; there are also hints of salt, lemon, and sweetness.

Tips—To prevent the phyllo dough from drying out and becoming difficult, cover the sheets with plastic wrap and a damp towel (or damp paper towels) until the second you begin using them. And have all your ingredients prepped and ready before you expose it to air.

8 TO 10 SERVINGS

FILLING

1 tablespoon ghee

1 tablespoon olive oil

1 pound ground lamb

Fine sea salt

4 medium shallots, 6 green onions (white and light-green parts), or 1 medium yellow onion, finely chopped

2 garlic cloves, minced (optional)

1 tablespoon Curry Spice Blend (page 352)

1 teaspoon honey

8 ounces lamb's-quarters or spinach, washed, dried, and finely chopped

½ teaspoon red wine vinegar or sherry vinegar

½ teaspoon lemon juice

½ cup finely chopped fresh dill or cilantro

ASSEMBLY

½ cup ghee, melted

Ten 13 x 18-inch sheets (8 ounces) phyllo pastry

1 tablespoon bee pollen (optional)

Flaky sea salt

continued

Prepare the filling: Preheat oven to 375°F. Heat a 10- or 12-inch sauté pan or skillet over medium-high heat. Add the ghee, olive oil, lamb, and 2 pinches of salt; cook, uncovered, stirring occasionally to break up the lamb, until the meat is a dark burnished brown, 8 to 10 minutes. Lower the heat to medium and add the shallots, garlic (if using), spices, honey, and another pinch of salt; cook until the shallots are translucent, about 6 minutes. Add the lamb's-quarter, stir to combine, and cover the pan. Once the greens are wilted, uncover and cook, stirring regularly so that the mixture doesn't stick to the bottom, until all moisture has evaporated (excess moisture can lead to a soggy pie)—about 4 minutes more. Off heat, stir in the vinegar, lemon juice, and herbs. Taste and adjust the salt, as needed. The filling can be prepared up to 3 days in advance; cover and refrigerate until ready to use.

Assemble the pie: Brush the bottom and sides of a 10-inch springform pan generously with melted ghee. Lay the phyllo dough in a stack on a rimless baking sheet and cut the stack in half crosswise, yielding 20 sheets, each about 7 x 9 inches. Be quick but gentle: center 1 sheet of phyllo across the springform pan and then ease it down to line the bottom, letting the ends drape over the sides; brush it—the entire piece—with melted ghee. Center another sheet across in the opposite direction, then ease it down to line the bottom; the 2 pieces will overlap in places, and that's fine; brush the inside of the sheet— bottom and sides—completely with melted ghee. Repeat this process, moving in a clockwise direction with the phyllo sheets fanning out and overlapping each other, until only 5 phyllo sheets remain.

Spoon the lamb filling into the pan, spreading it into an even layer. Add the remaining phyllo sheets to cover the filling, brushing each with melted ghee. Fold the overhang of the bottom phyllo sheets over the top and brush with a final, generous coating of melted ghee to seal. Transfer the springform pan to a parchment-lined rimmed baking sheet (the ghee is likely to drip out a bit as it cooks) and bake until deep golden brown—rotating the pan halfway through—about 1 hour. (Tent with foil if the phyllo appears to be getting too dark.)

Let the pie cool to room temperature for 15 minutes before releasing it from the springform pan and inverting it onto a platter. Cool 10 minutes more before sprinkling with bee pollen (if using) and a little flaky salt. The pie can be made up to 3 days in advance; cover and refrigerate. The pie tastes good cold (I've been known to eat it out of hand, like pizza), but if you choose to reheat it, dust off the pollen (it burns) and put it in a 275°F oven for 20 minutes.

SPICED LAMB CHOPS WITH BLACK VINEGAR AND HONEY

It's as if the combination of chile, cumin, and fennel was designed specifically for lamb. The recipe works a lot of flavor into the lamb during an overnight dry brine when the intense aroma of the spices slips into the meat. As the lamb browns on the stovetop, it gets basted with a mix of black vinegar and honey, just long enough for a deeply flavorful sweet-and-sour crust to form.

Tips—If you've never had lamb loin chops, seek them out—they look like miniature T-bone steaks. They are tender and flavorful and my preferred cut when not braising. Read through the recipe before starting, as it's one of those that moves quickly. And be sure to leave 24 hours for brining the meat.

2 TO 3 SERVINGS

2 chile de arbol or
1 teaspoon chile flakes

1 tablespoon cumin seeds, toasted

1 tablespoon fennel seeds, toasted

4 lamb loin chops
(approximately
1½ pounds), 1½ inches
thick, or individual rib
chops (unfrenched)

Fine sea salt

Olive oil

1 tablespoon black vinegar
(such as Chinkiang)

1 tablespoon honey

Using a knife, mortar and pestle, or spice grinder, grind the chiles and spices—make sure the chiles are pulverized, but don't go too fine. Season the lamb with salt and rub with olive oil. Give each chop a thick dusting of spices (you should barely see the meat), then massage the blend into the meat. Refrigerate uncovered, overnight.

Pull the lamb from the fridge 20 to 40 minutes before you plan to cook. Rub each chop all over with about ½ teaspoon (eyeball it) of olive oil; you'll disturb the spices a bit, and that is fine. In a small bowl, mix together the vinegar and honey until the honey dissolves; have a basting brush nearby.

Heat a 12- or 14-inch heavy-bottomed skillet over medium-high heat. Once it is hot, place the lamb in the skillet, leaving a little space between each piece (overcrowding prevents browning). Leave the lamb undisturbed for 2 to 3 minutes; if your stove heats unevenly, rotate the skillet halfway through. Use tongs to take a peek—if the first side isn't caramelized, give it another minute. Make sure you don't let the spices burn; lower the heat slightly, if needed. Using tongs, turn the lamb and cook until it's nicely browned on the other side, about 2 minutes more.

Now the lamb should be medium-rare, and ideally we don't want to cook it much more. Quickly brush the vinegar-honey mixture—trying not to disturb the spices too much—on one side. Place this lacquered side down and sear for 30 to 60 seconds, until deeply caramelized. Repeat lacquering and searing on the remaining side. I now take the time to sear the fat side and bone side—standing up the lamb chops and letting them lean on the skillet or each other, if needed. This takes about 30 seconds per side.

Transfer the lamb to a rack or cutting board to rest for at least 5 minutes before serving.

MOLE-SPICED BRISKET

The key to good brisket—as with any tough cut of meat—is patience, diligence, and ample, early seasoning. While that may sound like rigorous work, this dish actually comes together in a snap once the spice blend has been made. And if you cook more brisket than you need for a single meal (it's already huge, and easily scalable), it will give for days: shred the meat and stuff it into tacos; make sandwiches with Yogurt Mayonnaise (page 339); pan-fry some hash. When serving the full, rich cut as a main course, I suggest serving it alongside simple, fresh, unfussy sides, such as tomatoes dressed in olive oil, braised black beans, and/or a sprightly green salad.

Tip—Be sure to leave 24 hours for brining the brisket.

**APPROXIMATELY
6 SERVINGS**

1 large flat or first-cut beef brisket (approximately 5½ to 6 pounds), with ½-inch fat cap

Olive oil or neutral vegetable oil (such as cold-pressed rice bran oil or grapeseed oil)

2 tablespoons fine sea salt

2 tablespoons Mole Spice Blend (page 353)

¼ cup hot water

2 tablespoons red wine vinegar or apple cider vinegar

Cilantro, whole leaves and tender stems (optional)

2 limes, cut in half, for serving

Flaky sea salt, for serving

The night before you plan to cook, place the brisket in a deep roasting pan just large enough to hold it. Rub the brisket with just enough oil to coat. Season all sides generously with salt and mole spice blend. Turn the brisket fat side up and refrigerate uncovered, overnight. This is a dry brine, and it is essential for exceptionally moist and robustly flavored meat.

One hour before you're ready to cook (and at least 7 hours before you plan to serve it), remove the brisket from the refrigerator and let it temper at room temperature. Preheat oven to 300°F.

Add ¼ cup hot water and the vinegar to the roasting pan. Cover the pan tightly with parchment and then foil and then a lid (if you don't have a lid that fits the pan, a baking sheet works). Cook in the oven for 3 hours. Take a peek, and add another few tablespoons of water if the pan seems dry (there will certainly be fat but there must also be a bit of water). Cover again and return the pan to the oven for another 1½ to 2½ hours. It's done when a fork slides in without any resistance. If the meat resists, cook another 20 to 30 minutes or so, checking again and being careful not to let it dry out. (You can stop here, if you'd like, and cool the brisket to room temperature before refrigerating, well wrapped, for up to 3 days.)

When ready to serve, increase the oven temperature to 475°F. Return the pan to the oven, uncovered, until the top of the meat is caramelized, 20 to 25 minutes.

Let the meat rest 15 to 20 minutes after it comes out of the oven. Place on a cutting board and slice against the grain. Serve immediately with cilantro (if you'd like), lime wedges, and flaky sea salt.

PAN-SEARED RIB EYE WITH BLACK GARLIC GHEE

I believe two things separate a mediocre steak from a great one: quality of meat and technique. And my technique is always the same: dry brine, temper, pan sear, baste with ghee, then rest with more ghee. I do occasionally, however, vary the basting mix. Here, black garlic steps in, its molasses-like sweetness and subtle tang accentuating that intensely savory beefy flavor of the choice rib eye.

This recipe works alongside most vegetable dishes in this book, but especially dressed radishes (see Five Ways to Dress as Radish, page 112), Cucumbers with Crème Fraîche and Crispy Capers (page 121), or Celery Root Salad with Yogurt, Capers, and Tarragon (page 193).

Tip—Be sure to leave 24 hours for brining the steak.

2 TO 3 SERVINGS
One 1¾-inch-thick bone-in rib eye (approximately 1½ pounds)

Fine sea salt

4 black garlic cloves

⅛ teaspoon fine sea salt, plus more for seasoning the rib eye

3 tablespoons ghee or unsalted butter, at room temperature

1 teaspoon olive oil

Flaky sea salt

Season the steak generously with salt. Place on a rack set over a pan or plate and refrigerate overnight.

Put the black garlic in a small bowl; add a pinch of salt and use a fork to smash it into a paste. Add the ghee and use a spoon to mix thoroughly.

Pull the steak from the fridge 45 to 60 minutes before you plan to cook. Rub oil on the steak. Heat a 10- to 12-inch heavy-bottomed skillet, preferably cast iron, over medium-high heat for 1 full minute (it should be scorching hot). Cook the steak, turning every 3 minutes or so, until a dark brown crust forms on both sides and the internal temperature is a few degrees below your favored doneness (120 to 125°F for medium-rare), about 10 minutes.

Turn down the heat to medium and wait for about 30 seconds before adding 2 tablespoons black garlic ghee to skillet. Tilt the pan toward you so that the ghee pools on one side, and use a large spoon to continually baste the steak with ghee for about 1 minute. Transfer the steak to a rimmed plate or large shallow bowl and top with the remaining black garlic ghee. Let the steak rest 6 to 10 minutes.

Transfer the steak to a cutting board, reserving any buttery juices on the plate. Use a sharp knife to cut 1-inch slices of steak—always slicing against the grain. Pour the melted black garlic ghee from the rimmed plate over the steak and sprinkle with flaky sea salt.

Sweet Treats

DATES IN DATE SYRUP

Pictured on page 36.

These dark, sticky dates are reminiscent of caramel. They make a great end to a meal, alone or with a little Whipped Crème Fraîche (page 336). Spoon them on ricotta, cake, meringue, or ice cream. Or serve them as a snack or as breakfast, on Labneh (page 336), porridge, waffles, or generously buttered toast. There's nothing like the flavor and texture of fresh dates, but dried dates are lovely here too.

APPROXIMATELY 10 SERVINGS

1 pound Medjool dates, ideally fresh, halved lengthwise and pitted

½ cup date syrup

¾ cup water

⅛ teaspoon fine sea salt

Place the dates cut side up in a round or square baking dish just large enough to fit them snuggly (a 9- or 10-inch cake or pie pan does the trick). Place the lid for the dish nearby—this can be a baking sheet, a pot's lid, or a plate. Bring the remaining ingredients to a boil over high heat in a medium saucepan. Reduce heat and simmer 3 minutes, stirring once or twice. Immediately pour the simmering syrup over the dates and cover. Let the dates steep for at least 15 minutes. Serve warm or at room temperature. Refrigerate in an airtight container for up to one month; bring to room temperature before serving.

FUERTE BARS

Half energy bar and half candy, these treats were inspired by the puffed-amaranth-and-honey bars of Mexico, my favorite version of which is loaded with seeds, peanuts, and raisins. This was my go-to snack back when surf trips were a part of my life; often these bars were my only breakfast before paddling out at dawn, and they kept me going for a few hours. My recipe for "strong bars" (affectionately and aptly named by my husband) now fuels me through waves of a different sort—baby carrying, writing, cooking, cleaning, hiking, hanging—from an early lunch until a late dinner.

You can certainly improvise here, but the nut butter and puffed grain–and-seed mix should be a cohesive mass (no stray seeds, etc.) and this "batter" should remain in the same proportion to the melted chocolate. How you mold it is up to you too. Thick, thin, rectangular, circular—since this is a no-bake situation, you can choose the shape you'd like. I've even made tiny truffle-looking bars using silicone ice cube trays.

Tips— Be sure to leave 12 to 24 hours for refrigerating the bars.

If you don't feel like gathering seeds, nuts, and dried fruits, these are still fantastic without any frills. Just replace the collective 2 cups of such ingredients with 1 additional cup of puffed quinoa and proceed with the recipe as usual. Or if you want a more fanciful and richer bar, you can create a topping: In a small bowl, gather a ¾-cup mix of a few or all of the following: finely chopped toasted peanuts, sesame seeds, hemp seeds, currants, bee pollen, cocoa nibs, currants, and flaky sea salt. Melt an additional 6 ounces of 64%–74% dark chocolate and pour on top of the bars. Moving swiftly, before the chocolate sets, scatter your toppings to cover.

MAKES 16 BARS (½-INCH THICK)

2 cups puffed quinoa

½ cup protein powder of choice (I usually use pea protein) (optional)

¾ to 1 teaspoon fine sea salt, depending how salty you like your peanut butter or chocolate

1 cup mixed seeds (toasted sunflower, sesame, and/or pumpkin seeds; untoasted hemp and/or chia seeds)

½ cup toasted peanuts, salted or unsalted, coarsely chopped

½ cup currants or raisins

2 cups creamy unsalted peanut butter

12 ounces dark (70–74%) chocolate (I prefer Guittard or Valrhona)

Line a 13 x 9-inch rectangular pan with parchment. (I find it is best to oil the pan lightly with olive oil, then layer a cut-to-fit lengthwise strip before a cut-to-fit crosswise strip, then bend the overhang at the rim.) Alternatively, gather the silicone mold(s) of your choosing.

In a medium mixing bowl, use a flexible spatula or rounded bowl scraper to fully combine all ingredients except the peanut butter and chocolate.

continued

Place the chocolate in a medium heatproof mixing bowl set over a pan of simmering water, making sure the bottom of the bowl doesn't touch the water. (This is a double boiler, and it creates the conditions for gentle heating.)

While the chocolate melts, add the peanut butter to the quinoa mixture and stir to fully combine (it will be thick, and you can't overmix). Stir the still-warm chocolate into the peanut butter–and-quinoa mixture and combine fully. Scrape into the lined rectangular pan (or scoop into silicone molds, dividing mixture evenly); smooth the top as best you can, using an offset spatula, if you have one. Cool completely to room temperature and refrigerate overnight.

Use a serrated bread knife to the cut the bars: Cut the rectangle in half crosswise, then in quarters, and finally in eighths. Lastly, make one lengthwise cut through the middle. You should have 16 bars. Store the bars in an airtight container. They will keep at room temperature if it is cool, but I recommend refrigerating them—or even freezing them (they are soft enough to eat within 10–15 minutes of pulling from the freezer). Refrigerate for 1 month or freeze for up to 3 months.

EASY OLIVE OIL CAKE EIGHT WAYS

This recipe hits every note I like in a cake: moisture from olive oil and yogurt (that lasts for days), an interesting texture from an almond flour and sugar crust, and a certain *je ne sais quoi* courtesy of the modern larder. It's also quite forgiving and easily adapted to suit the season or mood. Along with the simple base recipe, I've shared seven of my favorite variations.

I am partial to plain, rustic cakes—they satisfy in a way other sweeter, richer, or more refined cakes don't. They can serve as a dessert, of course, but a slice will also beckon me to take a break, sit, chat, and collect myself midday. That said, you can easily turn this into a more fanciful, frosted celebration affair: double the recipe (and divide batter between two pans); prepare a batch of labneh frosting (beat 2 cups labneh—see page 336—with a pinch of salt and ¼ cup superfine sugar); and, once the cake has cooled completely, frost using the traditional layer cake method.

Olive oil cake also freezes well. Wrap freshly baked and cooled whole cakes or slices or portions of cake—unfrosted—tightly in three layers in the following order: parchment, plastic wrap, foil. Then you can freeze it for up to three months. Thaw the cake completely in the refrigerator overnight before unwrapping.

8 TO 10 SERVINGS

continued

½ cup olive oil, ideally something fruity, plus more for the pan

142 grams (1 cup) brown rice flour

75 grams (¾ cup) almond flour

30 grams (¼ cup) tapioca flour

150 grams (¾ cup) granulated cane sugar, plus 1 to 2 tablespoons for topping

1½ teaspoons baking powder

½ teaspoon baking soda

¾ teaspoon fine sea salt

¼ cup plain, full-fat Greek yogurt or crème fraîche

¼ cup liquid (see variations, or riff as you'd like, using one of the following: freshly squeezed and strained citrus juice, verjus, pomegranate molasses, milk, nut milk, or more yogurt or crème fraîche)

2 large eggs

Preheat oven to 350°F. Line a 9-inch round springform pan with parchment: take a sheet of parchment and lay it across the base of the separated pan. Clasp the springform round on top (there will be overhang, and that's fine). Lightly coat the parchment and sides of the pan with olive oil.

In a medium mixing bowl, whisk together the brown rice flour, almond flour, tapioca flour 150 grams (¾ cup), sugar, baking powder, baking soda, and salt. In a small mixing bowl or large liquid measuring cup, whisk the ½ cup olive oil with the Greek yogurt, ¼ cup liquid, and eggs. Add the liquid ingredients to the dry and stir until thoroughly combined (don't worry about overmixing). Pour the batter into the prepared pan. Sprinkle the top evenly with approximately 1½ tablespoons sugar.

Bake until the top is deeply golden brown and a little crackly, the center is firm to the touch, and a tester inserted into the center comes out clean, 55 to 70 minutes (variations with fruit take longer due to extra moisture). Transfer the pan to a wire rack and let the cake cool in the pan for at least 15 minutes. Slide a slim knife or small metal spatula around the edge of the cake to detach it from the pan. Cool completely before serving. Store tightly wrapped at room temperature for up to 4 days, or freeze for up to 3 months (see headnote).

OLIVE OIL CAKE WITH ALMOND AND ORANGE	OLIVE OIL CAKE WITH ALMOND, CITRUS, AND CORIANDER	OLIVE OIL CAKE WITH ALMOND AND YUZU	OLIVE OIL CAKE WITH ALMOND, CRÈME FRAÎCHE, AND CHAMOMILE	POMEGRANATE TEA CAKE WITH ALMOND AND ROSE
	COMBINE WITH THE DRY INGREDIENTS: 1 tablespoon plus 2 teaspoons toasted coriander seeds, finely ground	**COMBINE WITH THE DRY INGREDIENTS:** 2 teaspoons yuzu zest (use a Microplane for best results)	**COMBINE WITH THE DRY INGREDIENTS:** 2 tablespoons finely ground chamomile tea	**COMBINE WITH THE DRY INGREDIENTS:** Reduce granulated cane sugar to 125 grams (½ cup plus 2 tablespoons)
FOR THE ¼ CUP LIQUID: ¼ cup orange juice + ¾ teaspoon orange flower water	**FOR THE ¼ CUP LIQUID:** ¼ cup yuzu juice	**FOR THE ¼ CUP LIQUID:** 2 tablespoons lemon juice + 2 tablespoons orange juice	**FOR THE ¼ CUP LIQUID:** 2 tablespoons apple cider vinegar + 2 tablespoons water or milk	**FOR THE ¼ CUP LIQUID:** ¼ cup pomegranate molasses + ¼ teaspoon rose water

Fruit Additions

OLIVE OIL CAKE WITH ALMOND, PEAR, AND VERJUS

Use ¼ **cup white verjus** for the liquid. Peel, halve, core, and thinly slice **2 firm, ripe pears** (such as Bartlett or d'Anjou), keeping the sliced halves intact. Once the batter is in the pan, arrange the pear halves on top (no need to push them down—the cake will rise around them), with an inch or so between each (if the fruit is too closely packed, the cake underneath won't cook properly). Top with sugar and bake as directed.

OLIVE OIL CAKE WITH APPLES, HAZELNUT, AND MISO SUGAR

Replace almond flour with **hazelnut flour**. Use **2 tablespoons apple cider vinegar and 2 tablespoons water, milk, or apple juice** for the liquid. Replace the granulated cane sugar with **150 grams (¾ cup) Miso Sugar** (page 358). Once the batter is in the pan, arrange 2 small apples, cored and thinly sliced crosswise (from stem end to root end), on top, skin-side up— no need to push the slices into the cake, it will rise around them. Top with sugar and bake as directed.

TAHINI COOKIES WITH ALMOND AND HONEY

I almost gave up on these cookies. Finding the right ratio of ingredients to achieve sweet, salty, nutty, chewy cookie nirvana—without the use of gluten or dairy—was quite a feat. But I'm glad I persevered. Because—without any qualifiers—this is now my favorite cookie. Chewy, just sweet enough, nutty, a little salty.

MAKES APPROXIMATELY 20 COOKIES

165 grams (scant ¾ cup) well-stirred tahini, at room temperature

200 grams (1 cup) granulated cane sugar

¼ cup honey

1 large egg

1 egg yolk (from a large egg)

1 tablespoon water

1 tablespoon white vinegar

138 grams (1 cup plus 3 tablespoons) almond flour

110 grams (¾ cup plus 3 tablespoons) oat flour

30 grams (¼ cup) tapioca flour

3 tablespoons brown rice flour

3 tablespoons sweet rice flour

½ teaspoon fine sea salt

2 teaspoons baking soda

½ teaspoon baking powder

Approximately ⅓ cup sesame seeds or benne seeds (or more granulated cane sugar), for rolling

In the bowl of a stand mixer fitted with the paddle attachment, beat the tahini, sugar, and honey on medium-high speed for 1 to 2 minutes. Add the egg, egg yolk, water, and vinegar; continue to beat until fluffy, about 2 minutes more. Stop the mixer and scrape the sides of the bowl and the paddle; beat once more to thoroughly combine.

Meanwhile, in a large mixing bowl, whisk together the almond flour, oat flour, tapioca flour, brown rice flour, sweet rice flour, salt, baking soda, and baking powder. Add to the bowl of the stand mixer and beat on low speed until just combined. These cookies are too sticky to scoop straight away. Place the dough in the refrigerator (uncovered is fine) to chill for 30 minutes to 1 hour.

Preheat oven to 350°F. Line two baking sheets with parchment paper or silicone mats. Fill a small, shallow bowl with approximately ⅓ cup sesame seeds (or granulated cane sugar). Scoop golf ball–sized balls onto the baking sheets. Take each ball and roll lightly between the palms of your hands before rolling it in sugar or seeds. Return to the baking sheet and space at least 2 inches apart.

For a soft, pale, very chewy cookie, bake 12 to 13 minutes—they will no longer look wet but the center will be soft. For a crisp, deeply caramelized cookie with a slightly chewy center, bake 14 to 15 minutes, or until a deep golden brown. Repeat with the remaining dough, always using cold dough and a cool baking sheet. Let the cookies cool for at least 10 minutes before serving.

The cookies will keep in an airtight container at room temperature for up to 2 weeks; frozen in an airtight container, they keep for 2 to 3 months. Scooped, uncoated dough can be wrapped airtight and frozen for up to 3 months; defrost in the fridge overnight before rolling in seeds and baking.

LEMON-TURMERIC COOKIES

Pictured on page 305.

Sarah Owens is a friend, fellow cookbook author, and phenomenal woman. Her first book, *Sourdough*, won a James Beard Award. And she's written two more since. She teaches baking and preservation workshops globally—she even helped develop a bakery in Tripoli, Lebanon, working with Syrian refugees—and the baked goods she produces for her mail-order business make a strong case for using heritage grains, seasonal ingredients, and global spices. Sarah shared the recipe for one of her holiday treats with me—cheerful, golden whole grain cookies that seem like a familiar soft sugar cookie, yet they are bright with lemon and surprising with dimensions of turmeric and freshly ground cardamom.

Tips—Look for unsifted white stoneground pastry flour from specialty millers or use the freshest store-bought whole wheat pastry flour you can find. If you're gifting these over the holidays and want a little sparkle, roll the dough balls in coarse (demerara) or granulated sugar before baking. Be sure to leave 12 to 24 hours for refrigerating the dough.

MAKES APPROXIMATELY 20 COOKIES

220 grams (1¾ cup plus 1 tablespoon) white whole wheat pastry flour, preferably stoneground

1½ teaspoons baking powder

1 teaspoon ground cardamom

½ teaspoon dried ground turmeric

½ teaspoon fine sea salt

200 grams (1 cup) granulated cane sugar, plus more for rolling (if you'd like)

Zest of 2 lemons (use a Microplane for best results)

113 grams (½ cup; 1 stick) unsalted butter, softened, at room temperature

2 large eggs, at room temperature

½ teaspoon vanilla extract

In a medium mixing bowl, thoroughly whisk together the flour, baking powder, spices, and salt and set aside. Place the sugar in the bowl of a stand mixer and zest the lemons into the sugar. Using the back of a large spoon, squish the zest into the sugar, releasing the fragrant oils to create a thick, crumbly paste. Add the butter and beat with a paddle attachment on medium speed until the sugar and butter are fully creamed, about 5 minutes. The mixture will lighten in both color and texture. Scrape down the sides of the bowl and add the eggs one at a time, mixing in between. Add the vanilla. Continue to beat on medium-high speed until the mixture is thick and falls from the paddle in thick ribbons, 3 to 4 minutes.

On the lowest speed, add the flour in 2 to 3 batches (to encourage even mixing), scraping down the sides in between each addition. When all the flour has been added, continue mixing on low speed only until the flour has been completely incorporated and no dry clumps remain. Do not overmix.

Transfer the dough to a clean bowl and cover well with plastic wrap or a beeswax-coated cloth. Refrigerate overnight, or up to 3 days, to allow the whole grain flour to completely hydrate before baking.

Preheat oven to 350°F. Remove the cookie dough from the refrigerator about 30 to 45 minutes before you wish to bake the cookies, to allow it to slightly soften. Line 2 large baking sheets with parchment paper. Using a 1½-inch ice cream scoop, press the cookie dough into the scoop and release onto the prepared baking sheets, leaving a generous 2 inches in between. (If the dough balls have softened to a sticky consistency, allow to chill in the refrigerator or freezer until firm before baking.) Roll each cookie in sugar, if you'd like. Place 1 sheet in the refrigerator and bake the other on the middle rack for 12 to 13 minutes, rotating the sheet halfway in between. Remove from the oven before there are obvious signs of browning around the edges to ensure the cookies remain soft out of the oven. Repeat with the remaining dough, always using cold dough and a cool baking sheet. Let the cookies cool for at least 10 minutes before serving.

Once completely cooled, store in a covered container for up to 1 week; frozen in an airtight container, they keep for 2 to 3 months. Scooped, uncoated dough can be frozen for up to 3 months; defrost in the fridge overnight before rolling in sugar (if you like) and baking.

RED, WHITE, AND RYE
CHOCOLATE CHIP COOKIES

Pictured on page 305.

We could argue about whether or not the world needs another recipe for chocolate chip cookies. But let's not. Let's talk instead about more important things while we enjoy these. This cookie tastes familiar but upends our expectations thanks to a few key ingredients. They are rich, chewy, *and* crispy, and a touch salty. They're spiked with vinegar, and they boast the unique toasty primordial "grain" flavor that comes from heritage wheats and rye. Really, the flour makes all the difference.

This particular recipe was inspired by one of my favorite loaves of bread: Josey Baker's Red, White, and Rye. I took Josey's (rather romantic) idea—combining strong and tender, dark and light—and applied it to my tried-and-true cookie recipe. Then I took the chocolate-to-batter ratio to the brink—I doubt another morsel could make it in.

Tip: Be sure to leave 12 to 24 hours for refrigerating the dough.

MAKES 12 COOKIES

85 grams (½ cup plus 2 tablespoons) all-purpose flour, such as Hayden Flour Mills All-Purpose Flour (which is a blend of White Sonora and Red Spring Wheat)

65 grams (½ cup) spelt, farro, or einkorn flour

65 grams (½ cup) medium rye flour

1 teaspoon baking powder

½ teaspoon baking soda

¾ teaspoon fine sea salt

140 grams (10 tablespoons) unsalted butter, at cool room temperature

100 grams (½ cup) granulated cane sugar

100 grams (½ cup) firmly packed light or dark muscovado (or light or dark brown sugar)

1 large egg

1 egg yolk (from a large egg)

1½ teaspoons apple cider vinegar or white vinegar

6 ounces dark (70%–74% cacao) chocolate, chopped into chunks

Flaky sea salt, for finishing

In a medium mixing bowl, whisk together the all-purpose flour, spelt flour, rye flour, baking powder, baking soda, and salt; set aside. In a mixer fitted with the paddle attachment, beat the butter and both sugars together on medium speed for 2 to 3 minutes, scraping the paddle and bowl as needed. Add the egg, egg yolk, and vinegar; beat 2 minutes more. Turn off the mixer, add the dry ingredients all at once, then pulse the mixer a few times to begin blending the ingredients. Beat on the lowest speed until the flour has almost disappeared. Add the chocolate and incorporate by hand, using a flexible spatula; don't overmix.

Line a baking sheet with parchment or a silicone baking mat. Divide the dough into 12 pieces, roll each piece into a ball between your palms, and place on the baking sheet. Cover, and refrigerate the dough overnight, or up to 3 days.

Preheat oven to 425°F and position the rack in the center. Rearrange the cookies on the lined baking sheet, leaving 2 inches between each cookie (only half a batch will fit—keep the rest chilled while these bake). Sprinkle each cookie with a little lightly crushed flaky salt. Bake the cookies for 10 to 11 minutes (if you want a slightly crisper cookie, you can go 1 minute longer), then pull the baking sheet from the oven and, using a metal spatula, a pancake turner, or the bottom of a glass, tap each cookie lightly. Bake the remaining dough, always using cold dough and a cool baking sheet. Let the cookies cool for at least 10 minutes before serving.

The cookies will keep in airtight container at room temperature for up to 5 days; frozen in an airtight container, they keep for 2 to 3 months. Scooped dough can be frozen for up to 3 months; defrost in the fridge overnight before baking, and sprinkle with salt right before they go in the oven.

COCONUT RICE PUDDING WITH CARAMELIZED PINEAPPLE AND MAKRUT LIME

Helen Goh is best known as the mastermind behind the desserts at Yotam Ottolenghi's restaurants in London and as the coauthor of the bestselling cookbook *Sweet*. I also think of her as one of the hardest-working and most generous women in food—and, most relevant here, the reason many home cooks now consider crème fraîche, date syrup, tahini, rose, and typically savory herbs and spices a part of their baking larder.

Helen was kind enough to contribute a recipe to this book. She created this coconut rice pudding, imbued with makrut lime and topped with sunny, tangy pineapple whose punchy, tart flavor cuts through the rich coconut milk and sweet sugar in the pudding.

Tips—Use either Japanese short-grained rice or Italian arborio rice for the best texture. If you don't already have superfine sugar in your cupboard, simply powder 3 tablespoons granulated cane sugar in a (clean and dry) spice grinder or coffee grinder. Lastly, this rice pudding must be served warm (the coconut fat becomes granular when cold).

6 SERVINGS

100 grams (½ cup plus 1 tablespoon) short-grained rice

400 milliliters (1¾ cups) unsweetened, full-fat coconut milk

300 milliliters (1¼ cups) whole milk, or plain, unsweetened rice, oat, or nut milk

6 to 8 fresh makrut lime leaves

60 grams (½ cup) granulated cane sugar

½ vanilla bean

200 grams (1 cup plus 1 tablespoon) coconut cream

⅛ teaspoon fine sea salt

FOR THE PINEAPPLE TOPPING

350 grams (approximately ½ a small) pineapple

3 tablespoons superfine cane (or "caster") sugar (see headnote)

1 tablespoon lime juice

Preheat oven to 300°F. Place the rice, coconut milk, milk, lime leaves, sugar, and vanilla bean in an ovenproof baking dish or casserole dish, around 7 x 11 inches; stir to combine. Bake uncovered for 70 to 80 minutes, stirring every 15 minutes or so. When it's done, most of the liquid will have been absorbed and the rice will be cooked through but still holding its shape. Remove from the oven and discard the lime leaves; if you'd like, reserve the vanilla bean for pineapple topping. Fold the coconut cream and salt through the rice. If necessary, keep warm in a low (200°F) oven until ready to serve; if held for more than a few minutes, you may need to stir in a tablespoon or so of hot water, as the rice continues to absorb liquid as it sits.

continued

While the pudding is in the oven, prepare the pineapple topping. Remove the skin and core from the pineapple and slice or dice the flesh into pieces roughly ¾-inch tall and ¼-inch thick. If you'd like, cut the vanilla bean in half lengthwise and use a small paring knife to scrape out the seeds into a small prep bowl; set by the stove. Place the superfine sugar in a 9- or 10-inch sauté pan or skillet set over medium-high heat. Once it begins to liquefy, swirl and tilt the pan so the sugar melts evenly. When it is a deep amber color, remove from heat and gently add the pineapple and vanilla bean seeds (if using)—be careful, as the caramel may sputter and spit. Place the pan back on the stove and add the lime juice. Stir gently over low heat to coat the pineapple and melt the caramel if some of it has hardened. After a couple of minutes, increase heat to high to reduce the syrup slightly, about 1 to 2 minutes. Let the caramelized pineapple rest for about 2 minutes before proceeding.

Spoon the caramelized pineapple over the warm rice pudding, drizzling the syrup over the top. Serve warm.

VERJUS AND GRAPE SORBET

This may be my ideal dessert. It is delicate in both flavor and appearance. Bright, light—one small scoop is plenty, and I finish sated, with the slightest yearning for another bite.

Tips—Tapioca and corn syrup reduce iciness in sorbets. If you want to omit the syrup, add an additional 1½ tablespoons sugar and 1 tablespoon water instead—just know your scoop will be a bit icier. And it may seem unorthodox to season desserts to taste—when dealing with many ingredients, but especially fruit, it is important to adjust the sweetness, acidity, and salt based on the flavor of the ingredients you're using. Be sure to leave 6 to 24 hours for refrigerating the sorbet base, as well as an additional 3 hours for freezing after it has been churned.

4 CUPS

100 grams (½ cup) granulated cane sugar

½ cup water

1½ pounds (4 cups) seedless green grapes

½ cup white verjus

¼ teaspoon fine sea salt

1½ to 2 tablespoons tapioca syrup (see tip)

Combine the sugar, water, grapes, verjus, and salt in a medium saucepan and bring to a boil over medium-high heat. Reduce heat to a simmer and cook for 12 to 15 minutes, or until the grapes have softened. Puree in a blender until completely smooth, scraping down the sides, as needed. Add 1½ tablespoons tapioca syrup and blend to combine. Taste. Depending on the acidity of your grapes and verjus, you may need to add more tapioca syrup—keep in mind that the sweetness will mellow once the mixture is frozen. Once the mixture is seasoned to taste, chill in the refrigerator for at least 6 hours, or overnight. Stir, or—if you kept in the blender to chill—reblitz to reemulsify the mixture. Then process in an ice cream maker according to the manufacturer's instructions. Transfer sorbet to an airtight, freezer-safe container and freeze for at least 3 hours before serving.

YUZU ICE CREAM

I adore the combination of citrus and cream, and, as I've mentioned before, the lighter the dessert, the more apt I am to enjoy it. The clean, bright, and complex flavor of yuzu is just enough to cut the cream's richness, and the cream is just lush enough to foil the fruit's tang. This ice cream recipe is easier than most: there are no temperamental egg yolks or thickening agents such as gelatin, flour, or cornstarch to help the mixture thicken and set. I do ask you to think ahead, as mixing the zest with the cream the night before creates an infusion of flavor without heat. Alternatively, you can skip the straining step so that the zest—and all its essential oils—will remain in the finished scoop. And if you can't find yuzu, use Meyer lemons instead.

3 CUPS

1 tablespoon finely grated yuzu zest (from 2 or 3 yuzus; use a Microplane for best results)

2 cups heavy cream

¼ cup plus 2 tablespoons freshly squeezed yuzu juice (from 8 or 9 yuzus)

150 grams (¾ cup) granulated cane sugar

1 tablespoon plus 1 teaspoon tapioca syrup

⅛ teaspoon fine sea salt

The day before you plan to make the ice cream, combine the zest and cream; refrigerate overnight.

Set a fine-mesh strainer over a large mixing bowl. Strain the yuzu juice into the bowl, but keep the strainer nearby. Whisk together the juice, sugar, tapioca syrup, and salt. Gradually pour the cream through the strainer—about a ¼ cup at a time—into the yuzu-and-sugar mixture, whisking constantly. Continue to whisk until the sugar dissolves (until you don't hear or feel it scraping against the bottom of the bowl anymore).

Transfer the mixture into an ice cream maker and process according to manufacturer's instructions. Eat immediately or transfer to an airtight, freezer-safe container and freeze for a later date. If you don't have an ice cream maker, don't worry: this ice cream sets fairly well without one. Simply pour the mixture into an 8 x 8-inch square metal baking pan. Cover tightly and freeze until the mixture is solid around the edges and mushy in the middle, 2 to 3 hours. Stir well, cover once more, and continue to freeze until completely firm.

RASPBERRIES AND CREAM

One of the most elemental and essential desserts in my repertoire. Sweet, delicious mayhem.

3 TO 4 SERVINGS

8 ounces (scant 2 cups) raspberries

Splash (⅛ teaspoon) rose water (optional)

3 tablespoons to ¼ cup granulated cane sugar, divided

1 vanilla bean, halved lengthwise, seeds scraped and reserved (optional)

1¾ cups cold crème fraîche

Fine sea salt

Place the fruit in a medium mixing bowl and toss with the rose water (if using), 1 tablespoon sugar, the vanilla bean seeds and vanilla bean pod (if using), and a small pinch of salt. Toss and crush the berries with a fork. Set the mixture aside for about 10 minutes, then toss and taste. Add 1 or 2 teaspoons more sugar, if you'd like, until the flavor reminds you of a barely sweet jam.

Whip the cold crème fraîche, slowly adding 2 tablespoons sugar, until the cream forms soft, wet peaks on the end of beater when it is detached from the mixer and held upright. Fold in the fruit ever so slightly, leaving streaks of magenta and bright white visible throughout. Chill until ready to serve. This can be held in the refrigerator for up to 3 hours.

FROZEN YOGURT

I have a soft spot for soft serve. I was raised near a beach town in the era of step aerobics and SnackWell cookies, which meant a lot of visits to the local TCBY for a low-fat cup. Now I enjoy the cold, tangy, creamy treat for what it is—not as an alternative to something better.

Achieving a creamy and light frozen yogurt is difficult, since yogurt contains a fair amount of water. I tried many tricks, and this recipe—leavened and thickened with meringue—hit the mark. It may not have the silky, slight stretchy consistency of our childhood treat, but it is bright, lush, and creamy, and it begs for toppings.

Tips—If you don't already have superfine sugar in your cupboard, simply powder 200 grams (1 cup) granulated cane sugar in a (clean and dry) spice grinder or coffee grinder. Be sure to leave at least 2 hours for refrigerating the base, as well as an additional 2 hours for freezing the frozen yogurt after it has been churned.

4 CUPS (WITHOUT ADDITIONS)

200 grams (1 cup) superfine cane (or "caster") sugar (see headnote)

6 egg whites (from large eggs)

½ teaspoon fine sea salt

800 grams (3½ cups) plain, full-fat Greek yogurt

Mix-ins or toppings of choice (optional)

Preheat oven to 400°F. Scatter the sugar in a fine layer over a rimmed baking sheet lined with parchment and place in the oven for 5 minutes to warm.

Meanwhile, in the bowl of a stand mixer, beat the egg whites at medium speed, until frothy. Add the salt and continue to beat—now increasing the speed to medium-high—until white and fluffy. Tip the warm sugar, a few tablespoons at a time (I just pick up the parchment like a taco and pour from one end), into the egg whites, beating all the time at a moderately high speed. Continue for 5 to 7 minutes, until the mixture is stiff and glossy. The egg whites should stand in stiff, shiny peaks. Still beating, add the yogurt about ¼ cup at a time, and continue to beat until incorporated. Refrigerate until completely chilled, approximately 2 hours.

Pour the chilled base into an ice cream maker and process according to the manufacturer's instructions. When it reaches a soft-serve consistency, transfer to an airtight container and freeze for at least 2 hours before serving. Serve plain or with little bowls of various toppings alongside.

Or if you'd like to incorporate another flavor into the frozen yogurt, scoop one-third of the churned frozen yogurt into a 9 x 5-inch loaf pan. Top with one-third of the mixture of your choosing (make sure it is cold). Repeat this process 2 more times, then use an offset spatula or butter knife to swirl the mixture throughout the frozen yogurt. Wrap the loaf pan with plastic wrap and freeze until firm, at least 2 hours.

OPTIONAL TOPPINGS (Choose One or None)

- Chopped or torn honeycomb + bee pollen + flaky sea salt

- Candied fennel seeds or sesame seeds (see Candied Seeds, page 351)

- Sliced Dates in Date Syrup (page 296)

- Sweet Hazelnut Dukkah (page 356) + date syrup *(Pictured on page 294.)*

- Honey + walnut oil + chopped walnuts in walnut oil (page 137)

- Stewed Prunes with Caraway (page 149)

- Raspberries or chopped strawberries tossed with rose water + pinch of granulated cane sugar + sumac

Drinks

PINEAPPLE AND TURMERIC KVASS

Vibrant, refreshing, and brimming with beneficial enzymes and bacteria, fermented drinks have become mainstream in America. But while many folks are now keeping kombucha mothers and purchasing kefir grains, very few people speak of kvass. This Russian beverage is one of the easiest and most delicious home fermentation projects. The saffron-like hue of this particular kvass reminds me of some of the natural skin-contact (orange) wines I've had. Its flavor does too: sprightly, fruity, floral, funky, and a little bready.

It is essential that you use raw honey; the microbes in an unpasteurized jar act as a starter culture. I prefer kvass barely sweet; add more honey and/or coconut sugar if you desire a more soda-like result. Lastly, while spring water isn't a must, chlorinated tap water can slow the fermentation process.

For this recipe, you'll need to sterilize with boiling water an 8-cup (larger is fine) canning jar (such as Mason or Weck) with a tight-fitting lid, and 1 or 2 swing-top bottles (capable of storing at least 5 cups liquid in total). The swing top bottles will be used for storing the kvass after fermentation; the type of bottle is important, as they allow the ferment to give off small amounts of carbon dioxide, preventing unwanted explosions.

APPROXIMATELY 5 CUPS

1 medium, very ripe pineapple (approximately 2 to 2½ pounds), peeled and cut into a 1-inch dice

1 to 2 tablespoons finely grated fresh turmeric (use a Microplane for best results)

2 tablespoons raw honey

1 to 2 tablespoons coconut sugar or light muscovado

Pinch of fine sea salt

5 cups spring or filtered water

Place the pineapple, turmeric, honey, sugar, and salt in a food processor and pulse until a coarse mash forms. Place the mixture in a sterilized 8-cup canning jar and add the water (there must be at least 1 inch of headroom between the kvass and the jar's rim).

Tightly cover the jar with a lid. Keep in a fairly warm spot (near a window); give it a swirl and gentle shake a few times a day (this helps prevent bacteria from forming) and look for bubbles. When you see bubbles, carefully open the lid slightly to release some of the gas. Return the lid. In another day or two, you should see bubbles once again, in the still jar, rising as if in a glass of champagne (no shaking necessary). When these bubbles become vigorous, after about 6 days total, your kvass is ready. Refrigerate until cold. Strain through a fine-mesh sieve and funnel into swing-top bottles. Drink within 2 weeks.

KEFIR SMOOTHIE WITH
CARROT, ORANGE, AND GINGER

Bright in both color and flavor, this fairly unusual carrot smoothie is one I want often. The ginger and turmeric warm up its otherwise cooling effect, and the carrot and orange are a perfect pair.

1 TO 2 SERVINGS

1 navel orange, peel and white pith removed

1 large or 2 baby carrots, steamed or boiled

¾ cup plain, full-fat kefir or unsweetened coconut yogurt

¾ teaspoon finely grated fresh ginger (use a Microplane for best results)

1½ teaspoons finely grated fresh turmeric (use a Microplane for best results)

Pinch of fine sea salt

½ cup ice cubes

Place all the ingredients in a blender with ice cubes and puree until smooth. Any leftovers can be refrigerated in an airtight container for up to 2 days; shake well before serving.

RHUBARB AND ROSE LASSI

A springtime spin on a classic, this creamy and tangy beverage is perfect for perking up your energy during an afternoon slump or for cutting through the heat in a spicy meal (such as Coconut-Braised Chicken, page 268). If you can't find rhubarb, use an equal weight of strawberries.

3 TO 4 SERVINGS

1¼ pounds red rhubarb (7 long stalks), trimmed and sliced

½ cup granulated cane sugar

Pinch of fine sea salt

⅛ teaspoon rose water

1½ cups cold plain, full-fat Greek yogurt; plain yogurt; or unsweetened coconut yogurt

½ to ¾ cup water

Put the rhubarb in a medium saucepan with the sugar and salt. Cook over medium heat until the rhubarb has broken down into a rough puree, about 20 minutes. Off heat, stir in the rose water. Refrigerate until cold.

Blend rhubarb with the yogurt and enough water to achieve desired consistency. Drink immediately or refrigerate for up to 2 days.

TAHINI HOT CHOCOLATE

A rich, creamy hot chocolate without dairy, nuts, or soy. It doesn't separate like hot drinks made from most nondairy milks, and it has a purer cocoa flavor compared to a mug made with coconut milk. Even after a few sips, most people can't even name tahini as an ingredient. Coincidentally, the recipe is convenient for urgent cravings since the ratio of ingredients is easy to remember: for 2 servings, 2:2:2:2, plus a pinch of salt. Sweet tooths vary widely, as does the sugar content in various chocolates. Start with 1 tablespoon sugar and then sweeten to taste. I use Guittard's 74% "baking wafers," which I can add without chopping.

2 SERVINGS

2 cups water

2 to 3 tablespoons coconut sugar

⅛ teaspoon fine sea salt

2 tablespoons tahini

2 ounces dark (70%–74% cocoa) chocolate, chopped

Heat the water, sugar, and salt in a small saucepan, whisking to dissolve the sugar, until steaming. Off heat, add the tahini and chocolate; whisk until smooth. Taste—add more sugar or salt, if you'd like, and whisk once more.

SWEET-AND-SOUR ELIXIR WITH CHAMOMILE AND GINGER

I believe that with plenty of sleep, maybe an occasional short period of fasting, and some simple boosts through diet, our bodies can recover from ordinary daily strains without needing to rely on long-term "detox diets." This elixir is also known as oxymel, whose name means "acid and honey." It can be used as a base for tea—just add hot water to 1 tablespoon oxymel—or like shrubs, diluted with sparkling water, or tipped into dressings, marinades, and so on.

I encourage you to create your own concoctions too. How much of each ingredient you use is up to you. Just keep in mind that dried medicinal roots—such as angelica, burdock, and so on—are powerful; use these sparingly (for instance, ¼ teaspoon or so per pint of oxymel). If you're not sure how much you want of one thing or another, start light.

3½ CUPS

⅓ cup dried or fresh chamomile blossoms

One 4-inch piece fresh ginger, gently scrubbed and thinly sliced

2 tablespoon fennel seeds

Leaves from 2 sprigs rosemary

6 strips lemon peel

Pinch of fine sea salt

1½ cups raw apple cider vinegar

1½ cups raw honey

Place everything in a sterilized, quart-sized mason jar. Seal the jar and shake until well mixed. Place the jar somewhere cool and dark; shake a couple of times a week. (A little painter's tape stuck to the cupboard serves as a good reminder.) After 2 weeks, or up to 6 weeks, strain and pour into a glass jar for storage. Keeps indefinitely.

VITAMIN C TEA

Hibiscus and rose hips are both vitamin C power houses, and I like to add sumac for dimension and flavor. I love the pronounced tang and vibrancy of this tea straight, but feel free to sweeten if you prefer. The blend makes more than you need for 2 cups, because if I'm going to blend a tea, it's going to be a week's worth. It's easily doubled too.

    I use a mortar and pestle to crush the hibiscus and rose hips, but a heavy-bottomed skillet works too.

**2 SERVINGS,
PLUS MORE IF BREWED
A SECOND TIME**

3 tablespoons hibiscus, crushed

3 tablespoons rose hips, crushed

2 tablespoons barberries

1 tablespoon ground sumac

Combine all the ingredients and place in a container. Pour 2 cups boiling water over 2 tablespoons of the tea blend; steep 4 to 6 minutes, or longer if you prefer a stronger brew. Strain through a fine-mesh strainer lined with cheesecloth. Enjoy for multiple brews.

UME TONIC

This is my favorite home remedy, for everything from the flu, to hangovers (sugar or alcohol), to the common cold. It is thick and hot and not at all delicious, but it really can work wonders.

Tips—You can purchase umeboshi plums already in paste form, but I prefer to just use whole plums: scrape the flesh from the pit, and finely chop to a paste right before using; discard the pit. For 2 teaspoons, you'll need approximately 2½ umeboshi plums, depending on their size.

1 TO 2 SERVINGS

1½ tablespoons organic kudzu powder

1½ cups filtered water or twig tea

1 teaspoon umeboshi paste or ½ pitted umeboshi plum

1 teaspoon soy sauce (preferably nama shoyu)

1 teaspoon ginger juice (optional)

Dissolve the kudzu powder in 1 cup cold water or twig tea in a small saucepan. Add remaining ingredients to the pan and bring to a boil over high heat, stirring constantly with a whisk. After ingredients come to a boil, turn the heat down to low and allow to simmer for 1 minute. Once the liquid has turned from a chalky color to opaque, remove from heat. If desired, thin with remaining ¼ cup to ½ cup water or tea. Drink hot; or if you prefer a thicker consistency, eat with a spoon.

PLUM AND SHISO SODA

Whip up this soda in the summer, when plums and fresh shiso are both plentiful. It's sweet, tangy, assertive, and punchy. Serve it simply by adding 1 part syrup to 3 parts sparkling water. Or, if you're looking to use it in cocktails, the syrup is great in gin and tonics (the syrup replaces the need for tonic water—just use good club soda and lemon juice) or plum margaritas.

1 CUP PLUM-SHISO SYRUP; APPROXIMATELY 8 SERVINGS (AS A SODA)

1 cup granulated cane sugar

1 cup water

4 to 5 small ripe plums, preferably Santa Rosa (but any variety will do), halved, pitted, and cut into 6 to 8 wedges

Approximately 12 large shiso leaves, washed well and torn or snipped into roughly ½-inch pieces

Fine sea salt

4 to 6 cups sparkling mineral water or soda water, divided

In a small saucepan, bring the sugar, water, plums, shiso, and a small pinch of salt to a boil over medium heat; stir periodically to help the sugar dissolve. Remove from heat; cover and steep for 20 to 30 minutes. Strain through a fine-mesh sieve, pressing gently on the solids, and let cool completely; discard plum pulp and shiso. Chill syrup until ready to use, or refrigerate in an airtight container for up to 7 days.

To serve, chill a glass with ice cubes and add 2 tablespoons of the syrup. Top with ½ cup sparkling mineral water or soda water and stir. Taste, and add more water, if you'd like.

Foundations
+ Finishes

DRESSINGS

If you want good dressings, you must start with good ingredients. The quality of the salt, acid, and oil (or other fat) matters a lot— each component should taste stellar on its own. While I don't need to provide instructions on how to whisk things in a bowl, I do have a few more tips:

- When you can, let the salt sit in the acid for a few minutes so it dissolves, and your tasting will be accurate.

- If using alliums (such as shallot, green onion, or garlic), mellow their sharp pungency by letting them hang out in the acid-salt mixture for 5 to 10 minutes before adding any oil.

- If you like things a little sweeter, you can add a tiny bit of honey to your acid before adding the remaining ingredients.

- Once all the oil has been added, whisk in condiments, herbs, zest, and any other finishing elements, if using.

- Lastly, when tasting for balance and salinity, don't use a spoon or a finger—taste on whatever ingredient will receive the dressing, such as a piece of lettuce, a crouton, or a slice of radish.

The following dressings and vinaigrettes are my workhorses. I've provided measurements for one batch, but, if you cook regularly, I suggest doubling or tripling the amounts and refrigerating the dressing in an airtight container for up to 7 days; bring to room temperature before using.

¼ TO ⅓ CUP

BASIC BANYULS DRESSING

1 tablespoon Banyuls vinegar or shallot vinegar (see Quick-Pickled Shallots, page 348)

Fine sea salt

3 tablespoons olive oil

BASIC LEMON DRESSING

1 tablespoon lemon juice

Fine sea salt

3 tablespoons olive oil

YUZU KOSHO DRESSING

½ teaspoon Yuzu Kosho (page 343); if store-bought, use ¼ teaspoon, and then add to taste

Fine sea salt

1 tablespoon Banyuls or other red wine vinegar

¼ cup olive oil

CRÈME FRAÎCHE DRESSING

1 teaspoon lemon juice

Fine sea salt

¼ cup crème fraîche

1 to 2 teaspoons cold water (depending on desired consistency)

Tip—For **YOGURT DRESSING**, replace crème fraîche with plain, full-fat Greek yogurt.

PRESERVED LEMON DRESSING

Rind of ½ preserved lemon, finely chopped (⅛-inch dice)

1 tablespoon lemon juice

Fine sea salt

¼ cup olive oil

WALNUT DRESSING

1 medium shallot, finely diced

1 teaspoon sherry or white wine vinegar

1 teaspoon lemon juice

Fine sea salt

1 tablespoon olive oil

2 tablespoons walnut oil

UME DRESSING

1½ teaspoons umeboshi paste (from approximately 2 umeboshi)

2 teaspoons lemon juice or red wine vinegar, such as Banyuls

¼ cup olive oil

LABNEH

This dense homemade cheese is nothing more than cultured milk strained of whey until thick and creamy. It is used across many Mediterranean and Middle Eastern cuisines, but—like crème fraîche—it will seem at home on any table. Use it as the bed for roast vegetables or beans; as a spread, dip (page 59), or simple whipped dessert reminiscent of cheesecake (see Whipped Labneh, at right).

Save the whey for Savory Chickpea Flour Pancakes (page 130), poaching eggs (see Poached Eggs with Labneh and Chile, page 157), or any of the other applications mentioned on page 99.

APPROXIMATELY 3¾ CUPS

4 cups plain, full-fat Greek yogurt or plain, full-fat kefir
1 teaspoon fine sea salt (optional)

Mix the Greek yogurt or kefir with fine sea salt (if using) and let this mixture sit in a cheesecloth- or coffee filter–lined sieve set over a mixing bowl (pick a bowl that allows the base of the strainer to sit high above the whey that will accumulate) for 12 to 72 hours. The longer it drains, the thicker and drier it will become. (I prefer mine after 24 hours, when it is thick but still creamy.) Refrigerated in an airtight container, labneh lasts 3 to 5 days.

MARINATED LABNEH

Make labneh as above and allow it to drain for 3 full days. Then, roll it into balls, submerge them completely in oil (with herbs and chile, or left plain), and serve as you would marinated mozzarella or feta. Submerged in oil and refrigerated, the labneh is preserved for 1 month or more.

WHIPPED LABNEH

Whipping labneh transforms it into a luscious ingredient that is extremely versatile. It can be used in place of Greek yogurt, sour cream, or even crème fraîche in cold soups; as a topping for oatmeal, waffles, or pancakes; as a base for dips; and as is—with a dash of sugar and the right topping, it is the easiest impressive dessert I can imagine.

If making the sweet version, consider adding a splash of lemon juice or vanilla extract—or a few drops of rose water, even—along with the sugar.

APPROXIMATELY 1 CUP

1 cup labneh, store-bought or homemade (at left), strained 24 to 36 hours
⅛ teaspoon fine sea salt
Sweet variation: 2 teaspoons granulated cane sugar

Beat the labneh, salt, and sugar (if using) in a stand mixer fitted with a whisk attachment on medium-high speed (or whisk by hand) until silky smooth, stopping once or twice to scrape down the sides of the bowl with a spatula. Use right away or store in the refrigerator for up to 2 days. (If it separates slightly, simply give it a stir or drain off any liquid.)

WHIPPED CRÈME FRAÎCHE

Whipped crème fraîche is special stuff. It has a more beautiful sheen and a fuller flavor than whipped heavy cream, and it holds nicely for up to 6 hours—no more last-minute whisking for the last course! Not just for sweet treats, whipped crème fraîche can be used to top stuffed chiles (see Stuffed Poblanos, page 242), loaded potatoes, dips, soups, braised fish or chicken, and all egg dishes.

1½ cups crème fraîche

In a deep, medium mixing bowl, beat the crème fraîche with a whisk (or a stand mixer fitted with the whisk attachment, on medium speed) until soft peaks form (it aerates much faster than heavy cream). Cover and chill until ready to use, up to 6 hours.

HORSERADISH CRÈME FRAÎCHE

Horseradish is a pretty divisive ingredient, but I'm a big fan of the fresh stuff. Tart and fatty crème fraîche really tempers its bite, and, in turn, the horseradish provides a welcome edge to the refined richness of cultured cream. Serve this horseradish crème fraîche with fish, steak, or pork. Stir it into dips and plop it on hash (or any fried potato thing). Use it to dress beet salads (page 216), tomatoes, and cabbage dishes of all sorts.

APPROXIMATELY 1 CUP

One 6-inch piece fresh horseradish
1 cup crème fraîche
Pinch of fine sea salt

Use a Microplane to grate the horseradish into a small mixing bowl. Whisk in the crème fraîche with a pinch of sea salt. Taste and add more salt, if necessary. Refrigerate until you are ready to use. Horseradish crème fraîche keeps for up to 3 days in the refrigerator. The mixture will thicken slightly, and the mustardy bite will become a bit more pronounced.

BASIC TAHINI SAUCE

Out of all the sauces in this book, this is the one I use more than any other. Endlessly versatile, as every good book on the food of Jerusalem will show you (and, thankfully, there are a lot of these out there now), use it as a dressing for vegetables, grains, and leaves both raw and cooked; drizzle some over meats and seafood right before serving; or use it to create creaminess in dips and soups (pumpkin is particularly wonderful).

APPROXIMATELY 2 CUPS

1 clove garlic (optional)
1 teaspoon salt
Juice of 1 lemon, plus more to taste
1 cup tahini
¾ cup cold water, divided

Mince the garlic, if using, with half the salt until a smooth paste forms. In a medium mixing bowl, whisk together the garlic paste with the lemon juice and the remaining salt. Let sit for 10 to 15 minutes; this mellows the garlic and dissolves the salt. Even if you omit the garlic, let the salt sit in the acid for a few minutes. If the oil has separated in your tahini, stir it back together, then spoon approximately 1 cup (I say "approximately" because there is no need to dirty a measuring cup with thick, oily tahini) into a medium bowl. Use a whisk to start beating in cold water, ¼ cup or so at a time, until the mixture becomes smooth and creamy. At some point you'll think you're doing it wrong because it will look a mess—don't fear. Soon you'll see it start to emulsify, lighten in color, and become easier to stir. It will probably take about ¾ cup water total. Thin the tahini sauce with more water until you reach your desired consistency. Then taste and adjust the seasoning with more salt or lemon juice, as needed. Use immediately or refrigerate in an airtight container for up to 4 days.

TAHINI YOGURT

More of a ratio than a recipe, this is a very versatile sauce. Serve it alongside grilled fish, meat, or vegetables; toss with pasta; use it as a condiment for grain salads or baked eggs; thin it with a bit of water and use it has a salad dressing. It actually makes a great thickener for creamy soups too—try it with cauliflower or pumpkin.

    Mix 5-to-1 ratio, yogurt to tahini; season with salt to taste, thin with water, as needed, depending on use.

SPECIAL SAUCE

Don't doubt this combination. Believe in it. Double it. Make it when you know roast chicken and potatoes are on the docket, or when you want a simple but impressive salad (such as Kohlrabi Salad with Kefir and Caraway, page 186). Drizzle it over roasted cabbage (see Caramelized Cabbage for Many Occasions, page 226) or serve it with grilled steak or pork schnitzel (in both cases, a side of bitter or peppery greens is a must).

⅓ CUP

1 garlic clove, finely grated or minced
1 teaspoon apple cider vinegar or lemon juice
¼ cup plain mayonnaise, store-bought or homemade (at right)
1 tablespoon plain, full-fat kefir
1 teaspoon white miso
Fine sea salt

In a medium mixing bowl, whisk together all the ingredients. Add salt to taste.

MAYONNAISE

A staple in my kitchen, homemade mayonnaise befriends so many daily foods: greens, beans, bread, eggs, seafood (page 261), and roasted meats. If you fear breaking the emulsion, I understand—me too. So I recommend using a fine-tipped squeeze bottle for the oil and refrigerating it for an hour before you begin.

1 CUP

2 egg yolks (from medium or large eggs), at room temperature
1 tablespoon lemon juice, divided
½ teaspoon fine sea salt
1 cup neutral vegetable oil (such as cold-pressed rice bran oil or grapeseed oil) or good, buttery olive oil (ideally chilled for 1 to 2 hours)

Place a large mixing bowl on a wet paper or cloth towel (so it is less likely to slip). Add the egg yolks, half the lemon juice, and salt; whisk for about 30 seconds. While whisking constantly and vigorously, slowly drizzle the oil into the yolks, adding just a few drops at a time; wait until each drop emulsifies (appears to dissolve and disappear) before adding more. Continue this way until half the oil has been added.

Now that the egg proteins have sufficiently unraveled, the process can move forward at a faster rate. Take a break and do a little stretch. Then return to whisking, adding the second half of the oil at a steady, but very slow stream. Once all of the oil is incorporated and the mayo is thick, taste for seasoning, and see if you prefer more lemon juice or salt.

Transfer the mayonnaise to a small container, seal, and refrigerate until ready to use, or up to 3 days.

MAYONNAISE VARIATIONS

All these variations are versatile. Spread them on sandwiches or serve them in a bowl next to fries, chips, or raw or grilled vegetables. Toss them with shredded cabbage or julienned vegetables. Use as a bed for tartare and chilled seafood salads. Serve as a condiment for a simple roast chicken (page 264), Hard-Roasted Whole Fish (page 256), or braised beans and greens. Thin with kefir or buttermilk and use as a salad dressing.

- Substitute yuzu juice for the lemon juice

- Whisk in 1 tablespoon yuzu kosho, store-bought or homemade (page 343), to finish

- Whisk in 1 to 2 tablespoons Harissa (page 342), to finish

- Add 2 black garlic cloves, pounded to a paste; add to the yolks

- Decrease the salt to ¼ teaspoon and add 1 tablespoon minced salt-packed capers and 1 tablespoon finely chopped herbs, to finish

- Decrease the salt to ¼ teaspoon and add ¼ teaspoon fish sauce; add to the yolks

- Decrease the salt to ¼ teaspoon and add 1 tablespoon minced preserved lemon rind, to finish

- Whisk in 2 tablespoons crème fraîche or 1 tablespoon plain, full-fat kefir, to finish

- Add ½ teaspoon freshly grated horseradish, to finish

YOGURT MAYONNAISE

Compared to regular mayonnaise, this yogurt version is extra bright and nearly impossible to break. It's good on beans (see Slow-Cooked White Beans with Tomato and Curry Leaf, page 232), deli-style salads (potato, pasta, egg, chicken, tofu, celery root (193), and so on), or any number of sandwiches and savory toasts (see Toast Sweet and Savory, page 150, for ideas). It makes a remarkable rub for meat, enhancing both the flavor and browning. And it transforms an 8½-minute Soft-Centered Egg (page 144) into a satisfying snack: peel and halve egg lengthwise, smear on some mayo, and top with flaky sea salt and Aleppo-style pepper (or similar).

APPROXIMATELY 1½ CUPS

2 egg yolks (from medium or large eggs)
1 tablespoon lemon juice
¼ to ½ teaspoon fine sea salt
¼ cup plus 2 tablespoons labneh, store-bought or homemade (page 336)
½ to ¾ cup olive oil

In a medium mixing bowl, whisk together the egg yolks with the lemon juice, salt, and labneh. Slowly add the oil, whisking constantly (no need to go drop by drop—a steady stream is fine). The mixture may look curdled—just keep whisking, and it will come together. Once you've added ½ cup oil, taste and assess the viscosity. If you want your mayonnaise less bright and tangy, and perhaps a tad thicker, add a bit more oil until you reach the results you desire. This yogurt mayonnaise can be refrigerated in an airtight container for up to 4 days.

INSTANT "XO"

XO sauce is a brawny and dynamic condiment that originated in Hong Kong, China. Meaty, briny, salty, spicy, and sweet, it has gained popularity all over the world. Making traditional XO is a labor-intensive process that begins with sourcing a long list of relatively hard-to-find ingredients. The intrepid cook would never consider making their own and may even steer clear of store-bought versions. While I admit this recipe isn't exactly "instant," it takes a fraction of the time and calls for only 5 ingredients. I also like that—since it lacks ginger and other flavors that send an "Asian food" flag through the brain—this sauce is more versatile.

Use it regularly, but sparingly. And don't cook it too much—add it toward the end of cooking or to finish a dish off the heat. With a few drops or a drizzle, this "XO" is a welcome, punchy addition to noodles, beans, eggs, fish, meat, and practically all vegetables (see Caramelized Cabbage for Many Occasions, page 226; Green Beans, page 202; Skillet-Charred Beans, page 136)

APPROXIMATELY 2 CUPS

1½ cups neutral vegetable oil (such as cold-pressed rice bran oil or grapeseed oil)

4 ounces 'nduja

3 medium shallots, finely grated

5 oil-packed anchovy fillets, minced into a paste

2 teaspoons coconut sugar, muscovado, or rapadura

Place the oil and 'nduja in a small saucepan; set over medium heat. Cook the 'nduja—breaking up the meat with spoon—until caramelized and crispy, 10 to 13 minutes. Add the shallots and anchovies (be careful, hot oil will likely bubble and spit) and fry 1 to 2 minutes. Off heat, stir in the coconut sugar. Let cool completely. Transfer the mixture (oil and all) to a sterilized jar and refrigerate until ready to use; the mixture should sit for a minimum of 30 minutes to allow the flavors to meld. Label and date your jar (I use painter's tape); refrigerate in an airtight container for up to 1 month.

BAGNA CAUDA

Pronounced "BAHN-yah COW-dah," this "hot bath" can serve as a dressing, sauce, dip, spread, or marinade. It is particularly suited for bitter and/ or relatively bland foods (e.g., radicchio, kale, zucchini, cauliflower, pasta, etc.), all of which benefit from the sweetness of butter, the punch of chile, and the uniquely addictive quality of pounded anchovy.

APPROXIMATELY 1¼ CUP

½ cup olive oil

8 tablespoons unsalted butter or ghee

4 oil-packed anchovy fillets or 2 rinsed and boned salt-packed anchovies, minced; or 1½ teaspoons fish sauce

Fine sea salt

2 chile de arbol, stemmed and torn in two

6 cloves (preferably young and fresh) garlic, smashed, peeled, and finely minced

1 tablespoon chopped fresh thyme (optional)

Zest of 1 lemon (use a Microplane for best results)

Juice of ½ lemon

In a medium saucepan over medium-low heat, heat the olive oil and butter. Add the anchovies and stir constantly with a wooden spoon until the anchovies begin to dissolve in the fat, about 5 minutes. Reduce the heat to low and add a pinch of salt, the chile de arbol (seeds and all!), the garlic, and the thyme (if using). Continue to cook for 1 minute more. Turn off the heat and allow the garlic to finish cooking in the residual heat, making sure the garlic doesn't brown. Add the lemon zest and juice and stir to combine. Use immediately. Store any leftovers in an airtight container for up to 4 days.

continued

MISO BAGNA CAUDA

To make a vegetarian bagna cauda, nix the anchovies. Stir together 2 tablespoons white (or red) miso with lemon juice until it is no longer lumpy; add the miso-lemon mixture and zest as directed above. Use anywhere you would bagna cauda or Instant "XO" (page 341).

YUZU PONZU

This tangy, heady, smoky, umami-packed dressing can serve as sauce or dressing for fish (see Hard-Roasted Whole Fish, page 256), seaweed salads, cold noodles, pot stickers (especially mushroom-filled ones), and tofu.

APPROXIMATELY ¾ CUP

¼ cup Dashi (page 346)
¼ cup nama shoyu or white (shiro) shoyu
3 tablespoons mirin
¼ cup fresh yuzu or Meyer lemon juice

Combine the dashi, shoyu, and mirin in a small saucepan. Bring to a simmer over medium heat and simmer for 5 to 8 minutes (it should reduce slightly). Off heat, add the yuzu juice. Cover and refrigerate overnight, or for up to 3 days. Strain before using.

HARISSA

Whether you buy premade or make it at home, harissa in the fridge is like money in the bank—when times are tough, make a withdrawal and sigh with relief. My version is as complex and spicy as the rest, but, I think, better and more complex due to the addition of sesame and nigella seeds, coconut sugar, and Banyuls vinegar.

Use this red paste as a rub for meat (page 264), seafood (see Seared Squid, page 161), or roasting vegetables (potatoes and carrots are especially good). Add a dollop to sauces such as Blistered Tomatoes with Preserved Lemon (page 201). Make eggs and beans extraordinary.

APPROXIMATELY 1½ CUPS

16 small or 8 large dried guajillo chiles, seeds removed, torn into 1-inch pieces
8 chile de arbol, seeds removed, torn into 1-inch pieces
2 tablespoons sesame seeds or benne seeds
1 tablespoon nigella seeds
1 tablespoon coriander seeds
1 tablespoon caraway or cumin seeds
⅛ teaspoon coconut sugar
2 garlic cloves, thinly sliced
1 teaspoon sea salt
½ cup olive oil, plus more for storing
2 tablespoons Banyuls vinegar
1 teaspoon lemon juice

Place the guajillo chiles and chile de arbol in a large heatproof bowl and pour in boiling water to cover. Let the chiles soak until softened, 40 to 45 minutes; drain. Dry-toast the sesame seeds, nigella seeds, coriander seeds, caraway or cumin seeds, and coconut sugar; when cool, grind finely in a spice mill or with a mortar and pestle. Transfer the seeds and spices to a food processor and add the garlic and salt. Pulse until the garlic is very finely chopped. Add the chiles and pulse until they are evenly chopped. Add the ½ cup olive oil, vinegar, and lemon juice; pulse just until incorporated (mixture should have the texture of a coarse paste). Transfer the harissa to a container for which you have an airtight lid; spoon some olive oil on top to cover. Harissa can be refrigerated in an airtight container, submerged in a thin layer of olive oil, for up to 1 month.

UME BUTTER

Compound butters can add a clever wink to an otherwise elemental dish. Think toast (page 150), eggs, beans, rice, pasta, polenta, steamed fish, and grilled steak. I make versions with black garlic, dried lime, miso, yuzu zest, and yogurt or crème fraîche. One of the more unusual in rotation is this ume butter, delightfully zingy, salty, and rich.

Tips—To soften butter, simply leave it out at room temperature overnight. You can purchase umeboshi plums already in paste form, but I prefer to just use whole plums: scrape the flesh from the pit, and finely chop to a paste right before using; discard the pit. For 2 teaspoons, you'll need approximately 2½ umeboshi plums, depending on their size.

½ CUP

1 stick (110 grams) unsalted butter,
at room temperature
2 teaspoons umeboshi paste (see headnote)

Put butter in a medium mixing bowl and add the ume paste. Use a rubber spatula or wooden spoon to mix thoroughly. Cover and refrigerate for up to 2 weeks.

YUZU KOSHO

Yuzu kosho is a cute name for a powerful condiment composed of three ingredients: yuzu rind, chile, and salt. Somehow this trio combines to create a paste with incredible flare. Much like gremolata—the Italian condiment of herbs, garlic, and zest—yuzu kosho is versatile: you can use it anywhere you want a dish to really pop. It's spicy, grassy, bright, and it brings that special fermented funk. (One caveat, however: unlike gremolata, yuzu kosho can be very spicy; limit your dollop to a teaspoon or less.)

Incorporate yuzu kosho into vinaigrettes and marinades, or use it as a condiment for a plethora of dishes: noodles in all shapes and forms (especially good ol' chicken soup), short ribs or brisket, braised mussels or clams, raw oysters, chicken wings, and so on.

Since this condiment relies mostly on zest, juice the remaining yuzu flesh and use it in one or a few of the dressings, marinades, or desserts in this book. If you can't find yuzu, you can sub Meyer lemon, Buddha's-hand (with lemon juice), or a combination of citruses (think lemon, lime, mandarin orange, or grapefruit). And if you don't have the will or the time to make your own, store-bought is fine. This version is milder than any packaged product—if you want more heat, just increase the serrano until you're pleased.

APPROXIMATELY ¾ CUP

1 cup finely grated yuzu zest (from approximately 20 yuzus, use a Microplane for best results)
2 green serrano chiles, seeded and minced
1 teaspoon fine sea salt
¼ cup yuzu juice (from approximately 4 yuzus)
Pinch of granulated cane sugar

(I recommend wearing gloves.) Combine the zest, chile, and salt on a cutting board. Chop, dragging the knife blade at an angle across mixture, until a coarse paste forms. Transfer to a small bowl. Mix in the remaining ingredients. Transfer to a small jar, cover, and store in a dark, cool place for 2 days. Refrigerate for up to 1 month.

GREEN SAUCE

I find profound pleasure in a green sauce. Thin or thick, smooth or coarse, woodsy or bright and floral—this sprightly herbal condiment never fails to brighten, lighten, and complete a meal. Here are a few of my favorite versions that are just outside the realm of familiar.

While I give you measurements, know you needn't be precise. A little more parsley, a little less mint—whatever makes you happy. Since a green sauce is also a practical repository for any remnants in the crisper drawer, I encourage you to use up what you already have. As long as you taste and get the salt, acid, and fat in check, you can create by preference and taste.

Green sauce keeps well. Just spoon a little oil on top to create an air seal directly on the surface; cover the jar and refrigerate for up to 4 days or freeze for up to 3 months. Once you've got a batch, surely you'll dream of all the things you can spoon it under, over, and beside. Yes, it is a condiment to be served with grilled meats and seafood, fried eggs, and roasted vegetables, but don't stop there. Use the sauce as salad dressing (thin with a little acid, a little more oil, and perhaps some cold water); on sandwiches and toasts; in marinades and rubs (for vegetables as well as proteins); or swirled into dips, beans, soups, and stews.

First, choose a recipe from the opposite page. If the green sauce contains an allium—green onion, shallot, garlic, or green garlic—then let that mellow in the acid component (lemon, lime, or vinegar) with a pinch of salt (or fish sauce) and any sweetener (e.g., honey, sugar, etc.) for 5 to 10 minutes. If there are other aromatics such as zest or ginger, stir those in too. Add the oil before the herbs, as acid causes herbs to brown and we want the green sauce to be green (Nam Jim, which doesn't have any oil, is an exception).

Aiming for a coarse puree—and depending how finely you managed to chop things—stir to combine, pound in a mortar, or pulse in a food processor, scraping down the sides of the food processor bowl, as needed (and making sure the machine doesn't get too warm—also a cause of browning). Taste, and add more salt, acid, and/or oil until it tastes balanced to you. It helps to taste on something other than a spoon—a piece of lettuce, a nub of bread, or a slice of a vegetable. Green sauces thicken slightly as they sit, and you may need to add a little cold water and/or readjust seasoning right before use. To use by drizzling, aim for the consistency of heavy cream. To use as a dip, spread, marinade, or sauce, aim for the consistency of yogurt.

Transfer the green sauce to a container and spoon a little oil on top, creating a seal; cover with an airtight lid and refrigerate for up to 4 days, or freeze for up to 3 months. Bring to room temperature before using.

GARLICKY GREEN HOT SAUCE

8 to 10 stalks green garlic, finely chopped

1 teaspoon lemon juice

Fine sea salt

Rind of ½ preserved lemon, minced

2 teaspoons toasted cumin or caraway seeds, finely ground

¼ cup olive oil

1 to 2 serrano chiles, minced

3 cups cilantro (1 large bunch), finely chopped

1 cup mint, finely chopped

NAM JIM

1 stalk green garlic or 1 small garlic clove, minced or finely grated

Zest of 1 lime

Juice of 2 small limes

1 tablespoon fish sauce

1 tablespoon coconut sugar

One 1-inch piece fresh ginger, finely grated (use a Microplane for best results)

1 to 2 serrano chiles, minced or ½ to ¾ teaspoon ground chile de arbol

3 cups cilantro (1 large bunch), finely chopped

MAKRUT LIME GREEN SAUCE

Tip—Because of the relatively tough lime leaves, this green sauce is best when made in a food processor or blender.

1 stalk green garlic, or 1 small garlic clove, finely chopped

1 tablespoon red wine vinegar

1 tablespoon lemon juice

Fine sea salt

1 teaspoon honey

2 teaspoons toasted coriander seeds, finely ground

1 teaspoon dry-toasted fennel seeds, finely ground

6 to 8 tablespoons olive oil

½ chile de arbol, stemmed, seeded, coarsely ground

1 cup flat-leaf parsley (½ large bunch), finely chopped

10 makrut lime leaves, center stem removed, cut into thin ribbons and then diced

UME HERB SAUCE

1 stalk green garlic, finely chopped

2 tablespoons lemon juice

Fine sea salt

Zest of 1 lemon

8 tablespoons olive oil

½ umeboshi plum, pitted and minced into paste

2½ to 3 cups flat-leaf parsley (1 large bunch), finely chopped

2 very large handfuls of any seasonal, tender green (approximately 2 ounces), or a mix (dandelion, oregano, fennel fronds, arugula, watercress)

2 tablespoons rosemary leaves

Pinch of chile flakes (such as coarsely ground chile de arbol) (optional)

ANCHOVY GREMOLATA

More condiment than sauce, this punchy and herbaceous mix enlivens and emboldens. The uses for anchovy gremolata are limitless, but it is especially good on eggs, chicken, potatoes, brassicas, and sweet vegetables such as peas and favas.

APPROXIMATELY ¾ CUP

½ cup (loosely packed) finely chopped flat-leaf parsley

2 tablespoons finely chopped fresh thyme

2 tablespoons finely chopped chive (optional)

2 oil-packed anchovy fillets, drained and finely chopped

1 garlic clove, minced

1 scant tablespoon finely grated lemon zest (use a Microplane for best results)

½ to ¾ teaspoon crushed Aleppo-style pepper, Urfa pepper, or Marash pepper; or ¼ teaspoon coarsely ground chile de arbol

Small pinch of fine sea salt

Mix all ingredients in a small mixing bowl. Use immediately or cover and refrigerate for up to 2 days.

SIMPLE CHICKEN STOCK

This is more of an infusion than a stock. The absence of all aromatics and the gentle steeping yield an elegant, imminently useful broth.

APPROXIMATELY 12 CUPS

Chicken carcasses and/or parts—whatever and however much you have—cut with scissors or shears into roughly 6-inch pieces

Pinch of fine sea salt

One 2- to 3-inch piece kombu (optional)

Preheat oven to 400°F. Put the chicken bones and parts in a large, wide pot and roast, uncovered, for 25 to 30 minutes, or until most pieces are a light golden brown. Bring a kettle or pot of water to a boil. Pour the boiling water over the chicken, salt, and kombu (if using), submerge by approximately 2 inches; cover and steep for 30 minutes. Strain through a chinois or fine-meshed sieve lined with cheesecloth; discard the bones. Use immediately or cool quickly in an ice bath. Once cooled to room temperature, store in airtight container. The stock can be refrigerated for up to 4 days or frozen for 3 months.

DASHI

Both dashi and kombu stock (recipe follows) are mineral and light—they allow other ingredients to reveal their beautiful character. As such, I usually prefer them over rich stocks loaded with strong aromatics such as onion, celery, bay leaf, black pepper, and so on. That's not to say I don't enjoy a range of flavors. If I'm whipping up a single batch for something specific, I may add complementary and relatively subtle aromatics such as charred green onion, rosemary, dried mushrooms, ginger, or even toasted walnuts. If I'm tripling the recipe with the intent of freezing most for a later use, I keep the recipe pure—I can always alter the flavor later, when I'm reheating a few cups on the stove. It's fun to play around with infusions, and the briny, smoky quality of the bonito pairs kindly with many things.

> **Tip**—Be sure to leave 6 to 12 hours for soaking the kombu.

4 CUPS

Two 4-inch pieces kombu

4 cups cool water

1 cup (loosely packed) bonito flakes

Soak the kombu and water in a small saucepan overnight. Poach the kombu over medium-low heat for 20 minutes. Remove from heat, discard the kombu (or save for a "second dashi" or "second kombu stock"), and add the bonito flakes. Stir well and let stand for 15 minutes. Strain through a chinois or fine-meshed sieve lined with cheesecloth; discard the bonito or use for a second, lighter brewing (along with reserved kombu). Use dashi immediately or cool quickly in an ice bath. Once cooled to room temperature, store in airtight container. Dashi can be refrigerated for up to 4 days or frozen for 3 months.

VEGAN DASHI

If you want a vegan umami-packed broth with more flavor, color, and body than kombu stock, omit the bonito flakes and add 8 dried shiitake mushrooms and ½ cup of toasted walnuts to the water along with the kombu (soaking everything overnight). The smoky flavor is absent, but you could add a dash of smoked shoyu or olive oil, if you'd like (available online and from specialty grocers).

KOMBU STOCK

A prominent feature in my first book, kombu stock is the umami-rich backbone of much of cooking. And it is nothing more than kombu and water.

Like all sea vegetables, kombu is rich in many minerals and high in protein. Whenever I am feeling a little sick or stagnant, I turn to a bowl of this warm seaweed water; it consistently heals what ails me. As for a basic stock, it can't get easier or cheaper.

12 CUPS

Six 4-inch pieces kombu
12 cups water
½ teaspoon fine sea salt

Place the kombu, water, and salt in a medium saucepan and warm over moderate heat. When the first bubbles begin to appear, turn off the heat.

Cover the pot and steep for 30 minutes, or up to overnight. Strain through a fine-mesh strainer. Refrigerate in an airtight container for up to 3 days.

PRESERVED LEMON AND HERB OIL

APPROXIMATELY ½ CUP

1 bunch chives (approximately ½ ounce)
4 cups mixed fresh herbs (approximately 2 ounces) (such as flat-leaf parsley, dill, green sorrel, mint, fennel fronds, cilantro, etc.), thick or woodsy stems removed, gently washed
Rind of ½ preserved lemon
1½ cups neutral vegetable oil (such as cold-pressed rice bran oil or grapeseed oil) or good, buttery olive oil
⅛ teaspoon fine sea salt

Bring a large pot of water to a boil and add salt until it tastes of the sea. Prepare an ice water bath and set it near the stove. Line a fine-mesh sieve or chinois with a coffee filter or double layer of cheesecloth and set over a large measuring cup or small mixing bowl. Blanch the chives and herbs in boiling water for 10 to 15 seconds; use a fine-mesh spider to immediately transfer to ice water. When the herbs have chilled, remove any excess moisture by pressing them gently in a clean kitchen towel.

Place the blanched herbs, preserved lemon, oil, and salt in a blender. Blend just to a fine puree; stop before the blender heats up, as this can turn your herb oil brown. Strain the mixture through the prepared sieve—do not press on the solids or the oil will be cloudy (I'm impatient and want the maximum yield, so I put this whole contraption, uncovered, in the refrigerator and let it drip overnight). The herb oil can be made 1 week ahead. Refrigerate in an airtight container; bring to room temperature and stir or swirl before using.

CHILE VINEGAR

Unlike black pepper, chile flakes, and commercial hot sauces, this chile vinegar contributes a barely-there kick that hits the back of the throat at the end of a bite. Basically it is a fast and cheap way toward more interesting food. Of course, you can purchase a similar product, but making your own allows you to control both the level of heat (via the quantity of chiles, how finely they're cut/torn (finer equals hotter), and how long they infuse) and the type and flavor of the vinegar used. This recipe uses dried chile de arbol, which are available year-round. I usually splurge and use Banyuls red wine vinegar as the base, but white wine, rice, apple cider, and distilled white vinegar work well too.

1 CUP

15 chile de arbol, torn in half lengthwise, a few torn into roughly ½-inch pieces
1 cup vinegar of your choice
⅛ teaspoon sea salt

Place the chiles in a glass jar and add the vinegar and salt (the chiles should be submerged). Seal and let sit for 7 to 10 days. Strain through a fine-mesh sieve and funnel or pour into a fine-tipped squeeze bottle (or glass jar). It keeps indefinitely at room temperature. The resulting pickled chiles can be kept in an airtight container for up to 1 month. Slice thinly and use like chile flakes.

QUICK-PICKLED SHALLOTS

This is a simple process that leaves you with two products: an enormously versatile pickle and flavored vinegar. These shallots are tangy, pungent, and slightly sweet; they brighten and complicate any dish they touch. I always have these on hand and find endless uses for them.

APPROXIMATELY 1 CUP

10 small or 6 large shallots
¾ to 1 cup red wine vinegar (Banyuls is my favorite for this)
¼ teaspoon fine sea salt

Thinly slice the shallots crosswise; I use a mandoline. Toss the slices with salt and pack them loosely into a jar with a tight-fitting lid. Add enough red wine vinegar to cover by 1 inch (or more, if you desire more shallot vinegar). Set the mixture aside for at least 30 minutes, or refrigerate for up to 4 days.

CRISPY CAPERS

Croutons, breadcrumbs, and nuts aren't the only way to add texture to your food. Fried capers, Crispy Shallots (page 350), thinly sliced radish, puffed grains (page 76), fried or toasted buckwheat (page 21), Candied Seeds (page 351), and coarsely ground spice blends such as dukkah (page 356), are interesting toppers that contribute much-needed contrast. *(Pictured opposite.)*

¼ CUP

¼ cup olive oil
¼ cup salt-packed capers, soaked in cool water for 15 to 30 minutes, rinsed, and patted dry

Line a plate with 2 paper towels. Heat the oil and capers in a small saucepan over medium heat, swirling often, until the capers burst (as if blossoming) and are golden brown and crisp, about 5 minutes. Use a slotted spoon to transfer the crispy capers to the paper towels to drain. Use immediately, or keep uncovered at room temperature for up to 6 hours.

CRISPY SHALLOTS

In my kitchen, pickled shallots and crispy shallots are indispensable. Recently I've been grinding them into my spice blends (curry, baharat, berbere, ras el hanout) too.

My preferred method for caramelizing and crisping up thinly sliced shallots is relatively slow; it results in evenly golden, perfectly sweet little chips that keep for almost 2 days. You can certainly achieve consistent, thin slices with a sharp knife and a lot of practice. However, a mandoline makes it easy, delivering precision and speed simultaneously. *(Pictured on page 198.)*

APPROXIMATELY 2 CUPS

3 cups neutral vegetable oil (such as cold-pressed rice bran oil or grapeseed oil), pork fat, or other fat with a high smoke point
5 to 6 large shallots, peeled and very thinly sliced lengthwise

Line a baking sheet with a double layer of paper towels. Set a medium saucepan over moderately high heat; I use stainless steel so I can easily determine the color of the shallots as they cook. Add enough oil to reach a depth of 2 inches. Heat the oil until it reaches 350°F; I can tell by using a candy thermometer (a handy tool, if you plan to fry regularly) or by dropping in a few shallot slices and seeing if they bubble and jump right away.

Add the shallots and give them a stir with a slotted spoon or spider. Lower the heat slightly; the shallots should still be simmering. Cook, stirring once or twice, until the shallots are a light golden brown, about 15 minutes (they will continue to cook after removed from the oil). Use a spider or slotted spoon to remove them from the oil and transfer them to the paper towels to drain. Use immediately or store at room temperature in an airtight container for up to 2 days.

SHALLOT OIL

Strain the leftover frying oil through a fine-mesh sieve. Store at room temperature in an airtight container for up to 2 weeks. This delicious ingredient can be used to flavor dressings or marinades or to fry more shallots.

CRISPY CURRY LEAVES

Crispy, fragrant, and gorgeous, these fried curry leaves should adorn toast (page 152), poached eggs (page 157) or daal, roasted cabbage salads (page 226), and kale and yogurt dip (page 124).

If using frozen curry leaves, you can drop them straight from the freezer into the oil, but stand back a bit, as they will spit and sputter. Be careful not to burn the curry leaves—they are ready almost as soon as they stop sputtering (and will taste like burnt popcorn if taken too far). They will crisp up completely once they've cooled. *(Pictured on page 35.)*

MAKES 12 LEAVES

¼ cup olive oil
½ chile de arbol (optional)
12 fresh curry leaves
Fine sea salt

Line a plate or work surface with paper towels. Place the oil, chile (if using), and curry leaves in a small saucepan over medium heat and cook for 1 to 2 minutes or until the oil is warmed and the curry leaves are crisp; don't let the curry leaves burn. Use a small slotted spoon or a pair of tongs to remove the curry leaves and drain them on paper towels—salt them lightly while they are still warm. Use immediately, or hold uncovered at room temperature for up to 2 hours.

CURRY LEAF OIL

Strain the leftover frying oil through a fine-mesh sieve. Store at room temperature in an airtight container for up to 2 weeks. This delicious ingredient can be used to finish dishes, flavor dressings or marinades, or to fry more curry leaves.

CANDIED SEEDS

Make these crystalized seeds one afternoon when the thought of cooking is therapeutic. Then a few days later when you're feeling more harried and friends unexpectedly drop by and all you have is frozen yogurt (page 316) or some store-bought vanilla ice cream, these seeds will give you a low-fuss, high-reward dessert. They're also good on top of cakes and panna cotta or incorporated into cookie doughs—really anywhere a sweet crunch is welcome.

¼ CUP

2 tablespoons granulated cane sugar
2 tablespoons water
¼ cup small, fine seeds (such as sesame or fennel)

Line a baking sheet with parchment paper and set it by the stove. Heat the sugar and water in a 9- or 10-inch skillet over high heat until the syrup just begins to bubble. Add the seeds and stir constantly until the water evaporates and the surface of the seeds turns dry and powdery, 5 to 8 minutes. Use a heatproof spatula to pour the candied seeds onto the baking sheet, spreading them evenly. Let cool completely. Break up any big clumps and store in an airtight container at room temperature for up to 1 month.

TOASTED CHICKPEA FLOUR

Toasted chickpea flour is a surprising source of a nutty, toasty flavor that can define a dish (see Pomelo Salad with Chickpea Flour and Crispy Shallots, page 196). It can also function as a coating, binder, and thickener.

1 CUP

1 cup chickpea flour
¼ teaspoon fine sea salt (optional)

Place a heatproof bowl near the stove. Spread the flour and salt (if using) in a 10- or 12-inch heavy-bottomed skillet (if your chickpea flour has a lot of clumps, sift it into the skillet) and heat over medium heat. Toast the flour, stirring often, for 4 to 5 minutes, or until the flour has deepened to a light caramel color. Lower the heat and, stirring constantly, continue toasting the flour for another 6 to 8 minutes, or until another shade darker. Immediately transfer the flour to the bowl to halt cooking. Cool completely. Store in an airtight container for up to 3 months.

SEAWEED POWDER

Truly: if you want "seaweed powder," store-bought ground-up nori is great. But I like adding wakame for added nutrition and matcha, a sweet green tea, for the nice green hue it gives an otherwise obsidian mix.

APPROXIMATELY ¼ CUP

¼ cup wakame
¼ cup nori powder, store-bought or homemade (page 71)
½ teaspoon matcha powder (optional)

Place all the ingredients in a spice grinder and pulse until fine. Pass through a fine-mesh sieve. If you'd like, return large particles to the spice grinder and repeat the process once more.

DRIED SHRIMP POWDER

APPROXIMATELY ¾ CUP

½ cup dried shrimp
Fine sea salt

Soak the dried shrimp in cold water to cover for 10 to 15 minutes, or up to 25 minutes; rinse. Drain and pat dry. Toast the shrimp in a dry skillet over medium-high heat until dry and crisp, 5 to 8 minutes. Pulse the dried shrimp in a spice grinder or food processor until you have soft, irregular powder—mostly fine, but with some larger flakes. Toss with a pinch of salt. Store at room temperature in an airtight container for up to 2 weeks. *(Pictured on page 180.)*

SHISO SALT

APPROXIMATELY 1 TABLESPOON

1 ounce purple shiso leaves, washed, dried well, coarsely chopped
2 tablespoons flaky sea salt

Grind the shiso leaves and salt in a spice grinder or a suribachi (Japanese grinding bowl with a coarse, ridged interior) until finely ground. Leave uncovered at room temperature overnight. Store in an airtight container for up to 3 months.

YUZU SALT

Yuzu zest also makes a wonderful salt. Follow the method above but use the zest of three yuzus instead of shiso leaves.

CURRY SPICE BLEND

Home cooks all over the world keep a jar of their unique house spice on hand at all times. This is mine. It anoints everything from braised lamb to roasted carrots, egg salad to fried rice. Like the Mole Spice Blend (page 353), it is especially useful in those moments I don't have the time to peel a clove of a garlic or sauté a shallot—a spoonful of this burnished golden blend contributes enough flavor to render typical aromatics unnecessary. To start using your batch right away, check out the following recipes: Curried Fried Rice with Chickpeas and Cabbage (page 253), Lamb and Lamb's-Quarter Pie (page 285), Many Ways to Season a Chicken (page 264), Spiced Ghee (page 161), and Spiced Lamb Meatballs (page 273).

APPROXIMATELY 2 CUPS

½ cup toasted sesame seeds or benne seeds
⅓ cup coriander seeds
¼ cup cumin seeds
2 tablespoons brown mustard seeds
1 tablespoon fennel seeds
2 to 3 chile de arbol, stemmed (depending on desired heat)
2 tablespoons dried, edible rose petals
2 tablespoons plus 2 teaspoons ground sumac or 2 tablespoons dried lime powder (page 38)
1 tablespoon plus 2 teaspoons ground turmeric
1 tablespoon ground cinnamon (preferably true Ceylon cinnamon, not cassia)

In a 9- or 10-inch dry skillet, combine all the spices but the rose petals, sumac, turmeric, and cinnamon. Place over medium-high heat and toast, shaking the pan often, for 4 to 5 minutes. Do not burn the spices. Remove from heat and let cool to room temperature. Transfer to a spice grinder and add the remaining ingredients. Grind to a coarse or fine powder (you may have to do this in batches; or, if you have a large, high-speed blender, you can grind everything in one go), depending on the use. Store in an airtight container for up to 3 months.

I generally consider my spice blends to fall in one of two categories: those for cooking and those for finishing. When cooking with blends, I often "bloom" whole spices in warm fat briefly—either at the start of a dish (in which the ingredients will hit the same fat for their sauté) or as a finishing oil (which will be drizzled over a dish before serving; see Beets with Labneh and Curry, page 216). The fat extracts the aromatics while simultaneously seasoning the oil. Finer, more delicate spices—Urfa pepper or Aleppo-style pepper, turmeric, sumac, and so forth—as well as ground spices (alone or blended) can easily burn and should be handled with more care. When used as a rub (such as with the chicken on page 267), keep an eye on the heat and your nose on the job—if you start to smell burning, attend (and flip, turn, lower the heat). Or add the spices at the very end of cooking. Others are probably too delicate to see any heat all—rose, ground seaweed, and the like (and any spice blends containing them). Use them as you would flaky sea salt to finish a dish, or stir them into vinaigrettes for drizzling.

MOLE SPICE BLEND

Once you have this dark, spicy blend in your pantry, you're set for some minimal-effort, high-reward cooking. Apply as a dry rub to steak or brisket (see Mole-Spiced Brisket, page 290), chicken (see Many Ways to Season a Chicken, page 264), turkey, pork, lamb, grilled sweet potato, or oily fish such as mackerel and yellowtail. A small spoonful is also a shortcut to flavor in bean stews, braising collard greens, pumpkin tamales, meatballs (page 273), and stuffed peppers (page 242). (*Pictured on page 354.*)

APPROXIMATELY 1 CUP

2 dried Chilhuacle negro, Pasilla negro, or Cascabel chiles

2 dried ancho chiles

1 dried chipotle chile

1 to 2 chile de arbol (depending on the freshness and heat of yours and how spicy you like things)

1 tablespoon coriander seeds

1 tablespoon black sesame seeds

2 teaspoon cumin seeds

2 tablespoons dried oregano

1 cinnamon stick or ½ teaspoon ground cinnamon (preferably true Ceylon cinnamon, not cassia)

1 tablespoon cocoa powder

2 teaspoons coconut sugar

¼ cup toasted pumpkin seeds

1 teaspoon citric acid powder (optional)

Heat a 10- or 12-inch skillet over medium-high heat. Add the chiles and cook, turning once, until toasted, about 2 minutes. Once cool, stem and seed the chiles. Tear the chiles into roughly 1-inch pieces and put in a spice grinder. In the same skillet over medium heat, toast the coriander, black sesame, and cumin seeds, shaking and swirling the pan frequently, until they are fragrant and the coriander is a shade darker, 2 to 3 minutes. Let the seeds cool and then add to the spice grinder with the chiles. Add the oregano, cinnamon, cocoa powder, coconut sugar, pumpkin seeds, and citric acid (if using). Grind into a coarse powder. Store in an airtight container at room temperature (ideally in a dark cupboard) for up to 4 months.

SUNFLOWER DUKKAH

Dukkah is an everyday condiment that has been widely used in the Middle East since the ancient age of Egypt. Like *pesto* and *hummus*, the term is now used by many to generally convey a concept: a mix of nuts, seeds, and spices. It is a very pretty word, and now a familiar one, so I use it too. Dukkah not only adds a lot of flavor but also a pop of texture and color. And it can be a finishing touch for just about anything: bread, pizzas and flatbreads, pasta, beans, eggs, fish, vegetables, chicken, lamb, salads, soups, dips and spreads, fresh cheese, and yogurt.

Use this recipe, or choose your own combination of nuts, seeds, and spices. I never measure unless I'm recipe testing; once you get a feel for ratios, you'll be able to mix a batch on the fly. Use dukkah dry or stir it into olive oil or honey for drizzling. (*Pictured on page page 177.*)

APPROXIMATELY ¾ CUP

¼ cup sunflower seeds
¼ cup unsweetened dried shredded coconut
3 tablespoons sesame seeds or benne seeds
¼ cup coriander seeds
3 tablespoons cumin seeds
½ chile de arbol, stemmed
¼ teaspoon fine sea salt
2 tablespoons puffed quinoa (optional)

Preheat oven to 375°F. Place the sunflower seeds in an even layer on a rimmed baking sheet and toast in the oven for 7 to 10 minutes, or until brown. Place the coconut and sesame seeds on another rimmed baking sheet and toast in the oven for 5 to 7 minutes, or until a light golden brown. Meanwhile, place the coriander seeds, cumin seeds, and chile in a 10- or 12-inch skillet over medium heat and dry-toast, stirring constantly, until fragrant, 3 to 4 minutes. Let everything cool to room temperature, then transfer approximately half of the ingredients to a spice grinder or mortar, along with the salt. Grind into a coarse powder and transfer to a storage container with an airtight lid. Add the remaining mix to the grinder or mortar and pulse or pound until it is just coarsely chopped; add to the storage container and stir to combine. If using, stir in the puffed quinoa. Dukkah will keep in an airtight container at room temperature for up to 2 months, at which point its flavor begins to deteriorate.

SWEET HAZELNUT DUKKAH

(*Pictured on page 355.*)

APPROXIMATELY ¾ CUP

½ cup skinned hazelnuts or almonds
¼ cup sunflower seeds
¼ cup unsweetened dried shredded coconut
3 tablespoons sesame seeds or benne seeds
¼ teaspoon sea salt
½ cup finely chopped dates (optional)

Preheat oven to 400°F. Place the hazelnuts and sunflower seeds in an even layer on a rimmed baking sheet and toast in the oven for 7 to 10 minutes, or until brown. Place the coconut and sesame seeds on another rimmed baking sheet and toast in the oven for 5 to 7 minutes, or until a light golden brown. Let everything cool to room temperature, then transfer approximately half of the ingredients to a spice grinder or mortar, along with the salt. Grind into a coarse powder and transfer to a 2-cup storage container. Add the remaining mix to the grinder or mortar and pulse or pound until it is just coarsely chopped; add to the storage container and stir to combine. If using, stir in the chopped dates. Without the chopped dates, this dukkah will keep in an airtight container at room temperature for up to 2 months, at which point its flavor begins to deteriorate. Add the chopped dates right before using.

GREEN ZA'ATAR

I love za'atar and can cook my way through a bottle in under a week. Traditionally brightened with sumac, I sometimes reimagine the toasty, herby Middle Eastern blend with dried lime instead. It's a little funkier, and I'll admit I'm a sucker for a single-color palette. Sprinkle this on Labneh (page 59), softened butter intended for bread, radishes (page 114), green salads, charred cabbage (page 226), roasted potatoes, crispy eggplant, or fried zucchini; use it as a rub for seafood, lamb, and chicken (page 267). Really, it's hard to go wrong.

You can grind your own dried lime (page 38) or purchase it online. When ordering a bottle, insist on quality. Burlap & Barrel sells an exceptional product, but many others I've sampled aren't vibrant enough to be used in a finishing blend. If you can't find dried lime, you can always use sumac, or even a combination of lemon and lime zest.

½ CUP

¼ cup raw white or brown sesame seeds or benne seeds

¼ cup fresh thyme leaves, coarsely chopped

1 tablespoon ground dried lime, store-bought or homemade (page 38)

⅛ teaspoon fine sea salt

Toast the sesame seeds in a 9- or 10-inch skillet over medium heat, tossing constantly until they're fragrant and golden brown, about 5 minutes. Remove the skillet from the heat and cool completely. Add the thyme, dried lime, and salt, tossing to combine. Leave uncovered overnight (so the thyme can dry) before transferring it to an airtight storage container. Store at room temperature for up to one month. Always stir before using.

SUMAC-ROSE GOMASIO

Gomasio, or gomashio, is a seasoning blend commonly sprinkled on simple rice dishes in Japan. The word means "salt and pepper," as in someone who is handsomely graying; it's used to convey the traditional combination of black sesame seeds and white sea salt.

In this recipe, I've used the beautiful name, but taken creative liberties. I mix toasted white sesame seeds with magenta-colored sumac and dried rose. The combination pairs well with more than you might imagine: radishes (see Radishes with Crème Fraîche and Sumac-Rose Gomasio, page 112), lamb, fava beans (especially the spicy version below), fish, quail (and other game birds), grains and pilafs, chayote (with citrus and olive oil), pasta, cabbage, carrots, and on and on I could go.

½ CUP

3 tablespoons toasted sesame seeds or benne seeds

¼ cup plus 2 tablespoons ground sumac

1 teaspoon ground dried rose petals

¼ teaspoon fine sea salt

Toast the sesame seeds in a 9- or 10-inch skillet over medium heat, tossing constantly until they're fragrant and golden brown, about 5 minutes. Remove the skillet from the heat and cool completely. Transfer sesame to a spice grinder, mortar, or suribachi; pulse or pound until coarsely ground. Add the sumac, dried rose, and salt. Pound or pulse until just combined. Transfer to an airtight storage container and store at room temperature for up to two months.

SPICY SUMAC GOMASIO

Omit the rose. Add a scant ¾ teaspoon crushed Urfa pepper, Aleppo-style pepper, or other mild chile flakes.

SEAWEED GOMASIO

This spice blend sees a lot of action in my house. So many dishes benefit from its rich, nutty, briny flavor. It adorns eggs (see "Deviled" Eggs on Shiso, page 108 and Job's Tears "Stonepot" with Crispy Mushrooms and Jammy Eggs, page 247), fried rice and grains (page 253), salads (Little Gem, avocado, and cucumber is a favorite), and roasted vegetables of all sorts (see Crispy Sweet Potatoes, page 211).

If you are a fellow sesame lover, double this recipe. You can use a coffee or spice grinder and grind it in batches, or if you have a high-speed blender, use that to blitz the whole batch in one go. (*Pictured on page 210.*)

1 CUP

¼ cup plus 2 tablespoons black sesame seeds
One 2-inch piece kombu, torn into
2 or 3 pieces
1 sheet nori, torn or cut with scissors into roughly 2-inch pieces
2 tablespoons dulse flakes (purchase dulse already flaked, or use scissors to cut whole strips into ¼-inch pieces)
¼ teaspoon fine sea salt

Toast the sesame seeds and kombu in a 10- or 12-inch skillet over medium-low heat, stirring occasionally, until seeds are fragrant, 6 to 8 minutes (kombu will crisp up as it cools). Add the nori and dulse and dry-toast 1 to 2 minutes more. Let everything cool to room temperature. Remove a tablespoon or so of seeds and set aside. Pulse the remaining seeds and seaweed with the salt in a coffee grinder until coarsely ground. Stir in reserved whole sesame seeds.

Gomasio can be made 1 month ahead (it doesn't spoil, but its flavor deteriorates over time). Store in an airtight container at room temperature.

SPICY SEAWEED GOMASIO

Mix 1 cup seaweed gomasio and, depending on how spicy you want it, ¾ to 1 teaspoon ground chile de arbol.

FURIKAKE

Before grinding, add 2 tablespoons bonito flakes and 2 teaspoons yuzu (or Meyer lemon) zest to the mix.

MISO SUGAR

I can't explain why, but miso makes sugar taste more like sugar. As in sugarcane. This sugar is more fruity than savory (specifically, a strawberry-and-cream fruit leather, which might not be a thing), bright and subtly salty. You can, of course, sprinkle it here and there and incorporate into baked goods (page 303). Yet it's the kind of ingredient that invites whimsy and play, encouraging us to think differently about our daily kitchen routines. Sprinkle it on toast (*pictured on page 151*) instead of cinnamon sugar; stir some into warm applesauce and top the bowl with cold crème fraîche; shower it over your banana-topped oatmeal and then brûlée with a broiler or torch. The possibilities for this sugar are limitless. Make this a day or two before you want to use it; it needs time to dry out.

¾ CUP

¾ cup granulated cane sugar
2 teaspoons white miso paste

Put the sugar and miso in a food processor and pulse until well combined—the sugar will be an even light brown color and look like wet sand. Spread out on a baking sheet lined with parchment paper and rub the sugar between your palms to loosen up big clumps. Set aside to dry overnight. Once dry, break up the clumps that formed—either by hand or by passing through a fine-mesh sieve. Store in an airtight container, at room temperature, for up to 3 months.

ACKNOWLEDGMENTS

Every recipe in this book is marbled with ideas and ingredients that can source their origins in centuries-old foodways and cultures, found around the world. So, my deepest gratitude goes to the countless people—both known and unknown—who have contributed to my larder and to my cooking: chefs, food writers, growers, makers, and home cooks, past and present. We can eat well, happily, and creatively because of you. This book is, in the truest sense, a collaborative effort and belongs to us all.

To Michael: your support, humor, optimism, and love allowed me to make this book; it is as much yours as it is mine.

To the rest of my family and my friends: Your guidance, graciousness, encouragement, and appetites are invaluable. I love you all.

Thank you to Danielle Svetcov, my agent and career Obi-Wan: You're one of the finest humans I know. Somehow you keep me simultaneously psyched and calm. And you knew when and how to wrench this thing out of my hands.

Sara Bercholz, I'm immensely grateful to have a stage to create. Thank you, too, for your patience. And for sharing a passion for underdogs and umeboshi plums.

To Jenny Wapner, a brilliant editor: Thank you for all your hard work weeding and for showing me how to do it smart. You made this book much better.

To Rick Poon, for putting up with me and making the recipes come to life.

To Helen Goh and Sarah Owens: Your work has broadened the larder, and home cooking is better for it. Thank you, too, for contributing recipes to this book.

To my fearless recipe testers—Tara Duggan, Jaime Tjahaja, Kimberly Miramontes, Naz Sahin, Emily Geis, and Emily Olson: thank you for your time in the kitchen and all of your honest feedback.

To the entire team at Roost who shepherded this book to press (especially Audra Figgins, Emily Wichland, Kara Plikaitis, and Toni Tajima): Thank you for your extraordinary patience—and for every minute you gave to this project.

To the readers of this book: I am humbled and thrilled to share this work, five years in the making, with you. I hope it brings something new into your mind and onto your table. I hope it brings you joy.

INDEX

ABOUT THE AUTHOR

Michelle McKenzie is a professional cook, culinary instructor, food writer, food stylist, and recipe developer. She is the author of *Dandelion & Quince: Exploring the Wide World of Unusual Vegetables, Fruits, and Herbs*, nominated for both the James Beard and IACP Awards. Previously, she was the longtime program director and chef at 18 Reasons, a community cooking school in San Francisco.

Michelle graduated from the University of North Carolina at Chapel Hill with a degree in nutrition and a minor in biochemistry, giving her a deep understanding of food properties and their complex implications within the human body. She later graduated from The Natural Gourmet Institute for Health and Culinary Arts, where she immersed herself in health-supportive cuisine prepared from whole, organic, and seasonal foods. Michelle has worked at some of the best restaurants in the country, has been featured on the Cooking Channel, and has been a contributor for websites such as Food52 and publications such as *Sunset* magazine.

Photo by Daniel Dent